MOTHERS OF THE MILITARY

MOTHERS OF THE MILITARY

Support and Politics during Wartime

Wendy M. Christensen

ROWMAN & LITTLEFIELD
Lanham • Boulder • New York • London

Published by Rowman & Littlefield
An imprint of The Rowman & Littlefield Publishing Group, Inc.
4501 Forbes Boulevard, Suite 200, Lanham, Maryland 20706
https://rowman.com

Unit A, Whitacre Mews, 26-34 Stannary Street, London SE11 4AB,
United Kingdom

British Library Cataloguing in Publication Information Available

Library of Congress Cataloging-in-Publication Data
Names: Christensen, Wendy M., 1977– author.
Title: Mothers of the military : support and politics during wartime / Wendy M.
    Christensen.
Description: Lanham, MD : Rowman & Littlefield, [2018] | Includes biblio-
    graphical references and index.
Identifiers: LCCN 2018004648 (print) | LCCN 2018013708 (ebook) | ISBN
    9781538114247 (ebook) | ISBN 9781538114230 (hardcover : alk. paper)
Subjects: LCSH: Families of military personnel—United States. | Mothers of
    soldiers—United States. | Women and war—United States. | Parent and
    adult child—United States. | Mothers of soldiers—United States—Political
    activity. | Mothers of soldiers—United States—Social conditions—21st
    century. | Soldiers—United States—Social conditions—21st century. | Vet-
    erans—United States—Social conditions—21st century. | Support (Domes-
    tic relations)—United States. | United States—Armed Forces—Military
    life.
Classification: LCC UB403 (ebook) | LCC UB403 .C486 2018 (print) | DDC
    355.1/20973—dc23
LC record available at https://lccn.loc.gov/2018004648

*This book is dedicated to the
mothers of service members.
May it help make your burden less invisible.*

CONTENTS

ACKNOWLEDGMENTS

This book would not be possible without the mothers who opened their lives to me, describing their experiences of having a child in the military. They responded to questions and emails during often the most difficult moments of their own lives—when they were worried about their deployed children, or providing medical care to someone returned from deployment. To this day I remain in awe of their strength and grateful for their willingness to share with me.

This project has been shaped and supported by a number of mentors and colleagues. The project began as my dissertation research. Myra Marx Ferree was my mentor from the beginning of this project; she guided me through many incarnations and revisions with endless enthusiasm and support. Joey Sprague first asked me, years after I finished my dissertation, when the project would become a book, pushing me to write a prospectus. I am indebted to the mentorship of these and many other women in Sociologists for Women in Society.

Many others provided mentoring, feedback, and coaching throughout this process. My faculty writing group at William Paterson University read early chapters, assuring me that they indeed sounded like a book. My "Sunday Meeting" group (Denise Copelton, Laura Logan, Kylie Parrotta, and Trina Smith) supported my writing process from start to finish, encouraging me every step of the way.

I could not have written this book without the love of my family. My parents, brother, and sister have encouraged and supported every step of my education and academic career. And finally, my partner, Jo. She read every chapter from dissertation to book more times than I can count, providing feedback and editing. Jo cheered me on during the entire writing process, and kept me grounded and entertained when I needed breaks. I literally could not have written this book without her love and support.

INTRODUCTION

> My first thought was utter terror. How could my baby boy put him-
> self in constant danger of being killed? How could he do that to me?
> He told me he was thinking about his future, but all I could think
> about was why he wanted to fight in a war so many were dying in.
>
> —Barbara

When Barbara learned of her son's plans to join the armed forces, she was unsure how to react. Even though it was 2004 and the United States had been engaged in the War on Terrorism for three years, with no close relatives in the military Barbara admitted that she had never thought much about war. Chris's announcement was a shock and her immediate reaction was one of panic that her son was making the wrong choice and that he would be in danger.

Barbara is divorced, estranged from her ex-husband, and Chris is her only child. When Chris did not know what he wanted to do with his life, he dropped out of college and was living with his mother and working at a warehouse for minimum wage. Becoming a Marine was the first major decision Barbara had ever seen her son make.

He told her about his plans one afternoon before going to work, leaving a pamphlet on the kitchen table from the recruiter with whom he had been in touch for the past few weeks. The flyer for "Marine Parents" described the kind of success young people could have as Marines and included pictures of proud parents posed with their children in uniform. She did feel proud of his sudden sense of direction, but the panic and worry would not subside. She went to the website on the brochure to learn for herself what the Marines were about.

Barbara's story is typical for mothers of current service members. With the surge of military recruitment and enrollment after the 9/11 terrorist attacks, Barbara's reaction to her son's enlistment has played out the same way for thousands of military families across the country. Military families today may differ in terms of whether there are two parents, a history of military service, or knowledge about war, but the mixed reactions of panic, worry, and pride are nearly universal.

But during the current war these reactions are not experienced by all Americans. Unlike World War II, when the entire country was called on to play a role in the war—a "cast of millions" including everyone from schoolchildren to women—those connected to the War on Terrorism are a much smaller, more isolated segment of the population (only 1 percent of the US population has served since 2001).[1] The war in Afghanistan, now nearly two decades in, was initially supported by 90 percent of the population. But by 2013 support for the war dipped to only 17 percent.[2] Even the news media largely ignores the ongoing war.[3] The families of service members, especially those unlikely to live on military bases, end up feeling more and more removed from their neighbors, friends, and communities as they worry about their loved ones' lives in Iraq and Afghanistan. Most Americans go on with their lives as usual, while military families' lives are far from usual.

When Chris enlisted in the Marines, Barbara's life changed significantly. This book talks about the journey of change mothers go through when their children join the armed forces. Barbara may not have thought much about war or the military before her child's enlistment, but after his enlistment she found herself reading about basic training and learning military terminology and procedure.

Barbara was also not particularly involved in politics before Chris joined the military. When she voted, it was usually for Democratic candidates. Having a son in the military made her more aware of the war, though. She started to watch the news daily. She met a few mothers when she took Chris to boot camp and kept in touch with them by phone and email.

It wasn't until an incident at work that she started to talk with others about her son's military service. She had a photo of him in his dress blues at boot camp graduation on her desk. Every once in a while one of her coworkers would ask her about her son. She only had a few friends where she worked and not too many people knew her about her personal life. One day, a colleague from another department noticed the photo on her desk and said, "Wow, you must be really upset with the way this war is being run. W is such a liar." Barbara did not know how to reply to this offhand remark. She described how casual her coworker sounded, as if the war was distant from his own life and all he knew were the news media talking points. Barbara stammered as she struggled to get out the words that she was very proud of her son, regardless of the way the war was being run. Her colleague left, but she was unsettled by the exchange. She noticed that she felt defensive about not just her son, but the war itself. She explained, "The politics of it bothered me. What difference does it make who lied? My son still deserves respect and support."

This book is about the support Barbara believes her son deserves. For Barbara, like many mothers, that support is linked to respect—for her son's job and his sacrifice for the country. Support, in Barbara's mind, is not related to the politics of war. If anything, the politics of war distract from the support her son needs. For Barbara, the personal aspects of war (her son's service) are not related to the political reasons for war. He, and the rest of the troops, should be supported no matter what.

But, what does *support* mean? For Barbara, politics draws attention and focus away from supporting the troops. During Chris's deployment she voted in midterm elections but refrained from discussing for whom she was voting or publicly supporting any particular candidates. She volunteered with a group of mothers of service members to run bake sales and care package drives outside local public schools on Election Day. She knew the group was more conservative, as some wore campaign buttons for Republican candidates. Mothers in the group generally refrained from talking about politics, even on Election Day, but when they did, they spoke in support of the war and then president George W. Bush.

Barbara's story is one of depoliticization. It did not take Barbara long to learn that she should keep her left-leaning political views to herself while volunteering. To avoid uncomfortable conversations, she refrained from engaging in discussions about candidates and policy while working with the other mothers. In order to support her son she considered it her duty to support the war. During her process of learning the workings of the military, she started to quiet her own antiwar views and questions about the political reasons leading to war.

The mothers Barbara volunteered with represent another common position for mothers during wartime. For many mothers, supporting the troops means supporting their mission and the war itself. As Jody, another mother of a Marine, describes, "You can't be for my son and against the president at the same time. You have to support both." Voting to support the leaders of the military, including the commander in chief, the president, is considered a critical part of supporting the troops.

This is a book about the various and conflicting ideas of *support* during wartime. Support can mean moral, acknowledging and understanding the troops' sacrifice. Support can be deeply personal—providing approval and emotional support to deployed loved ones. Support can also mean political approval of war, either by campaigning in support of war, or silencing one's own questions about the war. Support can mean wanting the war to end and troops to come home.[4] Support is also material. Deployed service members need supplies, and those not provided by the military often come from community groups like the group of mothers with whom Barbara volunteered. Support has different meanings post-deployment. Returning troops need recognition of their sacrifice, and physical and mental health care. Through the experiences of mothers of service members, this book examines the kinds of support needed during war, who provides it, and what impact it has on engagement in the political process.

My interest in this project began in 2006. While researching another topic, I stumbled upon an online support group for mothers of service members. I was immediately struck by the use of patriotic images and language and strong maternal identity. The forum was covered in combat boots, hearts, and poems about mothers' love for their soldier-sons. I dug into the publicly accessible message forums, intrigued by the combination of care work for the troops (care package and holiday card drives), and vitriol against another mother of a service member who was making news headlines. Gold Star mother Cindy Sheehan, whose son Casey was killed in Iraq in 2005, was camping out at then President George W. Bush's Texas ranch, demanding that he meet with her about the reasons for her son's death.

In 2006, Sheehan's questioning of the war echoed doubts the public was also having. Just three years into the "war on terrorism," with the war already seeing a drop in public support, Sheehan had come to be known as the mother of the antiwar movement. Images of her at antiwar protests, in front of staged caskets or headstones of slain service members, were reminiscent of the powerful grieving mother images from previous wars. At demonstrations, Sheehan called for an end to war and for "not one more mother's son" to die. But the mothers in this online group wrote that she was "a traitor to her son" and "dishonoring his memory" in her protests. One mother even suggested Sheehan's son, Casey, was "probably rolling over in his grave." The mix of patriotic flags, bald eagles, and images of the World Trade Center struck me as toeing the pro-war line.

At the time I was personally active in marches against the continuation and escalation of the wars. Friends from high school were serving and their families were feeling the strain of multiple deployments. I had a yellow ribbon on my car, with the words "bring them home alive." I considered myself antiwar *and* pro-troops. But it seemed that on this website for mothers it was impossible to be both these things. The message forums I read were decidedly pro-troops and pro-war. I wanted to understand how mothers could support and encourage a war in which their children may be killed. What I found out is that mothers' relationship to war, and participation in politics during wartime, is much more complex than it seems on the surface.

Nearly two decades into the US War on Terrorism, the issues facing service members and their loved ones continue to be relevant. There are nearly 10,000 troops stationed in Afghanistan for the ongoing war against the Taliban. The United States pulled out of Iraq officially in 2011, but still has 5,000 troops stationed there as "advisors" working with Iraqi forces to fight the Islamic State.[5] While the ongoing war is far from most Americans' minds, service members continue their deployments, and military families continue to struggle with worry and isolation.

MOTHERS, GENDER, AND WAR

While women entering combat roles marks a huge shift in the relation-ship of women to war, women's role as mothers continues to dominate.[6] In 2013 the Department of Defense (DoD) lifted the ban on women in combat, opening some 33,000 combat positions to women.[7] But women are still only 14.5 percent of the All-Volunteer Force (AVF). Women's inclusion in combat positions has been met with ambivalence, confu-sion, and even hostility. Some argue that the battlefield is only for men, and women threaten the military order. Others argue that women, as citizens, should be protected at home to have and take care of children. Media accounts of women deployed to combat zones emphasize their motherhood and the children they leave behind to be cared for by a male spouse or parents. A *New York Times Magazine* feature story about women soldiers showed women in full combat gear, in poses of strength. But they were posed with their small children. The pictures emphasized the contrast between the strong, warrior poses and the women as mothers. They reiterated that the overwhelming depiction of a soldier, a warrior, remains that of a man.[8]

Mothers of service members are in the middle of these changes. On one hand, their role as mothers, providing care during wartime, is em-phasized by the military and in the media. And while women's emotion-al labor is often invisible in public, mothers become visible when they are grieving the loss of their children.[9] On the other hand, women are now warriors, deployed to a war zone and leaving children behind to be cared for by someone else (sometimes their husband). As warriors bal-ancing motherhood and deployment, women have become especially visible in the media. In this book I show that even though the inclusion of women into combat roles is a shift toward equality, the way war is carried out at home is still largely gendered, and the support burden still rests on women.

In the political sociology literature, depictions of mothers' experi-ences during wartime usually fall into two diametrically opposed cate-gories. On one hand, mothers are assumed to be against war because it is destructive to the human life they create.[10] On the other hand, moth-ers may blindly support state war efforts by offering up their sons (and now daughters) for war.[11] But the majority of mothers, like Barbara, do not easily fall into either of these categories. With a child deployed, they find themselves supporting the troops and wanting their children to be safe in the military. But they also live with the daily worry that their children could be killed in the war. As Barbara described,

> I'm not going to be one of those rabid protesting mothers chained up outside the White House demanding my son come home. But I want him to come home. I want the war to end. I think about that every day. I could protest. I could demand—as a mother!—that politicians should end the war, but I don't want our troops to be demoralized by demonstrations.

The image of Cindy Sheehan as a grieving antiwar mother is a familiar one. Throughout history mothers have been depicted as having privilege and moral authority as mothers to publicly grieve their children's death during war, and to speak out against war. As early as ancient Greece, mothers have been at the forefront of antiwar protests. The mothers in Aristophanes's *Lysistrata* cried out publicly against war. The Mothers of the Plaza de Mayo (mothers of the missing) in Argentina publicly protested as mothers against the disappearance of their children during the country's Dirty War.[12] In the United States, the Women's International League for Peace and Freedom was formed during the suffrage movement; activists considered women critical for giving and taking care of life. During the Vietnam War, women protested as mothers mourning both the US and Vietnamese lives lost in the war. Deeply impacted by the draft during the Vietnam War, mothers also protested draft policy and supported conscientious objectors.[13]

These images of mothers protesting align with the idea that mothers, given their maternal role in society, will support peace and not war. Mothers are inherently antiwar in that the everyday experiences of motherhood make the consequences of war—for families and the community—especially visible to them.[14] As mothers, they are not only more likely to support peace, but they are granted moral authority in the public to speak out against war.[15] As Cindy Sheehan's revival of the antiwar movement in the United States shows, the image of the grieving mother is a powerful tool in public relations to mobilize antiwar support.

But mothers, like the ones I encountered online, also actively support war. On this other end of the maternal experience during war, these mothers would be considered what political scientist Cynthia Enloe calls "fully militarized" so that their practices of caring for their children become a part of the war effort.[16] The state passively militarizes the pro-war mother to support war. One extreme version of this wartime mother is Nazi Germany's model of the ideal German mother. This ideal mother reproduced to further the Aryan race (women were given medals for the number of children they had), and proudly raised boys to defend their country, while assuming a sense of motherly duty to the country.[17]

According to Enloe, when mothers are "fully militarized" during wartime to support the war effort, motherhood becomes a critical part of the war. Motherly practices such as wanting their children to succeed, providing emotional support, sending care packages, and caring for wounded service members are folded into this war effort.[18] With "fully militarized motherhood," mothers have little agency in their militarization during wartime. They can choose how they support their children and other service members, but in supporting them as mothers, their motherhood is a part of waging a successful war. While they do have some choice in how they offer support during wartime, militarized mothers are ultimately passive cogs in the machine of war.

But when it comes to mothers like Barbara, neither explanation fits. Barbara's experiences as a mother have not led her to speak out against the war, as the inherently peaceful model of motherhood would suggest. And while she supports her son, and even avoids political conversations about war in order to support the troops, she would likely not see herself as a passive cog in the machine of war, as in fully militarized motherhood. The idea of the fully militarized mother leaves no room for Barbara's own complex ideas about what her son needs in terms of support during wartime. Even the mothers in the group with which Barbara volunteers would not see themselves as fully militarized. They chose to support the war because of their relationship with their child. Militarization is something done to mothers by the state, with little room for mothers' own ideas about politics and motherhood. As much as I might have assumed at first that pro-war mothers are militarized, blindly supporting the war, their experiences of war are that they are not passive political subjects.

The mothers in this book illustrate that the relationship between motherhood and war is much more intricate than the extremes of peaceful motherhood and militarized motherhood. Mothers make active choices about how to process their children's decision to enlist. Some—like Barbara—quiet their own antiwar views, while others—like Cindy Sheehan—make their own antiwar views more public. Both act in the name of keeping their children safe. Mothers make deliberate choices about how much they will participate in the political process during wartime. Some mothers decide not to concern themselves with the politics of war, while others take a decidedly political stance for or against the war. The question that arises is are these choices voluntary and deliberate on the part of mothers, or are they involuntary and shaped by their participating in the military institution? How and when do mothers adopt militarization when providing support, and how and when do they challenge it?

When mothers in this book make public political claims for or against the war, they describe these actions as part of motherly support, and not about politics. When their children return, wounded mentally and physically in battle, mothers take on care work as part of their mothering duties, and some become advocates demanding better treatment for their children and other veterans. The experiences of the mothers described here uncover ongoing tensions in the relationships between gender and politics, and gender and war.

WHY MOTHERS?

Mothers are in a unique position for examining the nuances of wartime support. While military wives and their wartime experiences are frequently the subject of research, mothers of service members remain largely unexamined despite their different relationship to war.[19] As mothers they are charged with nurturing service members, but as women they sit on the margins of war. Men are traditionally warriors and women are the caretakers of the home front.[20] Militaries rely on mothers to keep the home front running while men are fighting abroad, and for mobilizing war support at home. Women were charged with everything from running a frugal household, to saving household scrap metal, to working in factories, to taking on supportive military duties such as secretarial work and nursing.

While mothers have always been important to the state as suppliers of young men for war and caretakers of the home front, they are particularly significant during the current US War on Terrorism. As chapter 1 shows, the military recognizes the importance of mothers by directing the majority of their parental recruitment material to them. The military considers both parents to be key influencers in the decision to enlist, but fathers are usually assumed to be supportive of service and are even shown as conspiring with the child to "break the news" to Mom. Recruitment materials focus efforts on convincing mothers that service is the right choice for their child. Recruiters work to ensure that they acknowledge motherly worries, by building a sense of pride in the military and their child.

Mothers like Barbara are at the center of US War on Terrorism recruitment efforts for two reasons. Service members tend to be younger than the professionalized post-draft military of the first Gulf War. Younger service members are more likely to be like Barbara's son Chris, living at home with their parents (in this case, their mother) during, after, or in lieu of college. Compared with previous wars such as Vietnam where any male thirty-five years and under could be drafted, active duty service members in the all-volunteer military tend to be younger.[21] At age 18, US citizens can enlist in the military on their own and, at age 17, can enlist with parental consent. In 2009, the average age at recruitment for the Army was 22 for active service members, and 21.4 for reservists.[22] Furthermore, most recruits are single. When recruits are without their own families, mothers are key for newly serving members of the armed forces.

Compounding the younger age of enlistees is the fact young people today take longer to reach full adulthood. Markers of adulthood such as marriage and financial independence come much later for young people than they did a generation ago.[23] The majority of newly enlisted service members do not get married until four to six years after enlistment.[24] Chris is like thousands of other young people maintaining strong ties to his parents as an adult. Barbara is like many other mothers who still have influence in their young adults' lives, long after they turn eighteen. As of 2005, 33.3 percent of white males who are twenty-five still live with their parents, and 22.5 percent of black men live with their parents.[25] Institutions like colleges and the military are stepping in to ease young adults' transitions to independence. With more young adults in their twenties and thirties living at home, parents (and especially mothers) have more direct influence over the career and education decisions children make. For those who cannot afford college, the military may be a route out of poverty, or toward independence. As a result of the extension of "young adulthood," as well as declining enlistment numbers, the military now targets mothers in recruitment efforts as gateways to military service for their children.

INVISIBLE SUPPORT

Mothers are key to running a successful war, but their support work—like much of women's emotional labor—is often invisible.[26] Mothers of deployed service members provide a variety of physical, emotional, and moral support that the military relies on during wartime. Mothers, and other military family members, are emotionally connected to the troops and their connection is critical for troop morale.

The military supplies only items considered to be necessary, and counts on families, often led by mothers, to send care packages of supplies such as food, magazines and books, sunscreen, medications, toiletries, and clothing like warm socks to the troops during deployment. When on leave, the military relies on families to provide respite and care before returning to deployment. After deployment, military families, particularly mothers, are often the ones taking physical and emotional care of injured service members. The Department of Defense considers this kind of "auxiliary support" critical to waging war.[27]

Like many organizations in the United States, the group of mothers Barbara joined gathers donations to send care packages to the troops. Items such as powder, lotion, socks, hand sanitizer, vitamins, bug repellent, and hand wipes, not to mention entertainment items such as books, MP3 players, batteries, paper, pens, etc., are included in these boxes. In addition to helping put together boxes for as many as five hundred service members in a batch, Barbara sent her son individualized boxes during his deployment. She included comforting objects she knew he would appreciate—small packets of Chris's favorite condiments, photographs from home, allergy medicine, and sports magazines. She explained, "every mother I know sends care packages. It helps to know their child has some comforts from home in the sandbox. I'm always trying to think of what I can add to the next one."

Parents of service members are typically not visible to the public, except for when mothers are visible as grieving mothers. During WWII, families would display Blue Star, or Gold Star (if their children were killed in service) flags in the windows of their homes as a physical reminder of the ongoing war and the sacrifice their family was making. Care package drives (and holiday card drives, letter writing campaigns, etc.) are also ways for military families to rally the public around the ongoing war. But like many mothers, Barbara did not talk much about her son's deployment in her daily life. When it came up, she kept it brief, wanting to avoid "uninformed political comments." While some mothers I interviewed had stickers on their cars proclaiming things such as "proud mother of a Marine," Barbara did not work to draw attention to her son's service. The majority of citizens can all but ignore the ongoing war, and Barbara is happy to avoid conversation with those who are "uninformed" about it.

While there are in-person support groups available all over the country for mothers of service members, not everyone has access to one. But some mothers may turn to online support groups as a way to find other mothers and emotional support in addition to in-person groups. As an early form of social networking, online message boards connected people long before Facebook and other networks existed. Before 2008, less than 20 percent of US adults thirty to forty-nine were on Facebook, so anyone who needed to network with others would search for an online forum or message board.[28] Online message forums provide a kind of 24-7 support system and the feeling that "someone is always there," as another mother, Renee, explained.

HOME FRONT SUPPORT

It is not surprising that military family members like Barbara feel isolated from civilians who have no direct connection to war. As Barbara described, others—like her coworkers—can, and do, forget the war is happening, while she lives with the daily stresses of war. Mothers like Barbara feel alone because military families are a smaller segment of our citizenry than during previous wars.

Widespread drafts during WWI, WWII, and Vietnam meant the burden of war was spread somewhat evenly across the populace. Although many (often those who were white, upper class, and in college) were able to avoid the draft, in theory, every young man had the same chance at service, although black men ended up disproportionately represented especially in the front ranks. With 16 million Americans in active duty during WWII, and 9 million Americans (10 percent) in active duty service during Vietnam, the average American was likely to know someone who served—often multiple family members, friends, and neighbors.[29] However, since 2001, only 2.5 million military members have served in Iraq and Afghanistan—less than 1 percent of the population.[30] Their families are few and far between in the population at large. Unless they live on or near a military base, which is unlikely for military mothers like Barbara, they have little everyday interaction with other members of the military.

Some segments of the population are more impacted by the isolating experience of service than others. The All-Volunteer Force, in theory, means that anyone may select to join the services as an avenue to college or a career. In reality, those who join are more likely to be individuals with fewer other options after high school. The military does not have official race-based enlistment goals. But until the early 2000s when black enlistment dropped, the military relied on strong enlistment from black youth to meet recruitment quotas.[31] Black and Hispanic youth are more likely to consider military service, enlist, and make service a career.[32] Blacks are overrepresented in the 1.4 million active service members in the United States, making up 18 percent of the military and only 12.3 percent of the US population.[33] The branch with the highest proportion of black service members are in the Army, where 25 percent of soldiers are black.[34] There was a push in 2005 to raise black recruitment numbers (the military increased the recruiting budget 30 percent in areas with potential minority enlistees and renewed efforts to ensure recruiters are racially representative of the area where they work).[35]

The kind of support work Barbara and other mothers do intersects the personal realm of war with the politics of war. Mothers like Barbara find themselves at the center of the complex and contentious public discussions of what support means. While the troops need material support during war, the military also needs moral support during war. Military families ensure that their loved ones in the armed services are emotionally supported. The military needs political support from politicians and voters to engage in war, and needs continued political backing to sustain the war effort, and to be successful ultimately. The public is also called on to provide moral support in the form of thanking troops for their service, and respecting the sacrifices military members make for the country. Providing moral support to the troops makes it difficult not to support the war. Phrases such as "support the warrior, not the war" aim to place boundaries around moral support of the warrior, and politically questioning the war.

COMING HOME: SUPPORTING THE WARRIOR, NOT THE WAR

In order to support the troops during deployment, most mothers like Barbara speak out as mothers in support of war. Many consciously decide to not engage in the political process in order to support their children. But the mothers here do make claims of political authority when they rally for the post-deployment care of their children. Only when they perceive that the military has broken their promise to take care of their children by providing health care do mothers rally politically against the military for better care.

When Chris came back from deployment, Barbara became more political active. She bought a yellow ribbon for her car that said, "Support the warrior, not the war." Like many other mothers in this book, she was discouraged by multiple deployments of her son and his friends—"They're drained. How many more times can they be deployed?"

Chris was diagnosed with posttraumatic stress disorder (PTSD) soon after returning home. And immediately Barbara was disappointed with the provided PTSD treatment. She felt that he needed more support from the military to readjust to civilian life. The Veterans Administration (VA) group sessions on war trauma were not helping Chris and his insurance did not cover many psychologists in their area. Barbara started driving Chris a few hours away for weekly therapy and medication changes. She argued with the VA to have his condition classified officially as PTSD so he could receive more benefits. Frustrated with what she saw as inadequate mental health care, Barbara wrote letters to the local newspaper trying to raise awareness for PTSD. She joined a small group of women and wives to lobby the VA and politicians to change that care. Like Barbara, some of the women in this book take a political stance during wartime, especially when it comes to post-deployment health care when they feel "betrayed" by the military.

She described feeling angry that the VA made mental health care so difficult, saying "they owe them more support than what they're getting!" It was only then that she began lobbying for better veterans' care, and in doing so began to criticize the political decisions surrounding the war. In short, military mothers are an example of how a gendered identity like motherhood can lead to engagement, or disengagement, in the political process.

CHAPTER OUTLINE

In chapter 1, "The Bargain: You Made Them Strong, We'll Make Them Army Strong," I show how the military targets mothers for recruitment. I argue that recent shifts in demographics and military needs have shifted recruitment targets toward parents as a potential influencer of the decision to enlist. Specifically, I show how recruitment materials target mothers, and not fathers, in order to recruit. Advertisements, websites, and pamphlets all target mothers and when fathers are depicted they are assumed to be automatically supportive of enlistment. Fathers, according to the recruitment ads, will approve of enlistment and provide guidance during the process. Mothers, on the other hand, are assumed to be an obstacle to enlistment. Military recruiters assume that mothers will not want their children in harm's way, and thus work to convince them that it's "natural" to worry about their children's safety, and that military service is the right decision for their child. In order to manage mothers' worries, the military encourages mothers to take on the duties of providing physical and emotional support for their child, while promising, in turn, to provide training, education, growth, and a future career for their child.

Chapter 2, "Be All That You Can Be: Race and Class in Recruitment," brings in the dimensions of race and class to show that mothers do not equally assume the home front burdens of war. African Americans, increasingly Hispanics, and individuals from lower socioeconomic backgrounds are overrepresented in the service. This chapter shows how the military specifically targets these populations in order to boost recruitment numbers. I show that black single mothers are over-represented in recruitment materials. The military appeals to them through racial stereotypes about black families—that they are damaged and without hope for the future. The military describes itself as a patri-archal institution that can supply the direction and discipline sons are missing from their assumed-to-be absent fathers. Black single mothers are encouraged to be proud of their sons' responsible adult decision to enlist, and to be a part of their children's service as a kind of co-parent with the military institution. In doing this, I argue that the military not only furthers stereotypes of black families, but ensures that these fami-lies are shouldering more than their representative share of the war burden.

Part II turns from recruitment to the deployment stage of military service. In chapter 3, "'Half My Heart Is in Iraq': The Silent Ranks," mothers describe the daily experiences of having a child deployed in a war zone. For these mothers, war is an intensely personal experience. Some mothers ignore news about the war, while some follow everything they can. Like Barbara, these mothers feel separated and isolated from civilians who do not have a loved one at war. This isolation leads moth-ers to seek out groups of others who also have children deployed. Moth-ers, especially those who do not live near military bases, turn to the Internet to find camaraderie among other mothers. In these groups, mothers support one another through the daily stresses and worries of deployment. These online groups organize support drives for the troops, supplying everything from emotional support (cards, letters) to care packages of physical support. Some groups also organize "support the troops" events in their communities to raise awareness of the ongo-ing war. It is in these groups that mothers collectively work out the different meanings of support. Like the group I first encountered on-line, personal support of other mothers and of the troops is of primary importance.

Chapter 4, "'My Son Fights for Your Freedom': The Politics of Sup-port," examines the tensions in online support groups over what support and politics mean during war. The patriotic military images (like Army Moms' combat boots) on the websites mirror the way that mothers feel they are enlisted in the military along with their children. Every online group varies as to how much political discussion they allow, and what they count as political. Many groups have "no politics" rules enforced by moderators and other members. But pro-war discussions are regular on these boards, and are considered part of maternal support and do not count as political. Antiwar discussions, on the other hand, are considered political and harmful to the troops and the war effort. Mothers like Barbara learn to silence their criticism of the war in these spaces in order to provide unconditional love and support for the troops.

Part III is about the post-deployment experiences of mothers. Chapter 5, "Returning Home: The Invisible Burden of Caregiving," details the kinds of care veterans need when they return home from deployment. Mothers participate in two kinds of support for veterans. In groups, mothers ensure that veterans are thanked for their service and feel appreciated when they return home. In addition to this moral support, mothers are often the primary caretakers for wounded veterans. With tens of thousands of service members returning to the United States physically injured with incapacitating injuries such as amputations, and hundreds of thousands diagnosed with PTSD, service members from these wars need a tremendous amount of medical care. The mothers in this chapter make drastic life changes to provide health care for their veteran, sometimes giving up their jobs to provide twenty-four-hour care.

In chapter 6, "The Few, the Proud, the Forgotten," I look at what happens when mothers perceive that the military has not lived up to their side of the bargain to take care of the service member. After trusting that the military will care for their children by providing post-deployment health care, the mothers in this chapter are disappointed when their children do not receive the health care they need. Mothers who silenced their own criticism of the war and the military during deployment describe a sense of betrayal and speak out publicly in order to improve veterans' care. Here, mothers speak out politically, but do so as mothers who are caring for their children. The same sense of maternal duty that silenced their political activism during deployment becomes a means for protesting the VA, advocating for improvements that would help care for veterans with PTSD, amputations, and traumatic brain injuries (TBIs).

Part I

Recruitment

I

THE BARGAIN

You Made Them Strong,
We'll Make Them Army Strong

I had no idea Ben wanted to join the military. Not a clue. As a child
he was always a shy, quiet boy. I guess you'd call him a nerd. Kids
used to tease him, actually, because his grades were so good. I really
thought he would go to college. Maybe take a year off first, but go to
college.

—Cindy

Cindy is a forty-four-year-old married mother of three children. She
opened our correspondence about her son's military service by reflect-
ing on how she found out her son Ben wanted to join the Army. Her
father served in the Navy during WWII, but she had no other military
family history. Her husband, Ed, was an engineer, and she worked part
time as a teacher's aide while her children were in school. Her daughters were twelve and fourteen, and Ben was the oldest. She was surprised when he joined the military shortly after turning eighteen. Ed
was supportive of Ben's enlistment if it meant he would go to college.
Cindy's initial response was to wish that he would somehow not qualify
for service.

At the time I wished he had something that would disqualify him—
like ADD. See, for a long time in elementary school we thought he
had ADD, but he was never actually diagnosed. He had a fourth-

grade teacher who gave him lots of structure and helped him organize his school work and study habits. And he had some speech
therapy. He caught up with his peers and then started to surpass
them, grade-wise. He was reading at a high school level by sixth
grade! So he was not disqualified, passed his physical exam and did
well on the ASVAB. The recruiter was so happy to snatch him right
up.

But his test results were good and Ben enlisted. After his exam,
Cindy accompanied Ben to the recruitment center to pick up paperwork. She explained how apprehensive she was about meeting people
in the Army, particularly recruiters.

> I'd never been to that strip mall before. I must have passed it hun-
> dreds of times—multiple times a day—but never went in. It was
> strange to find the Army recruitment office next to an upscale light-
> ing store! Like, "pick up a new chandelier and then enlist!" . . . The
> recruitment officer was such a gentleman. He shook my hand, held it
> for a while in a friendly way. Then he sat me down to talk with me
> about Ben. He told me I should be proud of having "such a fine son."

Ben was never a top student. Cindy described him as someone who
"never applied himself" in school, "he's probably much smarter than he
thinks he is." She was never sure what he would wind up doing, or
whether he'd go to college. In praising her son and his decision, and
describing post-service college opportunities, the recruitment officer
made a positive impression on Cindy. He also took the time to answer
some of her questions about the training her son would receive, and the
kinds of careers he could prepare for. She described the recruiter as
"warm and personable" even in his full uniform. She left the recruiting
office feeling "much better" about his choice to enlist, and even proud
of the way Ben composed himself with the recruiter.

> I'd never seen him so respectful and courteous. Of course we raise
> our children to be those things but you're never sure how they'll turn
> out. Ben was so respectful. He looked the recruiter in the eye, and
> stood tall. That was really something to see.

Cindy's experience is exactly what recruiters want for mothers of
recruits. Parents are encouraged to be a part of the recruitment pro-

cess, but mothers are treated differently from fathers. Fathers are assumed to know more about the military, and are assumed to be supportive of enlistment. Mothers, on the other hand, can be either a barrier or a gateway to enlistment. Recruiters want to recognize and soothe mothers' worries, while convincing mothers that their children are making a good decision. Recruiters want the chance to explain the benefits of service, and make them feel proud that their children have made an adult, mature decision to enlist. This chapter details why and how mothers like Cindy are important in the recruitment process and how the military helps them feel as if they are part of the process.

FILLING THE RANKS

> Ma'am, I'm SGT Ring, John's Army representative. The reason I'm calling is to discuss the many opportunities available to John in today's Army. Ma'am, do you happen to know what John's planning to do after graduation?" (Response) "Ma'am, that's exactly why I'm calling. The Army offers guaranteed state-of-the-art skill training that will help him get a good job and education programs that can pay for his college education. I think it would be worth John's time to hear what the Army has to offer, wouldn't you agree? Ma'am when would be a good time to catch John at home?
>
> —*U.S. Army Recruitment Manual*, 2007

The most basic need of the military is troops to fill the ranks. Since the end of conscription and the beginning of the AVF in 1973, the military has been concerned with maintaining adequate troop levels. To do this the military spends six billion dollars on advertising and recruitment efforts. Recruitment efforts include hiring the advertising firm McCann Worldgroup, researching how to reach those with a "high propensity to enlist," and staffing local recruitment offices with personnel trained vis-à-vis training manuals and scripts, like the one above, to recruit in the most effective way possible. In short, recruitment of new enlistees is vital to the military, and is treated with the same strategic effort as any other military mission.

Recruitment advertising messages are crafted to meet the concerns and ambitions of each generation. Just as the sample script above emphasizes job skills and education, recruitment after Vietnam specifically de-emphasized the battlefield, drawing attention to the benefits to college and careers. The Vietnam conflict was considered a loss, casualty rates were high, and Americans experienced gruesome images of war at home on their televisions. After Vietnam, instead of focusing on battles, advertisements emphasized military technology and on service as an opportunity for education and a career. Common recruitment themes in the 1980s were appeals to patriotism, desire for adventure, and travel opportunities—"see the world"—with little mention of war itself.[1]

If the military was a choice after conscription then recruitment materials maximized the message that it was a choice that came with benefits, including higher social status for those who enlist. In the 1990s, the military amplified the themes of humanitarianism ("change the world") and personal development ("be all that you can be") in campaigns.[2] The focus was on individuals who wanted to reach their full potential, while using their personal achievements to help others.[3] Recruitment advertising focused on what the military could do for an individual—how the military could transform an individual into "An Army of One." This often included talking to key influencers—teachers, parents, clergy, etc.—but the primary target of recruitment was the individual making the decision to join the military and to change himself or herself in the process.

Recruitment levels remained constant until the late 1990s, when enlistment numbers dropped across all branches. By the late 1990s the military began to struggle to meet recruitment goals. As a result, the military began to adapt recruitment tactics to meet the needs of the current generation of enlistees. New strategies included targeting potential enlistees with military video games, increasing the military's presence on the Internet and in social media, and further encouraging influencers (parents, teachers, coaches, etc.) to support, and even suggest, service as a pathway to college and a career. As the recruitment script above illustrates, talking to parents became a crucial part of the enlistment process.[4]

US WAR ON TERRORISM RECRUITMENT STRATEGY

Recruitment strategies shifted again in the early 2000s. Despite a small bump in enlistment immediately after the terrorist attacks of September 11, 2001, after several years of war in Afghanistan and Iraq, the military was missing recruitment goals. Initially, recruitment advertising after 9/11 was bolstered by a renewed focus on patriotism as an appeal to enlist. Recruitment ads centered on the themes of national pride, belonging to the military (as part of a team), and protecting the nation that was attacked.[5]

By 2006 casualties were high and public support for the War on Terrorism was trending down for the first time since 9/11.[6] Therefore, five years into the War on Terrorism, the military drastically altered recruitment strategy by hiring the advertising firm McCann Worldgroup to develop a new multibillion-dollar marketing campaign,[7] and commissioning research organizations like RAND to produce a series of strategic reports on recruitment and youth demographics.[8]

The new advertising campaign not only developed a series of television and print advertisements for recruitment, but also embraced online technologies as part of the strategy for reaching youth.[9] For example, recruitment websites included options such as "talk to a virtual recruiter" or "ask a soldier" where recruits could interact in real time with the military, asking questions and getting personalized information. The military also began to utilize Web 2.0 technology, developing Myspace and Facebook pages for each branch, and adding their advertisements and informational videos to YouTube.[10]

With casualty numbers mounting in the War on Terrorism, military recruiters started to recognize that showing images of service members fighting a war against terrorists "in the sandbox" was no longer working for recruitment. Images of urban warfare and vehicle ambushes emphasized the dangers of war. Advertisements began to focus less on the dangerous "excitement" of war (like a video game) and more on the opportunities of service for education and career. Advertising also began to focus specifically on parents who would be more invested in personal and professional growth than in (potentially dangerous) adventure. Each branch developed web pages for parents of recruits. The Marines encouraged parents with images of young people lined up in uniform with the tagline "Your Son. Your Daughter. Our Country" and the page categories "Making Marines" and "Developing Strong Citizens." The Army developed a companion campaign to their new "Army Strong" campaign just for parents, with a tagline acknowledging parents' work in raising soldiers: "You made them strong. We'll make them Army Strong."

TARGETING PARENTS

John, I realize this is an important decision in your life and you would like to discuss it with your parents. I would like to be there with you to answer any questions they might have.

—A "contingent close" script in the
U.S. Army Recruitment Manual, 2007

When recruiters begin to talk with a young adult like Ben about enlistment, they create what's called a "blueprint" detailing the potential enlistee's road to the military. Parents figure prominently in recruitment blueprints as "potential obstacles" to enlistment. Recruiters are trained to engage directly with parents, sometimes even before speaking with the potential recruit. Heading off or "calming" any "fears or apprehensions" mothers like Cindy might have is a key part of recruiting successfully. As the suggested "contingent close" dialogue shows, recruits are even encouraged to include the recruiter in the conversation when they talk with their parents about the armed services. Cindy was so impressed with her son's recruitment officer, she came to think of him as her connection to the military, calling him with questions about where her son would be deployed—"He couldn't tell me what Ben's deployment would eventually be, but he gave me examples of the kinds of work Ben might do. That made me feel better and made me look forward to seeing what he was capable of."

Targeting parents is a significant change in how the military perceives military service. While military service has always been a family affair, these advertising strategies extended to the recruit's parents. Indeed, for most recruits, their parents are their immediate family members, as most are single at the time of enlistment. Previously, a service member was more of an "Army of One," sometimes with spouses and children to support. Recognizing the importance of service members' immediate families, the military created spousal support structures, family health care, and childcare services during the 1980s and 1990s.[11] In 2005 the military ended the "Army of One" campaign, replacing it with the "Army Strong" campaign that included more family members—like parents—in recruitment efforts. At the same time, new en-listees are younger than they were in the past. In 2015, 62 percent of Army recruits and 73 percent of Marine recruits were between seven-teen and twenty years old at the time of enlistment.[12]

Part of acknowledging parental involvement in recruitment is the military responding to the increasingly delayed transition to adulthood among young people.[13] In previous generations, leaving home after high school (and marrying and having children soon after), was the marker of adulthood. Now, adulthood consists of "five core transitions": "leaving home, completing school, entering the workforce, getting mar-ried, and having children";[14] these core transitions are happening later in children's lives than previous generations, so that children might not reach these transitions until their twenties or thirties.[15] More young adults are living at home into their twenties and thirties, so that parents continue to have direct influence over the career and education deci-sions they make. Institutions like college and the military become step-ping-stones to ease young adults' transitions to independence, and par-ents remain a key influence in their children's life. Military enlistment usually signals adulthood, but with younger recruits, and markers of adulthood that come later, recruits today are in a sort of suspended state of young adulthood.

With increasing influence over their not-quite-adult children, by 2005, parents are very real obstacles to recruitment. Not only has public approval of the war slipped; parental support for military service has dropped. But potential recruits still identify parents as key players in their decision to enlist. Recruiters found themselves "vexed by a gener-ation of more activist parents who have no qualms about projecting their own views onto their children" (i.e., discouraging enlistment).[16] In 2004 only 25 percent of parents would encourage their children to go into the military—a number that dropped significantly from 42 percent of parents who would encourage service in 2003.[17] As a result of less parental support, the military tripled the number of advertisements targeting parents, and worked to counteract parents' hesitations about military service with information about the benefits of military service for their children.[18] As a gateway to recruitment, the military focused on bargaining with parents—offering to take care of their children and provide them with personal growth and opportunities, in exchange for sending their children to a war zone.

PROUD FATHERS AND WORRIED MOTHERS

> FATHER: She's a typical mother, worried about her child leaving her.
> MOTHER: I was worried about him at first; number one, he's never
> been away from home. And we have been real protective of him.

Military advertising campaigns launched in 2005 focused on mothers and fathers, but targeted each parent differently. As the short conversation above from an online recruitment video shows, parents' reactions to potential enlistment are depicted as gendered. Military advertisements assume that fathers would be automatic supporters of military service, whereas mothers are assumed to be unsupportive of putting their children in danger. Fathers are portrayed as having pride in their children's decision to join, but mothers need to be convinced of the benefits of service for their children before they are portrayed as proud of his or her enlistment.

From 2006 to 2009, 97 percent of all advertisements and model stories online feature mothers, and like the conversation example above, 44 percent of those also feature fathers. When fathers are present, they are portrayed very differently. Stories about mothers coming to terms with the recruit's decision are the most prevalent part of parental recruitment websites (they make up 71 percent of stories online). The advertisements, like the one above, featuring mothers present them as "typical" if they "worry" about "her child leaving her," that she's "protective" and "he's never been away from home." This example conversation is one of the few times that the recruit is described as a "child" instead of a recruit, or soldier, Marine, etc. Referring to the service member as a "child" highlights the gendered role of the "typical mom" worrying about her son. The father refers to her motherly worry, but does not express any worry himself. The assumption is that he already approves of the decision to serve.

A television commercial for the "You made them strong, we'll make them Army Strong" campaign also shows the dynamic between the automatically supportive father and the mother who needs to be convinced.

> DAD: Listen, son: I just want to check. I thought the plan was for you
> to go to college. [As the son begins to speak, his mother enters the
> room and stands behind him, listening in.]

SON: Dad, this is all part of the plan. The army is going to help me. What's more, the training and experience that I get—it'll change my life. I'll become stronger.
DAD: I know.
SON: So can we go and talk to her?
[The mother smiles and approaches the son.]
DAD: We already have.

The son initially approaches his father for support to join the military, and to help him break the news to his mother. The son's trepidation about telling his mother illustrates the assumption that mothers of potential recruits will initially resist enlistment based on their emotions and lack of information about the military. Another commercial for Today's Military titled "Game Day" similarly illustrates the automatic support of fathers and the assumption that mothers will need to be convinced.

[The son, in a football uniform, talks to his father who is sitting in a truck, with a football field behind him.]
DAD: How was practice?
SON: Coach said I was a leader.
DAD: [nodding] You are.
SON: [pauses] That's what they look for in the military.
DAD: Was that his idea?
SON: No, mine. I like being part of a team, and the physical challenge. I think I'd be good at it.
DAD: You would be. But, I've got some questions. [pause] And I think someone else might, too.
SON: Mom? [chuckles]
DAD: [chuckles] Get home early.

In addition to showing that mothers will need to be convinced that the military is a good choice, this commercial also shows an alliance between fathers and sons. Fathers and sons are assumed to have a common bond in making the decision to serve, and that disparages the mother's role in decision making. The father knows his son would be good at military service, but the mother will have questions and concerns. Her approval is a kind of afterthought to the father-son conversation and decision to enlist.

Given that convincing mothers is a primary goal of recruitment advertising, it seems contradictory that mothers are also depicted as an afterthought to the decision to join the service. This contradiction illustrates the gendered assumptions about military service. Not only are mothers assumed to be initially non-supportive of service; they are also assumed to not understand the military. As women, traditionally left out of the armed services until only recently, mothers are the ones who will need to be educated about the masculine military institution through their sons, husbands, and recruiters. Fathers may have some questions and concerns (as Ed did about Ben prioritizing college) but they are not expected to stand in the way of service as mothers may, so their worries need less military intervention during the recruitment process.

OVERVIEW OF RECRUITING THROUGH MOTHERS

For mothers with no other military family members, each step of the process of enlistment, training, and recruitment is a new experience. The mothers I interviewed describe a steep learning curve with the large and complex military institution. Through their parental relationship with their child, mothers go through a process of becoming a part of the military institution—a part of an extended military family. In recruiting material, the military depicts mothers going through a transitional process of understanding their recruit's decision to serve. Mothers such as Cindy are initially apprehensive about giving up their children to military service, so they must be convinced by recruiters and recruitment materials that the military is the right choice for their child. During the process, mothers are asked to make a bargain with the military. They agree to let their children join and support their children during service, and the military promises to provide the opportunities and transformation that will make their children successful adults.

This process has three steps. First, mothers are convinced by military recruiters and their children that the benefits of service (education, training, and career benefits) outweigh their worry. Second, after they see their children's growth (often referred to as "becoming a man") during training mothers are depicted as proud of their children and their service. Finally, as part of the process of building pride, mothers are encouraged to feel as if they too are a part of the military. Part of this co-enlistment is to feel that they and their support for their children are vital to military success. Cindy described feeling as though she could help make her son, Ben, successful during his service—"Ben needed me to get him ready for training, and I knew he would need me to be strong during deployment." The support the Department of Defense asks mothers to provide is unconditional support not just for the troops, but also for their mission. Unconditional support for the military as an institution and for all its particular actions becomes the only way, in Department of Defense materials, that mothers of service members can hold up their end of the bargain by taking care of their children.

MANAGING MOTHERS' WORRY

> As a mother I had so much anxiety about my son enlisting. How will he do in Basic Training? Will he be able to specialize in something that helps him in his future career? Our Army recruiter made sure I had the information I needed to feel better about his enlistment.
>
> —Go Army Parents website

As this quote from the Army Parents website shows, the military begins by acknowledging the anxiety that mothers in particular, and not necessarily fathers, have about their children going to war. Mothers are shown needing reassurance that the military is a good choice for their child. As one recruiter explained,

> We can provide the information they need to assure them that the recruit is making the right decision, and that they should feel proud. And usually it's the Mom we spend the most time talking with. She's the one who has the most concerns. Dads might also be concerned, but they don't really show it. They're more resolute about it. Dads don't require the same kind of convincing.

Recruiters are both a source of information and socialization into the military, and encouraging pride is a key part of discouraging worry. Fathers are described as irrelevant in this process of turning worry into pride. Their concerns are either more concealed—"they don't really show it"—or like Cindy's husband, Ed, more pragmatic. They may be more concerned with pragmatic decisions like making sure college is part of the plan, instead of the emotional worry of mothers.

By drawing a strong division between fathers' and mothers' concerns, recruitment advertising reiterates gender difference in parenting, showing fathers and mothers as parental opposites (mothers as emotional, fathers as pragmatic). Providing quotes, like the one above, from nervous mothers is one way that recruitment materials show mothers that they are not alone in their worry, that it is natural for them to be nervous and have concerns. This both acknowledges mothers' worry, and dismisses any worry fathers might have—as the recruiter above explained, fathers may even feel they should hide their concerns.

The parent-child relationship in recruitment advertising is also shaped by gender difference. The majority of recruitment advertisements focus on sons; with rising rates of female enlistment, daughters are sometimes included. The relationship between parents and daughters in the military is presented slightly differently than that of parents and sons. Fathers display pride in their daughters' decision to join just as they do for sons, and mothers are initially apprehensive. The difference lies in how the recruits are portrayed. Male recruits, especially nonwhite ones, are often portrayed as needing the direction and discipline the military provides. The military is seen as a remedy for "guy culture," channeling sons' interests in adventure (and potential mischief) into productivity through education and work opportunities.[19]

On the other hand, daughters who enlist are presented as ambitious—they want to change the world, or do something good with their service. Female enlistees more often join the military after completing their college education, and therefore do not have the same need to transition to adulthood within the confines of the military.[20] Women recruits tend to be older than their male counterparts are when they enlist, tend to have shorter careers in the military, and tend to use the military to further their education and get a better job.[21] In short, male recruits are portrayed as *needing* the military to become adults, and female recruits are depicted as already making adult decisions.[22]

COMBATING WORRY WITH INFORMATION

> Your son mentions enlistment and a million things rush into your head. We're hoping one or two of those things are facts.
>
> —Today's Military advertisement

One of the primary goals of recruitment advertising is to help mothers understand the opportunities and benefits of military service so that their pride for their children overshadows their worry. Mothers' anxiety about their recruit going to war is also portrayed as a kind of gendered ignorance about the military. If they learned more about the military, they would support enlistment; as the mother above explained, "Our Army recruiter made sure I had the information I needed." Fathers are shown as knowing all they need to know about military service. Mothers are assumed to be uninformed in general, and particularly uninformed about the opportunities and benefits of the military. Even though going to war is dangerous for their children, recruitment materials show mothers who do not yet know enough about the military to be fully supportive of their child.

The idea is that once mothers learn the education, training, and career benefits—once they know "the facts"—they will be accepting, supportive, and proud of their children's decision to join. The Today's Military "Make it a two-way conversation. Get the facts" campaign, quoted above, starts by acknowledging worry and fear, and then encourages mothers to get facts by going online to learn more about service. The ads ran in women's magazines such as *Ladies Home Journal*, *Reader's Digest*, and *Good Housekeeping*. One of these ads shows a mother and son in the car together. The text states, "Talking with your son about the Military has you anxious and emotional. It's times like this, facts are reassuring." These ads depict anxiety and worry as a first stage, uninformed response by mothers of new recruits but override it by focusing on "facts." For example, text on the TodaysMilitary.com website quotes Sherrie, a mother, describing how her head (the facts) eventually won out over her heart (worry and emotion): "Upon considering the educational, financial and travel opportunities the Military had to offer, Sherrie put it best, 'My head won out over my heart.'"

In order for mothers' "heads to win out over their hearts," the military provides information about how military service will benefit recruits. The majority of military recruitment web pages are devoted to explaining the education and career opportunities offered by the military (64 percent of the Marine Corps web pages, and 72 percent of Army web pages). Each Department of Defense website, like Todays-Military.com, has specific information pages for parents about the opportunities the military offers. The Today's Military website suggests facts as an antidote to worry and fear. The web page for parents opens with the following:

> When considering the Military, your child may look to you for support or advice, so it's important to know the facts. The resources presented here will give you the information you need to keep the conversation going.

The "facts" presented online focus on the non-war-related aspects of service such as pay, health care, money for education, and post-military career training opportunities. Material for parents of new recruits focuses on their military as a career, providing both short-term and potentially long-term employment. These websites often begin discussions of military opportunities by addressing how the military can fulfill the recruit's aspirations, and parents' aspirations for their recruit. The Todays Military website splash page for parents asserts that their children can reach their "potential" "no matter what" their career aspirations are.

> No matter what your son or daughter's career aspirations, chances are we offer a job and the training that will help them realize their potential. And if they don't have any career aspirations yet, we can help guide them in a positive direction.

Implicit in this quote is that the recruit may not be heading in a "positive direction" before choosing to serve in the armed forces—that mothers fear their children do not have the opportunities they should. This illustrates how military resources work to soothe mothers' fears about their children enlisting by invoking less explicit worries that parents might have about their children without directly naming them. For example, referring to the benefits of money for a college education and job training targets mothers' fears of being able to afford their children's education. Furthermore, explaining the economic opportunities (signing bonuses, futures in technology and other marketable careers), speaks to mothers' worry about their children's present and future economic stability. When the military describes the benefits of direction and discipline for the recruit, they address mothers' unnamed worries about their children's continued adolescence and irresponsibility.

MAKING THE BARGAIN

Through the recruitment process parents are asked to support their children's decision to serve, and in exchange, parents are promised that the military will provide training, education, and career opportunities. For example, the website for parents of potential National Guard recruits includes a frequently asked questions (FAQ) section that includes the following entry.

> Some parents are surprised—even shocked when their child announces they want to join the military. So many questions. So many concerns.
> Rest assured: the Army National Guard will give your child the skills, confidence, leadership, and discipline it takes to succeed in life. They'll grow physically strong in basic training. They'll train for the career of their dreams throughout their service. We'll cover college tuition and expenses, and give them the real-world experience employers look for on resumes. It's a competitive world out there. Explore these links and find out how the Guard can give your child the edge and help them fulfill their potential.

The entry itself echoes the anxiety and emotion ("surprised" and "shocked") experienced when parents learn that their children want to join the military. While the gender-neutral term "parents" is used here, the content is directed implicitly toward mothers: the picture accompanying the entry is of a mother, and the sidebar of the page includes quotes from other mothers concerned about their sons "fulfilling their potential." In response to worry, the military urges mothers to "rest assured" that this choice is best for their child.

The military promises parents that their children's "dreams can be pursued" in the military by describing all the benefits of service. Websites for parents go into the technology, training, and career options that each branch offers. FAQ sections detail signing bonuses and money to attend college. When stories refer to what an enlistee can achieve in the military, it is often to set parents (especially mothers) up as potentially standing in the way of those goals by not letting them join. For instance:

> LET YOUR CHILD PURSUE HIS OR HER DREAMS. Law enforcement. Engineering. Law. Medicine. No matter where your son's or daughter's interests lie, the Army offers expert training in a wide range of careers: 120 in the Army Reserve and 150 in active Army. Whether they choose to explore a new career or strengthen their current one, hands-on experience will give them an edge.

In addition to describing the benefits of service for success in a civilian career, mothers' concerns about their children enlisting are also countered by describing military service as a job. Describing the military as a civilian job moves the focus away from the dangerous aspects of service (i.e., deployment and war). For example, the Army website's descriptions of "active duty" and "enlisted" emphasizes that military service is like a full-time job (with free time off), and that working for the Army is similar to being an employee of a company:

> Active Duty is similar to working at a full-time, civilian job. There are hours when Soldiers must be training or performing their jobs and then there are off-hours when Soldiers can do what they like. In Active Duty, terms of service range from two to six years.
> Enlisted Soldiers put plans into action. Much like employees at a company, they perform specific job functions and have the training and knowledge that ensures the success of their unit's current mission within the Army.

Defining military service as "similar" to a full-time civilian job aims to make mothers feel better about their children choosing to do something that is potentially dangerous.

Sometimes military service is even depicted as better than civilian employment. Unlike most civilian jobs, military service includes on-the-job training, money for education, and worldwide travel opportunities. For example, a quote from the "Life as a Marine" section of the Marine parents' website compares being a Marine to a nine-to-five job, arguing that the Marine Corps offers benefits and opportunities "not found in the private sector."

The Marine Corps lifestyle is about as far from a 9-to-5 job as one could imagine, with travel, adventure, and opportunities for advancement and leadership not often found in the private sector. Marines also receive a host of benefits, including free on-base housing, full medical benefits, free- or low-cost educational opportunities, and more, from a grateful nation.

A similar description of service refers to "amenities" and an excellent "quality of life" on the air force website:

As a member of the U.S. Air Force, your son or daughter will have more opportunities than they ever thought possible! As an Airman, your child will have access to more than just a wonderful career; their quality of life will be excellent due to our outstanding base amenities, living quarters, travel opportunities, and recreational activities.

The military is arguing that service is similar to a nine-to-five civilian job, but it is also better than one because it offers more valuable opportunities and benefits. Comparisons to civilian employment normalizes military service for mothers and takes the focus off the realities of war (that military service means using weapons and killing people, or being wounded or killed). Painting military service as a safe job makes it more likely mothers will want to support enlistment.

Just as recruitment websites discuss jobs, training, and education instead of the dangerous aspects of service (deployment), parents are assured repeatedly that military service does not always mean combat. The Army National Guard/Reserve website includes the following in the questions and answers section for parents:

What are the chances that my young adult will be deployed to support the Global War on Terrorism?

It depends on the Army branch the Cadet chooses and the unit to which he/she is assigned. However, Army missions and challenges are always changing, so there's no way to know in advance which specialties and units will be needed where. All Soldiers in the Army or Army Reserve face the possibility of deployment at some point during their careers. But all Soldiers are fully trained and proficient in the tasks and drills of their units. And Officers are specifically trained to make the right decisions so that missions can be carried out safely and successfully.

This answer downplays whether the recruit is deployed in the war on terrorism by explaining that deployment depends upon many factors—the branch, the unit, their specialties, and the mission at hand. Despite all those variables, mothers are told that if their recruit is deployed, they have the best training and the best officers that will work to keep him or her not only safe, but also successful in the mission. Notice how safety is linked with success in this quote. Tying success in the mission (winning the war) with the safety of the recruit (the recruit returning home alive) makes questioning the war difficult for mothers. The safety of their children depends on the success of the mission.

Part of making a bargain with mothers is to convince them that they can trust the military to keep their children safe, something that seems counterintuitive to potentially dangerous service in the armed forces. For example, a smiling mother on an Army recruitment page explains:

> As far as the training and the Army and the program and the units and how they handle themselves, I've always been impressed with the lengths that the Army and the entire military go to keep Soldiers safe.

Recruitment materials try to convince mothers that they do everything they can to keep service members safe. They focus on training and technology and deemphasize participation in war in order to alleviate mothers' fears. Instead, they assure mothers that they can trust the military to prepare their children for whatever—unnamed—activities they might encounter. For example, on the Army Reserve website a mother describes, "There's no doubt in my mind that the Army Reserve has prepared Naomi for deployment; to teach her to be the best Soldier that she could be." Similarly, the Army website describes a mother who "felt a mixture of pride in her son and trust in the Army [that] offset Cathy's anxiety. If John was prepared, she could be too." Building this trust in the military, however, also makes it difficult for a mother to question the military without being perceived as questioning her child's own accomplishments. The military institution and the child's training and accomplishments become intricately tied.

Another way the military downplays war and sells itself as an institution that takes care of service members is by describing military service as similar to college. For instance, each branch's website for parents includes a section, much as one would find on a college website, describing service members' everyday lives during training and deployment. The "daily life" section on the Army website shows pictures of on-base facilities such as dorms for single soldiers, common rooms, dining halls, and fitness facilities. Websites even list sample menus for food during basic training, ensuring parents that their children will receive balanced meals. The following quote, for example, could easily be found in a college brochure (just replace the word "training" with "studying").

> When your son or daughter is done with the day's work or training, the rest of the day is theirs to do whatever they like: work out, shop, do laundry, go to a movie or hang out with friends, just to name a few.

As in college admissions material, the military is also described in terms of quality-of-life opportunities. This reflects a similar trend in college recruiting to include more information about quality of life; parents are increasingly involved in the daily lives of students as "helicopter parents."[23] Just like college students, recruits are adults but still need to be taken care of during their training and deployment, so quality-of-life issues matter for parents. This also suggests that parents continue to "raise" their children along with the military—that mothers and the military (especially for single African American mothers, as I describe in the next chapter) are co-parenting recruits. Enlisting may be a sign of adulthood, but the military can help the recruit grow up.

PRIDE AND SUCCESSFUL PARENTING

Recruitment websites contain stories of mothers going through transformations—from initially worrying about their children's enlistment, to becoming proud of his or her decision and accomplishments. One story, featured throughout the Army website, is about Deb, a mother who describes being initially "shocked and scared" that her daughter, Jodie, wanted to join the Army. Through a series of pages complete with photos and quotes, the website takes readers through the stages of Deb's transformation. She starts out scared, then learns the benefits of service for her daughter's future career, and finally is shown as proud of her daughter's accomplishments in basic combat training (BCT).

The recruiter is a central part of the story. He includes Deb in the recruitment process and provides information to counter her concerns. Deb's questions about her daughter's enlistment are eased by the recruiter, who stresses the opportunities that the Army offers Jodie—opportunities that include paying off college loans, training, and experience for her career. Deb's story is told on the Army Parents website:

> Deb began to feel more comfortable when they met with Army Recruiter Tom Brown. He grew up near their family in Maine, and she saw how the Army had strengthened him. His honest answers helped ease her concerns.
>
> Tom explained how the Army would give Jodie the advanced training she needed for a better career, the leadership opportunities she wanted for a better future and the financial assistance to pay off her college loans. The concerns were still there, but now so was Deb's support. The decision was Jodie's to make—a decision that could give her just what she'd been searching for.
>
> In Jodie's letters home, Deb could track her daughter's progress: from doubting her ability to realizing her goals to achieving success. That success was on full display at Jodie's BCT graduation– a day the entire family will remember for a long time.
>
> Beyond their daughter beaming with pride, the first thing Deb noticed at BCT graduation was Jodie's newfound sense of honor, respect and responsibility—a reflection of the Seven Core Army Values, the true distinctions of a Soldier.

Deb's story shows how the military encourages mothers to be a part of their children's progress and accomplishments in the military. Deb is shown as involved and supportive of her daughter through training—she tracks her progress through letters from Jodie. Finally, at BCT graduation Deb notices how much her daughter has grown during basic training—that she has taken on a responsible adult role. As a result of this newfound growth, Deb "beams with pride," without any of the worry she might have initially had about the armed services.

The pride that parents gain from watching their children grow up within the military is a significant benefit of service. On recruitment websites mothers are described as witnessing their children's transformation as a move into the adult world. As the "You made them strong, we'll make them Army Strong" slogan suggests, the army picks up where parents left off, helping their children transition into adulthood. The new, successful recruit is a reflection of successful parenting. The Marine Corps website encourages parents to recognize and be proud of the "first adult decision" their child makes to join the military. Mothers describe first seeing their children as adults when they make the decision to enlist, and then seeing them as a new person—an adult and often specifically a man—at the end of basic training.

After not seeing their children during the months of training, this transformation is especially striking. For example, a mother on the army website is shown beaming with pride standing with her son in his army uniform at graduation. For this mother, the army "helps you grow up."

> I think the Army is a great opportunity for a young man or woman because it gives them the time to really see what they want to do. I think it helps you grow up, whether you stay in just for two years or three years or you make a career of it.

This particular mother describes to potential recruits how the military helps them grow whether they stay in it as a short-term option or as a lifetime career. Another example from the Marine Corps website emphasizes how parents will see the process of transforming recruits into Marines—independent adults with "self-discipline, leadership skills, and courage."

> During the 13 weeks of Recruit Training, your son or daughter will be transformed into a Marine.
> As a recruit, he or she will be physically and mentally challenged every day. During 13 weeks of Recruit Training, they will be transformed into Marines. As a Marine, your son or daughter will have self-discipline, leadership skills, and courage—qualities that will help them both in and out of the Corps.

Emphasizing the gendered relationship between mothers and sons, mothers are often depicted as having pride not in their recruit's transformation into an adult, but in their son's transformation into a man. A mother in a TodaysMilitary.com video explains this about her sons:

> When they came home I had to look at both boys as not being boys anymore, but being men. I think that the way I started treating them was more mature. . . . I had to stop seeing them as just teenagers. They've earned the right to be treated as adults.

For this mother, the military not only helped her sons become men; it changed her relationship with them because they had "earned the right to be treated as adults." Another featured story titled "Finding His Own Way" tells of a mother watching her son join the Air National Guard and becoming "self-sufficient," "thinking for themselves," and "managing their own lives." She explains,

> Even though I was nervous, I was a little scared about it, I knew it was good for Eric. I knew that he would come out of it being a better person, and being a better man. A man able to support himself and his future family.

Here, part of the process of becoming a man also has to do with being "self-sufficient" financially, and even being able to support a future family. The military provides (male) recruits with job opportunities and training that will help them live up to the gendered expectation that as men they will be the ones supporting their families in the future.

ENLISTING MOTHERS

There is a bit of a paradox, however, in encouraging mothers to recognize their children's transformation into adults. The recruit is depicted as strong enough to make an adult decision to join the armed forces. In some cases, the decision to join is the first adult decision a recruit makes. The recruits might become adults during training and deployment, but they still need family support during enlistment, deployment, and veteran's care. The military relies on families to supplement supplies with care packages and to bolster troops with emotional and moral support. Recruitment material encourages mothers to feel that they are a part of the enlistment process, and then relies on them as a necessary part of the military support system when their children enlist.

To encourage this co-enlistment, recruitment advertisements depict mothers also going through a transformation in the military. Mothers who worry when their children first announce that they may enlist come to learn about the military institution and what it can do for their children. Mothers are shown going through the emotions of training and deployment along with their children. They come to share their recruits' pride in their service to country and learn that they can help in that service. For example, the introduction page of the Marine Parents website tells mothers that it is something they "can be a part of."

> With service to country comes the highest level of training and success—both in defending our country and in a Marine's personal life. Marines win battles and develop into quality citizens. It is a difficult road, but one you can be proud your son or daughter is considering. It is also something that you can be part of.

For mothers, support of their enlisted children during wartime means being unconditionally supportive of their children's decision, and giving up certain parental rights by sharing parenting with the military. As the Go Army Parents website explains,

> Your Soldier has chosen this profession. While it's natural for you to worry, your Soldier still deserves your full support because your nation's security is now in your Soldier's well-trained hands.

Here, the choice the soldier makes to enlist deserves "full support" from parents. Full support is also linked to national security. In other words, parental support is key for the troops to be successful at their important job—keeping the nation safe. Here, physical and emotional support are connected to moral and political support for war, and the suggestion is that parents cannot supply one without supplying the other. This makes it more difficult for mothers to potentially question the moral and political rationalization for war.

Being a supportive mother—providing emotional support—begins with supporting her child's decision to serve. For example, in these quotes on the Marine Parents website, mothers describe themselves as "having to stand behind" and "support" their children's decision to serve:

> MOTHER #1: When I really realized that Walt had made his mind up to join the Marines, then as a mother I had to stand behind him.

MOTHER #2: He seemed absolutely certain in his mind and heart that that is what he wanted to do. So I had to support him.

Emotional support and political support for war become intertwined in recruitment material. "Standing behind" their service members also means standing behind the war effort. Mothers learn to trust their children's decision to serve, and the military institution. Questioning the political reasons for war, or military war policy, is not a part of being supportive of their children.

For example, military websites often include information for parents on coping with their children's first deployment. Mothers are reassured on these pages not only that their children are well trained (i.e., safe) but that their children believe in the mission they have been given. One mother who is quoted on the deployment frequently asked questions for the Marines Corps explained, "I think what helped me is Ryan was very confident in himself and he really believed in what was happening. So that helped me get through it." The Go Army Parents website also includes advice from the mother on coping with training and deployment.

> Regardless of where you come from, your race, religion or political views, you need to realize how important your Soldier is to our Army and to our country. You may have mixed feelings and emotions about all of this, but above all you should be bursting with pride. You should be "lump in your throat, goose bumps on your arms, and tears in your eyes" proud!

This mother advises new army mothers that they should not only be "bursting with pride" in their children's choices and achievements, but also that this pride should come "regardless . . . of political views." This prescription for "tears in your eyes proud" relies on understanding that the service member is important for the military and for the country. Recognizing this importance in order to be proud of their children makes questioning military or war policies seem akin to questioning their children, and thus untenable for mothers of service members.

CONCLUSION

This chapter uses recruitment materials to examine the place of mothers during the enlistment process. The goals of recruitment go beyond enlisting new service members. Recruitment is also about socialization, bringing family members into the military, giving them a sense of pride and purpose in supporting their loved ones during training and deployment. During recruitment, support means that the parents provide approval of the decision to enlistment, and that the military provides training, career options, and help in making their children adults, but this bargain looks very different for mothers and fathers. The next chapter looks at how enlistment and military socialization vary by class and race.

Recent changes in recruitment combined with the economic challenges for young adults make mothers particularly important for military recruiters. Using slogans such as "You made them strong, we'll make them Army Strong" and a network of websites aimed at convincing mothers that service is right for their children, military recruiters sell the military as an avenue where children become adults and productive citizens.

Recruitment materials draw heavily on gendered understandings of fatherhood and motherhood, appealing to each differently. When recruitment materials show fathers, they assume that they will approve of their children's enlistment. The military calls on fathers to be proud and provide guidance during the process. In contrast, they spend a lot of time addressing mothers' emotions and perceived misconceptions about the military. They assume that mothers do not understand the military institution (as women), and will "naturally" worry for their children's safety (as mothers). One way that the military tries to manage these worries is to encourage mothers to take on the duties of providing physical and emotional support for their children, and all the troops, during the war. The military, in turn, agrees to provide support for the enlistee in the form of training, education, and personal growth.

Making sure that mothers feel comfortable with military service and building pride in their children's decision to serve brings mothers' support to the process of recruitment, deployment, and post-deployment health care. This home front support is critical for successfully waging war. The tasks of supporting the troops are not distributed evenly, however. With black and Hispanic Americans overrepresented in the armed forces, the burden of familial support falls disproportionately on their shoulders. In the next chapter I turn to the issues of race and class inequality in how mothers experience war.

2

BE ALL THAT YOU CAN BE

Race and Class in Recruitment

Patricia is a single black woman in her mid-forties. She raised her son, Eddie, and his younger sister mostly by herself with the help of nearby relatives. When Eddie was in middle school, she had to move from the city where she had family (a sister, who watched the children for her) to a more urban area halfway across the country for work. The opportunity of a better job, and moving up in the medical records company she worked for, was too much to pass up. With her busy work schedule, she did not have much time to make close friendships, and largely felt isolated in her new city. When Eddie started high school, she worried about all the free time he would have after school before she came home from work. She encouraged him to join sports and clubs, but nothing appealed to him. "I wanted him to have some passion to occupy his mind and his time. You know, that's good for kids his age. To have a purpose. To keep him from hanging out with other kids trying to figure out what mess they could get themselves into." In his sophomore year, he surprised her by bringing home a permission form for the Junior Reserve Officer Training Corps (JROTC) program.

> Eddie actually brought home a form for me to sign so he could join JROTC. I nearly fell to the floor I was so surprised. I had given up on him finding any passion a long time ago. He brought me a brochure about it, too. I read that it wasn't about preparing them for war; it was about learning skills, developing leadership, and becoming a

proud citizen. It seemed to me like Eddie could benefit from all that and then some. Being around responsible adults and other students with goals in their heads seemed like a good idea to me. It was only later I wondered if it meant Eddie might want to enlist someday.

Eddie stayed in the JROTC program, becoming a cadet colonel. And he did enlist after graduation.

I guess I knew he would enlist when he turned eighteen. His life just clicked in JROTC. He had purpose and focus. He made great friends and started doing his schoolwork and getting good grades. They weren't the best grades, but they were good enough to maybe even go to college. What I really want for him is a college education.

When Eddie told Patricia he wanted to enlist, Patricia had concerns about whether service would make it more difficult for him to attend college. "I didn't want him to take time off between high school and college—what if he never wanted to go back inside a classroom?" She talked with the recruiter on the phone, and the recruiter offered to come over and answer her questions in person. At Eddie's insistence, she took the recruiter up on his offer.

The recruiter was very nice. Actually, I guess it's OK if I say he was also very handsome! He reminded me a bit of a younger version of Eddie's father. He was very polite and sat and talked with us for over an hour. What stuck out to me was how happy Eddie was talking with Jack [the recruiter]. Jack asked about his hobbies—you know, video games are what Eddie's into and Jack seemed to know them all but then gave Eddie a hard time for letting those games disrupt his schoolwork. I was like "huh, this is what it's like to have a man in the house." Not that I've ever needed a man around, but sometimes it comes in handy when raising a boy to be a man.

Patricia's story is typical for many military mothers, but is also specific to nonwhite families in the military. Just like any mother, Patricia wants her son to grow up and be successful. Recruiters and recruitment advertising focus on people who are most likely to join the service, or in military-speak, individuals who have a "high propensity to enlist."[1] The military's objective is to reach enlistment goals and fill the ranks with the most highly qualified individuals.

Eddie fits the military's definition of a youth who has a high propensity to enlist. He is from a single-mother family. He lives in a lower-income community and attends a school where few students go to college. As his mother describes, he shows little passion or direction for his future, and could easily end up hanging out with other teens and getting into trouble. His mother is a single parent, with little means to provide Eddie a college education.

Another mother, Tamara, described similar circumstances when her son, Lionel, joined the Army, but Tamara encouraged his enlistment from the beginning.

> I have no way for my son to go to college. Maybe community school I could afford, but not without loans. A friend of mine, her son joined the Army and got to go to school that way, so I always hoped Lionel would want to enlist. Her son serves stateside doing communication, so maybe Lionel could do that, too. And be safe from deployment. When Lionel was seventeen I mentioned it to him, and wanted him to check out the JROTC. But he didn't do Junior ROTC. He did enlist at eighteen, right after graduation. I knew it was also what he wanted, too.

Tamara is a single mother, and Lionel is her only child. They live in a lower-income suburb of Chicago. For most of Lionel's childhood, Tamara worked two or three jobs at a time to afford rent and childcare. She described how much she feared he would not go to college. Tamara had "only a technical degree," and "very much regretted" not attending college herself.

> I didn't have much going for me after high school. I didn't think I could afford college so I got a technical degree in accounting. It was all online. My parents never went but they wanted us all to go to college. My brother went to community college, and he told my son to make sure he made something of his life. We all just wanted him to make something of his life.

So Tamara encouraged Lionel's enlistment, and was proud when he completed basic training. When asked if she was worried about deployment she explained,

I didn't think too much about him being in a war zone. We didn't discuss it during recruitment and I didn't think about it after. I wanted him to go into either medical or communications work, and he did end up specializing in communications. But then he was deployed to Afghanistan and I was a little worried. Maybe I should've thought of that sooner, but I didn't.

Instead, Tamara told Lionel to keep his goal in mind during deployment—to go to college.

I told him he had to come home safe and go to college and get a good degree and job. Even if he wanted to stay in the military as a career, that would be okay, as long as he got that degree! The Army means money for college. Not taking advantage of that would be such a shame.

Like Patricia, Tamara wanted her son to go to college and saw the military as a stepping-stone for him to get there. Coming from limited means, money for college means a future for their children. The concerns that Patricia and Tamara have for their sons are reflected in, and amplified by, military recruitment materials. The military wants to find the highest quality recruits possible, while also recognizing that those recruits may come from economically disadvantaged areas.

To accomplish this, military recruiters capitalize on the concerns all mothers have for their children, but stress particular concerns—like potential delinquency, unequal access to college, missing fathers, difficult job prospects—when addressing the black community. Recruitment messages make appeals not just to mothers who might have concerns about their children making successful transitions to adulthood, but specifically to African American single mothers in situations where they make less money and are less likely to attend college. By recruiting through race and class inequalities, the military exploits citizenship obligations for already precariously positioned families. This targeting of minority populations for recruitment means that the burden of service still falls disproportionately on minority communities.

RACE AND CLASS IN THE US MILITARY: OVERVIEW

African Americans are overrepresented in the armed forces. Black Americans make up 18 percent of the 1.4 million active service members, and only 12.3 percent of the population.[2] The Army has the highest proportion of black service members, where 25 percent are black.[3] One reason African Americans are overrepresented is that those with the highest propensity to enlist are often disadvantaged youth with few options after high school.[4] African Americans are less likely to attend college than whites and have a lower median income than their white counterparts.[5]

Socioeconomic status is a strong predictor of enlistment potential and recruits tend to come from areas with median incomes less than the US average.[6] While the military does not make economic background information about recruits available, studies looking at the geographic location show that recruits tend to come from areas with median incomes less than the US average,[7] and that those from lower income areas are more likely to enlist in the military.[8]

College attendance after high school also affects enlistment. While recruitment aptitude tests are used to weed out recruits from lower socioeconomic backgrounds, score thresholds were lowered in 2005, opening the doors for those with lower educational backgrounds.[9]

The JROTC program offers a pathway into the military for middle and high school students like Lionel and Eddie. In 2006, more than 18,000 seventeen-year-olds enlisted through the JROTC's Deferred Enlistment Contract program. According to a 2008 ACLU report, JROTC programs like the one Eddie joined target middle- and low-income communities where fewer students go to college.[10]

Military JROTC programs tend to be in schools with high race and ethnic minority populations, and lower numbers of graduates attending college. The ACLU documented recruiters' use of coercion and deception with students and their parents to convince them that leaving the military program was not an option later on (even though they have the right to).

JROTC programs encourage enlistment by emphasizing education and career opportunities to avoid becoming a "social problem." As Patricia learned, JROTC programs serve as a support system for young men struggling in the process of becoming adults.[11] Such programs provide structure, discipline, and parental figures for youth. Eddie's recruitment is a direct result of what the ACLU found in their large-scale study of JROTC programs—that the military aims to increase recruitment of specifically low-income and African American youth by targeting the two highest predictors of recruitment—race/ethnicity and college plans.

The military's focus on recruiting individuals from lower-class areas, who are less likely to go to college, means that the burdens of war are not equally shared across the United States. Lionel and Eddie, as young black men, are perfectly situated for enlistment into the armed forces. Appealing to their mothers is a key part of their enlistment. When targeting Tamara and Patricia, the military capitalizes on the worries they might have for their sons, as black single mothers. With black fathers assumed to be absent, the military works to convince mothers that they will provide the discipline and guidance their sons need—in short, to act as surrogate fathers. The military sells itself as providing the opportunities for black youth to become respected citizens, while expecting black single mothers to see the military as a co-parent, supporting their children unconditionally. Appealing to black mothers establishes a specific support relationship between these families and the military institution—one that relies on assumptions about race and class differences and demands more support work based on inequality.

Racial inequality also continues after enlistment. Senior officers in all branches are more likely to be white; 77 percent of active-duty senior officers are white, only 8 percent black, and 5 percent Hispanic.[12] Historically clustering blacks in lower ranks contributed to high rates of casualties among black service members,[13] but that is not the case today. They are now more likely to select career-focused support positions when they enlist, so casualty rates are lower than in previous wars.[14] Nevertheless, the war burden still falls disproportionately on minority families, and these families remain an important target of recruitment efforts.[15]

"DIVERSITY IS OUR STRENGTH"

For all intents and purposes, the US military looks like the picture of diversity—an integration success story.[16] Military YouTube videos tout "diversity is our strength," showing successful service members and their happy families in a rainbow of colors. For example, a video from the US Military Academy boasts, "We draw strength from our diversity. At the United States Military Academy, cadets come from across our nation, from all races and walks of life." Another video "celebrating 60 years of diversity in the military" shows individuals of all racial groups training, graduating, and working together. An advertisement for recruitment shows different colors of service members, lined up in front of an American flag: "How strong is our diversity? Army Strong."

Videos and advertisements like these celebrate the history of blacks serving the armed forces as one of inclusion in the citizenry. Military service is a measure of equal rights and citizenship.[17] Serving one's country is often considered one of the highest forms of citizenship for men and doing so signifies belonging to the collective nation.[18]

Citizenship is a legal status, but it is also based on productivity and belongingness.[19] Through systematic, institutionalized racism, black families have been excluded from citizenship and national belonging.[20] Black families, particularly lower-class black families, are construed as a "menace" dependent on the State.[21] Including blacks in welfare programs initially for whites only was a step toward equal citizenship, but it led to demonization of the poor.[22] Black mothers became the "undeserving poor" who "deserve" poverty.[23] When Welfare Reform in 1996 ended the right to benefits, the "welfare queen" became a non-citizen subject, her life open to public scrutiny, denying her equal citizenship.[24]

One route to belonging as citizens is to volunteer to fight—and potentially die—for the country.[25] Service promises a way to public recognition of productive citizenry for minority youth and their families.[26] Along with education and career opportunities, the military provides an alternative to poverty, dependency, and/or prison.[27]

Black Americans have fought in every US war since the Revolution, but not always as free and equal citizens. African Americans served in the highest percentages during WWII, but did so in racially segregated units. After WWII, in 1948, President Truman ended racial discrimination in the military, outlawing racially segregated units.

But the unevenness of the Vietnam draft rules ensured that blacks were drafted in higher numbers. Black Americans were less likely in the 1960s and 1970s to be enrolled in college and qualify for deferment.

During the 1980s and 1990s, blacks continued to be overrepresented among enlistees, and became more likely than whites to make the military a longtime career.[28] The military relied on the strong enlistment numbers from black youth to meet recruitment quotas until the 2000s, when black recruitment numbers dropped.[29] The decrease in enlistment came, in part, from the growing unpopularity of the war, particularly among African Americans, and a growing distrust of the government's ability to care for black communities after Hurricane Katrina.[30]

In response to lower enlistment rates, the military increased the recruiting budget 30 percent in areas with high numbers of minority enlistees,[31] and added guidelines to ensure that recruiters themselves are diverse and represent the population of the area in which they work.[32] Recruitment levels rose slightly after the terrorist attacks on September 11, 2001, but returned to low levels by 2003. Since that wartime slump, the recruitment focus has been to fill the ranks with those whom they assumed most willing to serve.[33] These recruitment efforts succeeded in raising the rates of black recruitment by 2006, but not back to 1990s levels. During the same period, Hispanic enlistment also increased steadily.[34]

Even though research shows that the targeting of minorities during the recruitment process is one source of racial segregation and overrepresentation in the military, the military does not focus on specific disadvantaged groups for recruitment.[35] Instead, military reports describe recruiting African Americans strategically as building a military that is "representative" of society as a whole.[36] The military's Leadership Diversity Commission advises recruitment efforts with the aim of increasing the diversity of service members at all levels of service.[37] In fact, some celebrate the military as one of the few American institutions to achieve integration.[38]

The military markets itself as an avenue to successful citizenship for underprivileged youth, much as integrated military units were a pathway to equality for African Americans decades ago. In military recruitment terms, young minority men fit the model of individuals who have a "high propensity to enlist." They frequently lack options after high school; they have few job prospects and little money for a college education.[39] Serving in the armed forces is a responsible choice to serve one's country (instead of potentially taking from one's country) and ultimately to become an adult and successful citizen. Military service epitomizes the rights and duties involved in citizenship, especially for men.[40] Service is sold as an alternative to high rates of imprisonment for black male youth. As a result, black men continue to recruit at higher rates, particularly when they are from lower socioeconomic backgrounds.[41] Making up about a third of black service members, black women are also overrepresented in the military.[42]

MILITARY PATERNALISM

One recruitment narrative frequently focused on African American mothers like Patricia and Tamara is that the military can lead to a better future for their children. Recruitment websites list every possible training and career option for that particular branch of the military. Sounding much like college recruitment materials, they describe signing bonuses and health benefits, and detail college aid and loan programs. This information, and the quotes and stories from real parents that accompany it, assure mothers that their recruits' "dreams can be pursued, no matter what." For example, the Army website tells the story of Tanya, another African American single mother with a son in the Army. In various video clips, Tanya describes how her dreams for her son came true in the military, and the result was a good job in the civilian world. Notice the emphasis in her story, as in others, on the non-dangerous aspects of military training (i.e., intelligence activities, computer consulting, information technology).

> It's a dream she always had for her son, to become a man. Jonathan is stationed at Fort Riley, KS, and works as a Fire Support Specialist. This job specialty requires Jonathan to work as a member of an artillery team used to support infantry and tanks. He is also responsible for leading, supervising, or serving in intelligence activities. The experience Jonathan has gained and skills he has learned can help him pursue a career in the civilian world in computer consulting, information technology support or data processing.

Dreams—the ones mothers have for their children, and the ones children have for themselves—are a common theme in military websites. Tanya's dreams suggest that she may have been concerned that her son was lacking direction toward becoming a man. As a mother,

Tanya's dreams for her son are that he will learn to work in a team, to supervise, to be responsible, and to gain skills that will help him have a career when he leaves the military. Single mothers from lower socioeconomic backgrounds, who are worried about the future of their children, like Patricia, are especially susceptible to these appeals. With a strong school-to-prison pipeline for young black men in particular, and few resources for attending college, black mothers are particularly concerned about their children's, and more specifically about their sons', futures. [43]

Only black single mothers are portrayed in recruitment materials as needing the military to co-parent in the place of the absent husband. These stories assume that without the father, the military is necessary to help their sons become men. An Army commercial features a black teen having dinner with his mother.

> MOTHER: Something good happen today?
> SON: Found someone to pay for me to go to college.
> MOTHER: [stops eating and looks up]
> SON: Ok, now before you ask, Mom, I already checked them out and I can get training in just about any field that I want. And besides, it's time for me to be the man.
> MOTHER: [smiles at her son]

Initially the son seems to expect his mother to argue with his decision, but she does not. Instead she smiles and acknowledges that her son needs to be—not just a man—but the man in the house, and that by joining the military he has taken the first step.

Patricia's story is one that would work well on a military recruitment website. These websites show mothers first seeing their children as adults when they make the decision to enlist. Like Patricia, single mothers are described as worried that their sons will not become men without a father figure at home. A lot of recruitment material focuses on a mother's happiness when seeing her son at the end of basic training; she sees him as a new person—an adult, and specifically, a man.

Like Patricia, Tamara saw tremendous changes in her son after enlistment. Tamara's son, Lionel, completed a community college degree with his GI benefits after his service ended. Lionel was happy with his community college experience and degree, and got a job working for a private security firm. Tamara was proud of his associate's degree and job, but still hoped he would do more:

> I'm hoping he goes back to school. I wasn't buying his serving at first, but he gained so much confidence in the military. That first time he came to me and said "Mom I want to do this!" I couldn't believe it, you know? He wasn't joking! He's serious and focused now, and such a hard worker. I don't want to see him stop with his two-year degree. But he has a good job now, good pay, and health care benefits. So he's happy. And I am so proud of him. He's made good decisions, and as a mother I can't complain about that!

Like other mothers, Tamara didn't "buy" his service at first. She was worried that Lionel would deploy to a war zone. But she saw his decision as an adult one ("he wasn't joking!") and was proud of his ensuing hard work. Part of her recruitment journey was recognizing her son as making an adult decision to enlist. For example, in a television advertisement for Todaysmilitary.com, an African American son discusses military service with his mother. His initial tone in the commercial is defensive as if he assumes his mother will not be supportive of service. He is assertive about his decision and tells his mother "It's what I was meant to do."

> SON: [Sitting on the couch watching TV] Hey, Mom. You know I haven't changed my mind about joining the military.
> MOM: [In the next room doing her daughter's hair] I didn't expect you would. I just wanted to make sure you thought things through.
> SON: I did, and I know for me this is the right decision. It's what I was meant to do.
> MOM: I believe that.
> SON: Then why'd you want me to keep thinking about it?
> MOM: Because I'm your mom and that's my job. [Looks at her son and smiles]
> SON: [Smiles to himself and sighs]
> Text on screen: It's a big decision. Talk about it. Todaysmilitary.com

This particular commercial shows single mothers that making a decision to join the military is an adult decision—one that means their children are on their way to becoming successful adult citizens. It also reiterates the military's prescription that mothers are involved in the decisions their children make—it's their job to help their children make the right decisions (by getting "the facts"). In this short exchange, a "mom's job"—a single mom's job—is to make sure her child makes an informed, adult decision about military service. But he is presented as bothered by her "mothering" because he is now an adult. She trusts him to make this decision as he indicates to her that he is growing up. Validating her child's decision to serve is a key part of becoming proud, and doing a mother's job by helping him make that decision is part of being supportive. As a quote from a single African American mother on the splash page of the Army recruitment website for parents states, "He obviously had put a lot of forethought into this. It wasn't a quick decision that he'd made. But I do confess that I started to cry."

Another "success story" on the Army website details the story of A.J., and his mother's involvement in his recruitment and training. His mother, Danielle, is described as finally feeling "real good and real comfortable" with her son's decisions. The implications are that she might not have been happy with his decisions in the past, but now the military—with her help—has changed A.J. into someone who balances the military and college:

> A.J. is first and foremost a Soldier. Yet he also has to balance his Army job with college studies–all while keeping an eye on the future. And his mother is making sure he stays firmly focused.
>
> "Everything is lined up and I feel real good and real comfortable about his decision and continuing on with his education," she says. "I can see a career young man sitting right next to me." "I'm very proud of the choices that A.J. has made. Seeing him now, a young man with a bright prospect for his future, I've just seen a fantastic change."

Single mothers are shown having pride both in the adult decisions the recruits make to enlist and in witnessing the transformation they go through in the service. Tamara describes how Lionel was "a different person" after basic training.

> I swear he grew like two inches over those ten weeks! He was taller and thinner, and so handsome! I went to his graduation with my sister, and she didn't even recognize him at first. I don't know what happened to him over those weeks, but he came out a different man. And a man, and not a child.

Recruitment materials tell stories of mothers like Tamara seeing their children as adults—and specifically men—at the end of their training. For another African American mother, Shirley, the military made Eric a man and "brought out" his adult manners. Her son transformed from a boy to a man in boot camp, where she noticed he was no longer the "little boy" she had sent to boot camp but was "such a man." Shirley said proudly,

> Transformation is the biggest and best word you can use. On Christmas day when I saw him, he wasn't the little boy I sent to boot camp. He was such a man. And the manners. I knew they were in there somewhere, and the military brought it out.

Boot camp graduation day is a point where mothers notice the changes in their sons, and can feel proud of their accomplishments. As the story about Shirley and Eric continues, Eric's graduation was a special day for Shirley:

> Seeing him graduate, I was just so proud of him. Because look at this kid who's turned into a man, in a matter of weeks. It was like the kid you always wanted. You wondered back when they were teenagers and the "where'd I go wrong" thing. You didn't go wrong. It was just a phase like everyone said. But, yes, transformation, absolutely. And he likes the transformation. He's happier with himself.

Recruitment materials define moving into the adult world as gaining education, a job, and a career—all things that the military offers. The military is there to help transition the child to adult, and in that way the military is an extended partner in parenting. The "you made them strong, we'll make them Army Strong" slogan suggests that the Army picks up where parents left off. Their parents brought them part of the way by making them strong, but the military will continue their parenting and make them stronger. But, the parents continue to be a part of the process. For example, an African American mother on the lead page of the Go Army Parents website states, "I went to Shenique's graduation and that day was the proudest day a mother could have other than the day she was born." There is a bit of a paradox, however, in encouraging mothers to see their children's transformation into adults. The recruit is depicted as strong enough to make an adult decision to join the armed forces, becoming an adult during training and deployment, but still needing family (the mother's) support for that decision. As the "you made them strong, we'll make them Army Strong" trope shows, while the military may take on some parenting duties, parents need to provide ongoing support for the adult soldier.

As Tanya describes on the Go Army Parents website, the military turned her troubled teenager into a responsible man:

> Throughout the next year, Tanya observed her son become a strong Soldier and mature into a "wonderful man." She recalls how handsome Jonathan was in his uniform when he graduated from basic training and how he even looked taller standing at attention. Tanya was amazed at how the Army had helped transform Jonathan mentally and physically into a more responsible individual.

Focusing on sons becoming men emphasizes a gendered relationship between mothers and their sons. As sons transform "mentally and physically" into "responsible men," mothers do what they can to support them during their training and deployment. Without a man at home, sons are in need of masculine role models. Through military service, they are able to break away from home and are provided with discipline and adult skills. But they still need to rely on their mothers for emotional support during their training and deployment.

RAISING SUCCESSFUL CITIZENS

Single black mothers, as sole parents, are encouraged to be an active part of the decisions their recruits make to serve. Through building a sense of pride in their children's decision and in the military itself, mothers are depicted as enlisted along with their recruits. They also become a part of the military institution. For example, a story on TodaysMilitary.com about Sharlene, whose two sons join the military, shows that mothers can assist their recruits in making good decisions when they enlist. The mother, Sharlene, is depicted as involved in her sons' decisions so that they have good career opportunities after leaving the military and become successful citizens. As a result of the paths they chose, Sharlene is proud of her sons:

When the boys enlisted, Sharlene spoke to them about the importance of choosing the right job specialty. She wanted her sons to
acquire skills that would benefit them in the Service and thereafter.

"It seemed like a shame to spend all this time and energy learning
something that could only be used in the Military," she commented.
She was pleased that her sons settled into fields that could develop
into rewarding civilian careers: David in medical administration and
Adam in satellite communications.

Sharlene is proud of both of her sons, the experiences they have
gained, and how they have grown.

By depicting mothers as proud of their children's growth in the
military-as-parent, recruitment materials accomplish two things. First, a
mother is going to be proud of her recruit's growth during his or her
training and deployment. This is especially the case for African
American single mothers who are portrayed as having few other options
for their children. Second, a mother is going to be supportive when her
child acts and makes decisions like an adult instead of a child, both in
joining the military and while a part of the military. Growth and deci-
sion-making skills reflect the mothers' own success at raising their children and this is amplified in recruitment material.

Being a part of these decisions helps build a sense of pride for
mothers in their children and in the military. Sharlene is shown as
proud of the paths her sons took to have civilian career opportunities
after service. The reward of the enlistment process is that both Sharlene
and her sons become successful citizens.

Black single mothers are in the position where their citizenship is
under scrutiny and they can be "sold" potentially successful citizenship.
Selling them military service as an avenue to success means speaking
about their families as deficient, lacking potential. While all enlistment
material (aimed at both white and nonwhite recruits) draws on the
narrative of success to recruit, black mothers in particular are targeted
as benefiting from the military in unique ways. Black families, through
the potential success of their children as service members, are encouraged to prove their family's worth in society.

Both Tamara and Patricia described how much they wanted their
children to be successful citizens, but the terms they use are slightly
different. Patricia describes success in terms of contributing to society:

> I don't want my son to be a taker. I don't want him needing a
> handout or needing help. I've needed help in the past and I know it's
> demoralizing. It makes you feel lower than dirt. I want a son who can
> hold his head up and say he supports himself and his family. He's
> contributing to society, not taking from it. And that makes me feel
> like I did something good. I raised a kid who's a giver and not a taker.

For Patricia, needing help, or being a "taker" is the opposite of
contributing to society, or being a good citizen. Her own citizenship is
bolstered by his successful citizenship—that she raised a "giver and not
a taker." Patricia also emphasized the military as a sign that her son
wanted to do more than "just make money." His successful citizenship
comes from wanting to make the country better through military service, not just buying nice cars and clothes.

> He wants to make this country and the world better, and I applaud
> that in him. That makes me proud. Lots of kids his age want to make
> money. They want the cool cars and clothes. They want to go and
> blow money on trips and concerts. That's not my Eddie. I guess he
> was never focused on materialistic things even as a child. He wants to
> make things better. Make this country better. So the military seemed
> like the best choice for him.

Mothers like Tamara and Patricia inhabit a precarious position in the
United States. As women, they shoulder the majority of the burden of
raising children. As black mothers, they carry the cultural baggage of
blame for (mythical) social ills such as crack babies and welfare fraud.[44]
As black Americans, they are charged with proving their worth as citizens and contributing members of the community. With so many black
fathers either unemployed or in the prison system,[45] two-thirds of
African American women are single mothers at birth, while only one-
quarter of white mothers are single at the time of birth.[46] Single African
American mothers have fewer economic and institutional support resources to access while raising their children.[47]

African American single mothers are especially susceptible to fears
of parenting failure.[48] The military has a variety of negative images of
black mothers to draw on in recruitment material. For example, the
Reagan administration successfully sold the American public the image
of the "welfare queen," a "lazy, greedy, Black ghetto mother" who lived

off the system and made no contributions to the country.[49] Cultural images such as the "welfare queen" serve to control black women's behavior by "otherizing" their struggles in life and parenting as different from "normal" Americans. With Welfare Reform in 1996, citizens were no longer entitled to benefits and the "welfare queen" became a kind of "non-citizen."[50] The archetypal black welfare mother is labeled a "bad mother" who fails to pass on good work habits to her children.[51] Black mothers became the face of the "undeserving poor" who actually "deserved" their lives of poverty.[52] They are demonized as pariahs undeserving of the welfare system, which in turn controls their lives.

For these mothers, the military provides a route to both successful citizenship and successful motherhood. Instead of their sons ending up in the prison system (a sign of failed citizenship and another system of control), they can contribute to the country.[53] The role of black mothers does not end with successful recruitment; the military needs parents and families to support service members and wars. Mothers must make sacrifices to support their children's decision. The military also shows mothers how, by supporting their children, they implicitly support war in a way that makes criticizing the military difficult. This creates a new kind of docile black subject. As mothers "enlist" along with their children, they are discouraged from exercising full citizenship that allows them to criticize the military and political/military leaders.

Another single black mother in a video online describes being worried despite the fact that she describes herself as "pro-military" and "patriotic":

> I am very pro-military. I'm very patriotic. But I am a mother and I don't know any mother out there who wouldn't have their heart just bend with the thought of their son or daughter being in a place where there's nothing you can do.

This video, like others, reassures mothers that they are not alone in feeling nervous, and that it is natural to be worried about their recruits being somewhere dangerous where they cannot help them; this quote reassures mothers that *every* mother has to overcome these natural feelings. Not only does every mother have these feelings; those feelings are positioned against being patriotic and pro-military. While any mother might resist her child's enlistment ("but I am a mother" even though she is "very patriotic"), the narrative points to the necessity for single mothers to accept, and even celebrate, the decision. They can manage their worry through increasing their trust in the recruits (it is "their decision" rather than a response to recruitment pressures) and trust in the military itself.

UNEQUAL BURDEN OF WAR

Just as the all-volunteer military is not representative of the country's demographics, mothers do not equally assume the home front burdens of war. Racial minorities (African Americans, and increasingly Hispanics) and individuals from lower socioeconomic backgrounds are overrepresented in all branches of the service. While this is partly the result of fewer educational and work opportunities for these young people, recruitment strategies also contribute.

Military advertising appeals to black single mothers in order to foster an environment where their sons are encouraged to enlist and supported during their military careers. By using images and stories of black single mothers in recruitment materials, the military perpetuates the overrepresentation of black service members in the ranks, without achieving actual equality. Since military units were racially desegregated in 1948, the military has celebrated "diversity [as] our strength," but in reality, military ranks are not so much *diverse* as they are *unequal*.

This continued inequity is partially the result of the military's use of the current system of race and socioeconomic inequality. By specifically targeting single black mothers, the military strategically draws on the precarious racial and socioeconomic position these mothers occupy. Black women are usually either absent from public discourse or are the face of government dependence and failed citizenship. The military is depicted as an avenue not only for education and career advancement, but for successful citizenship for a segment of the population typically viewed as failed citizens. The military reverses this depiction and uses it to encourage children from single-mother families to fulfill citizenship duties by serving. Those with a high propensity to serve are young black men; the military targets them, and the support of their mothers, for recruitment in a way that limits their mothers' engaged citizenship.

Appealing to black mothers establishes a specific support relationship between these families and the military institution, one that relies on assumptions about race and class differences and demands more support work based on inequality. Recruitment narratives take advantage of the worries that black single mothers may have for their children—that their sons have few college and career opportunities and may end up making poor choices as they grow up. White recruitment narratives show the father as supportive of service, but fathers are absent from depictions of black families. Instead, the military works to convince mothers that they will provide the discipline and guidance their sons need—in short, to act as surrogate fathers. The military sells itself as providing the opportunities for black youth to become respected citizens, while expecting black single mothers to see the military as a co-parent, supporting their children unconditionally. Mothers are expected to defer to the male parents' decisions, and support not only their children but the war itself. By advertising for new recruits in this way, the military exploits mothers' desire to raise successful citizens, while reaffirming cultural stereotypes and other beliefs about the black community, families, and single moms.

Part II

Deployment

3

"HALF MY HEART IS IN IRAQ"

The Silent Ranks

When Rob told me he wanted to join the Army I was so proud. I was scared for him and scared that it meant he was really growing up and leaving me, but I was really proud. He talked to a recruiter on his own at school, and made his own decision to serve. He brought me pamphlets about what he could do in the Army. Some of my girl-friends didn't get it because their children were going to college and they think college is better. But he's always wanted to be a mechanic so college was never in his head. . . . If I talked to them about being worried, it justified their own worry. So I just stopped talking to them about Rob's service.

—Joanne

Like Barbara from the introduction, Cindy from chapter 1, and other mothers without family in the military, Joanne was surprised when her son Rob told her he wanted to enlist. Rob was only seventeen at the time, but Joanne readily signed his enlistment papers so he could join when he turned eighteen, a month after graduating from high school. She never expected Rob to go to college, so the military seemed a wise alternative. She was also proud of "his own decision to serve"—it meant to her that he was becoming an adult—but she was worried about his safety. "I had a few reservations but they were only because I wanted him to be safe. I wanted someone to guarantee me his safety, but no one could."

   When Rob enlisted, Joanne spent time learning about service and the military institution. Through flyers and conversations with the recruiter and other mothers in her area, she was socialized into the institution, learning everything from military acronyms to customs.

> I'll never forget the first time I met a mother of another soldier. I asked her how her son enlisted and she explained how his father and grandfather were both Marines. She went on a sort of rant about her son enlisting in the Army instead of the Marines, and it was the first I had heard of this rivalry, with the two branches. I think I did something stupid like call her husband a soldier and she immediately corrected me. He was a MARINE. I never made that mistake again! We did become friends, despite that awkward conversation.

   When Joanne's son finally left for training she learned about another part of military life: the constant worry.

> Basic training was basically not being in touch with Rob for ten weeks. He couldn't call very often. And when he did, he said he was having a hard time sleeping with his back [an old back injury]. That was hard. I hated the idea of him being in pain and not getting help. I didn't know how they were treating him. I wrote letters but he only had time to write a few back. I suppose it was training for deployment. I mean, for me, it was training for when he would be deployed. And I would worry.

   Another mother, Kelly, described how "idiotic" she felt when she went to her first luncheon for Army Moms.

> My son's recruiter told me about this group of other mothers who had lunch once a month or so. The first time I went, the women were so nice. I really felt like I was being welcomed into a family—a sisterhood, actually. But then they started talking about "digies" and "NCOs" and "AFAPs" and "CONUS." I felt idiotic because I had no idea what they meant by anything and I didn't dare ask. Well I did ask about "CONUS" because one of the woman said her son would be stationed there, and it means "Continental US." Boy, did I feel silly. But, why not just say the US? It's like they want to make people feel like outsiders!

As Kelly and Joanne were meeting new people and learning about the military, they also describe feeling more separated from nonmilitary friends. Worried about where her son would be sent after basic training, Kelly found more comfort in the monthly group of mothers than with other friends. "Their sons were going to college, and I just couldn't relate. I was sending my son to do something potentially dangerous, not worrying about which towels to get for his dorm!" After Rob joined, Joanne felt the rift grow between herself and her friends who did not have children in the service. She was nervous about Rob's deployment, and had no one to talk with about it. Like other military mothers, Joanne described how civilians did not understand how proud she was of her son, or why enlistment was a good choice for him.

> My civilian friends just didn't understand. They talked to me as if I was preparing Rob to just go off to college, instead of preparing him for training and service. The only people who got it were the other mothers. I found a group of mothers online and chatted with them daily about everything, from our fears to the details of what we would do to make sure our sons had what they needed when they did deploy.

By the time their children go through training and are deployed, mothers describe themselves as part of a military family that is separate from the civilian world. Before Rob went to basic training, his recruiter gave Joanne a brochure for a group of military mothers that met locally. She attended a meeting at a coffee shop with five other women with children in different branches of the service. "I instantly felt like I knew them," she described. "All the experiences, fears, and questions I had came spilling out. We spent three hours at that coffee shop! I knew I made friends for life." From the women, she learned how to contact her son in training, what he could bring with him, what she could send, and what was not allowed. She was able to ask some questions about things that worried her. She was embarrassed to ask the recruiter whether her son could be physically disciplined (hit) by a drill sergeant, or how often physical violence against new recruits occurred. She asked the other mothers how illness and injuries were handled during training. She had wanted to ask the recruiter but her son was embarrassed she was "acting so much like a mother."

Mothers sit at the intersection of the public political issue of war and the personal issue of having a child in harm's way. This perspective is what isolates them from civilians. Like Barbara, who found that her coworkers did not understand the ongoing war from her personal perspective, Joanne found she could no longer relate to some of her friends. The group of mothers she met with encouraged her to join a larger group of mothers online—the Mom2Mom message board. When her son was deployed to Germany and then to Afghanistan a few months later, she found these connections to other mothers an invaluable part of surviving the stress of deployment. She explained her bond with mothers online: "We [military mothers] understand why we try to be strong but automatically cry when we see the foot powder display at Wal-Mart."

This chapter is about the online communities that mothers like Joanne and Kelly use to connect with other mothers, to share stress and worry about their children during wartime. While some mothers have access to in-person support groups, many do not, or they supplement in-person groups with mothers online. Sometimes these groups, such as Semper Fi, are recommended explicitly by recruiters in order to help mothers learn about the military and feel supported during recruitment.

In groups such as Mom2Mom, mothers lean on each other for daily support while learning to navigate the military institution. Collectively the women in these groups describe themselves as the "silent ranks," shouldering the home front burden of war. They organize drives to supply moral support (letters, cards) and material support—everything from equipment (batteries, body armor), to clothes (extra socks and underwear), to medicines and toiletries (cold medicine, baby wipes, foot powder) for deployed troops. They describe the support they provide as an extension of their unconditional love for their children, but it is actually also critically important to the military and the war.

The process of providing material support further separates mothers from other civilians whom they perceive as having the luxury to avoid war. "Supporting the troops" comes to mean something significantly different for military mothers than for other civilian citizens. They see their support for the troops (and for some, the war itself) as not an option but as a moral imperative if they want their children to survive, while nonmilitary families can all but ignore the ongoing war. Some mothers argue that providing the troops necessary material supplies is an extension of their personal connection to war and is not connected to politicians or their own roles as citizens. As one such mother explained, "it's not about politics, it's about foot powder."

When their newfound awareness of war makes them feel different from those with no connection to the military, and makes them feel vulnerable to news reports of casualties, message boards help mothers be strong together and focus on their pride for their children. These needs for personal support under shared circumstances, however, provide an inroad to teaching mothers how they can be helpful and feel important (how to feel proud, help the troops, educate the public, etc.) during wartime. Based on their common connections, mothers learn what kind of support is appropriate during wartime—that they must unconditionally support the troops and their mission, and leave political decisions up to others.

MOTHERS AND AUXILIARY WAR SUPPORT

Family members provide critical supplies and support during deployment. While the military supplies basic goods for service members, they often still need "extras" like warmer socks, medications, comfort items, entertainment items, and small food items. After deployment, the military supplies health care for soldiers and their families, but families are expected to take over the care of soldiers who may be experiencing posttraumatic stress disorder and/or recovering from medical procedures.[1] As Segal says, the military is a "greedy institution" during wartime, making demands on military families during the time when they are under the most stress.[2]

The Department of Defense has a long history of relying on mothers like Joanne to supply physical "auxiliary support" that includes everything from assisting the deployed troops, to supplying home comforts like foot powder, to postwar support for their loved ones.[3] Mothers' auxiliary war support has a long history in the United States. Women were "camp followers" during the US Revolutionary and Civil Wars. While some camp followers were prostitutes, women also followed their husbands' and sons' units and provided nursing and other kinds of support (such as cooking and laundry) in exchange for half a soldier's rations.[4]

During WWII women supported the war effort at home by collecting goods (scrap metal, cooking oil) for the war effort, and/or working civilian war jobs.[5] The group Blue Star Mothers was also formed during WWII to bring mothers of service members together to provide physical and moral support to the troops during wartime. Blue Star Mothers continue to be active today, organizing care packages and letter-writing campaigns for service members. But participation in organized Blue Star Mothers groups has decreased since WWII when 30,000 mothers were involved in local chapters. Now, the organization has only 7,500 members.[6] This drop in membership reflects the smaller population that service members come from, and the presence of online support groups for mothers.

The gendering of support during wartime is also built into our ideas of citizenship. Women's citizenship is measured in terms of reproduction of the nation, raising future children who will be soldiers.[7] Defining women in terms of motherhood during wartime typically means conceptualizing mothers as inherently peaceful or fully militarized. Mothers in this chapter fit the idea of inherently peaceful motherhood; their home front experiences of war show the consequences of war for themselves and their families—fear, worry, and stress. But by connecting with other military mothers and focusing their energy on how to support the service members, these mothers can be seen as typifying militarized motherhood. In militarized motherhood, the acts of mothering (caring, nurturing, worry, etc.) are co-opted for the war effort. By socializing one another into the military family, these women are participating in the war effort through their role as mothers. This chapter begins to complicate this binary by showing how mothers negotiate wartime support while beginning to place boundaries around what that support means (i.e., not participating in politics).

ISOLATION AND THE UNEVEN WAR BURDEN

Once Rob shipped out, I didn't relate to a lot of my friends anymore. It was sad. They were worried about things like planning birthday parties, and I'd try to listen to them all the time thinking "my son is

in a war zone and could die." I mean I didn't care about their birthday parties or the latest show. All I could think about was my son.
And they didn't understand that. . . . So I called them less and less.

What Joanne describes is the isolation that comes from being a part
of a small subset of the American population connected to war. Unlike
during WWII, where the entire country was called on (called "a cast of
millions") to take part in the war effort in their everyday lives, military
families bear the brunt of the war burden today. Even during Vietnam,
widespread conscription and the possibility of being conscripted meant
that more Americans felt connected to and invested in the war. But as
the drop in Blue Star Mothers' membership shows, fewer families are
connected to the military than in past wars. The current war burden is
largely invisible. Helen, the mother of a Marine, for example, explained
that at one time war had just been "a passing thing that was going on"
but was now suddenly "intimate" to her.

Then Jesse joined the Marines and my life changed. Now [war] was
more than a passing thing that was going on. It was my life because
my son would be a part of it, intimately. Mothers without sons and
daughters serving have no idea of what it is like to send a child off to
war. My life has changed forever. I can never go back to being just a
mom. I will always be a mom of a Marine, a Marine that served
during a war.

The daily experiences of war that separate mothers from civilians
also create larger gulfs in public knowledge and support for war. Since
the war in Afghanistan began in 2003, public war support dropped from
73 percent to 38 percent. The public was also less aware of US military
casualties than their military family counterparts. By 2008 only 28 percent of Americans were able to reasonably guess the number of US lives
lost at the time of the poll (~4,000) whereas 55 percent were able to do
so in 2004.[8] In 2008, approval of then president G. W. Bush hinged
upon whether an individual knew someone deployed. Those who did
not know anyone serving had a higher probability of disapproving of the
president than those who did know someone serving, or had lost someone in the terrorist attack of September 11.[9]

When her son deployed to Iraq in 2005, Naomi described how she
became "obsessed" with sending care packages, thank-you letters, and

supplies to the troops. Unable to communicate with her son (who was on a special mission and out of communication for over six months) she threw herself into becoming a public reminder of war. She covered her car with "Marine Mom" stickers and talks to "everyone that'll listen and those that won't" about the war and how to support her child's service:

> I announce my volunteer work to everyone that'll listen and to those that won't. When people ask what they can do, I direct them to the care package program for fund raising and have since organized the "Wear Red on Friday" for our department.

Mothers often describe the war as "out of sight, out of mind" for Americans who do not have a direct familial connection to the war. They see themselves as symbols of the valuable work of service members volunteering to fight to protect others' freedoms. However, as these mothers remind others of the value of the work their children do, they also cast the war as "protecting" others in a way that assumes the war is beyond debate. For example, Gail, a mother with a son in the Army, described her wartime role as "to keep others aware of his (and all soldiers) sacrifice and not to forget them. I am supporter, cheerleader, counselor, anchor." Similarly, Helen described,

> I've noticed (well before now) that Americans in general don't worry about something until it's in their own backyard, and bore easily. As the mother of a deployed Marine I felt my job is to keep people aware that there are still people over there dying and being wounded every day. I went to a meeting once and mentioned my son was deployed and one of the people, kind as he is, said "Wow, it's been a long time since I thought about it . . . sometimes I forget we are at war." I was visibly stunned and vowed to support all our troops, not just my son, and I never forget that somebody is in harm's way.

Helen, like many other mothers, sees herself as the reminder "that there are still people over there dying and being wounded every day." She describes her shock that a colleague had forgotten that the country is at war. The fact that others might not think much about the war, or even forget that we are at war, is for mothers the same as forgetting or ignoring their children's (and all the troops') service and sacrifices.

REMINDERS OF WAR

Mothers like Naomi take on the task of helping their deployed children and the war effort by encouraging widespread public support. As Hanna, another mother, described, "I know the ultimate sacrifice a mother can make for her country. I am the face of this war and wear my 'Proud Marine Mom' tee every place I can." Other mothers told me about similar public displays—talking about yellow ribbons and Army Parent bumper stickers and lapel pins. Natalie, a pro-war mother, was nicknamed "Camoqueen" for her public display of Army fatigues.

> My truck is fully decked out Army, from bumper stickers, to personal license plates that says ARMYMA. I love camo, so much that I was nicknamed Camoqueen, my son gave me his spare dog tags, I wear with his class ring, and a silver cross, I got a tattoo in the shape of a Christian fish, with the name Army inside the fish and the cross at the tail, my way of having the good Lord watch over the Army.

Mothers often see themselves as physical reminders of a war that civilians may actually forget about. Like Hanna and Naomi, mothers wear clothing and pins, and put stickers on their cars in order to remind others of the ongoing war. Common bumper stickers read "Land of the free, Courtesy of the brave: Proud National Guard Mom," "Sleep well America: My Marine has your back" and "My son protects your freedom: Proud Army mom." The message from mothers to civilians is that they and their children make daily sacrifices for their rights—for the country and the greater good. Their public role is one of an educator, combating negative media portrayals of war and educating people about "what is really going on in the sandbox." As Hanna, whose son is serving in the Army, explained,

> I see myself in the role of an educator to those who have no idea what is really going on in the sandbox. I believe the news media never gives the whole story and what information that they usually provide is negative. Then they wonder why so many people have a standoffish attitude toward our servicemen and women.

Acting as the public face of war is necessary for "correcting" media portrayal of war that only focuses on the negative aspects of war. Laurel,

another Army mother, echoed Hanna's view that mothers need to counter what they see as inaccurate information in the news.

> A military mom has to make people aware of what is going on be-
> cause the news media twists everything and ignores the truth and the
> good. She is a fundraiser and volunteer. My role is to make sure my
> child and his buddies are supplied with everything they may need or
> want. I am a prayer warrior for him and those he serves with. I am a
> surrogate mother to many. I am his voice.

Laurel describes herself as her son's "voice," making sure that civilians know the good that service members do. She also describes feeling
compassion that all military mothers do for the troops as a "surrogate
mother to many." As a militarized mother, however, she translates this
feeling of compassion into needing to make sure others know about the
troops' good work.

For Naomi, taking on the role of public educator about war is also a
matter of silencing others' potentially oppositional views. Naomi's public volunteer work, like many military mothers, is aimed at not only
educating the public, but also making sure that the troops know they
are widely supported—by the civilians in addition to their families. As
Naomi went on to explain the reasons for her public activism,

> They need to feel as though Americans support them and are behind
> them, 100 percent. They do not care why we are in this conflict, nor
> do they need everyone's opinion about it.

Politics (having opinions) is irrelevant to troop support and separate
from the military tasks of waging war. Not only do the troops "not care
why we are in this conflict"; publicly displayed oppositional opinions
about war are not needed, and are potentially dangerous to the troops'
safety.

ONLINE SUPPORT COMMUNITIES

> *I wear no uniforms, no blues or army greens*
> *But I am in the Army in the ranks rarely seen*
> *I have no rank upon my shoulders—salutes I do not give*
> *But the military world is the place my son lives.*

I'm not in the chain of command, orders I do not get
But my son is the one who does, this I cannot forget
I'm not the one who fires the weapon, who puts my life on the line
But my job is just as tough. I'm the one that's left behind
My son is a patriot, a brave and prideful man,
And the call to serve his country not all can understand.
Behind the lines I see the things needed to keep this country free.
My son makes the sacrifice, but so do his siblings and me.
I love the son that I bore, soldiering is his life
But I stand among the silent ranks known as the Army Mom
      —Adapted by a mother from the "Army Wife" poem

The poem above was originally written for a soldier's wife, but was adapted by an online participant and posted to the homepage of Mom2Mom. Since the wives (and husbands) of soldiers are considered a part of the military institution along with their husbands and children, it makes sense that this poem talks about wives as the "silent ranks"— not the "one who fires a weapon" but the "one that's left behind." Mothers adapting this poem for themselves, and adopting the idea of also being in the "silent ranks" shows how they consider themselves enlisted along with their children in the military. Along with this enlistment goes a certain kind of support—not being able to "forget" they are serving, understanding "what is needed to keep this country free," and making a sacrifice along with the soldiers.

Mothers are drawn to online support groups by their isolation and new role as reluctant public educators. Building a strong sense of community among parents is a key part of making families feel a part of the military, while also pointing parents to what the Department of Defense deems are appropriate organizations from which they can receive support. One way they do this is by encouraging mothers to join networks with other military parents. Like most recruitment websites, the Marine Corps website suggests early on in recruitment material that mothers join online communities and support groups with other Marine parents in order to feel like a part of the Marine family (the "be part of"—part of the discourse). These websites are endorsed, and sometimes even sponsored, by each branch of the military. They are part of the larger military community that families are encouraged to join. For instance, the Marine website advises parents,

There are a number of groups and online communities for parents of Marines. They provide an open way to exchange information with other parents, and learn about what your son or daughter is doing for the Corps. Click on the "In Your Community" and "Websites" links on the navigation bar on the left for information about these resources.

The wider military community, as the Marine Corps website advises, provides parents and family members with information and support while their children are in the Marine Corps. This includes online support groups.

During their height in 2006–2008 (before Facebook caught on with adults beyond college age), there were dozens of message boards online aimed at mothers of service members. The message boards in this book are ones I was able to access with permission from the moderators and/or from members themselves (see the appendix). Although some of the websites no longer exist, or the groups exist in other forms, I obscured names and details of the message boards to maintain the privacy of participants.

The message boards described here are as follows.

Mom2Mom: This is the group Joanne joined, and the only one that covers all branches of the military. Mom2Mom is a simple message board website. The homepage is pink with patriotic images and a poem about mothers of soldiers. This message board has about one thousand members who add about fifty posts in total each day. Members can only access posts online (not through email), and many are on the message board multiple times during the day and night. The message board posts are accessible to everyone and open to the public, but one must be an approved member to post. There is little, if any, moderator intervention in the posts.

PAMs (Proud Army Moms): PAMs is a smaller group with only about five hundred members. The homepage is covered in Army fatigues and includes images of combat boots and hearts. The message board is inaccessible to the public, and mothers must be approved as members before posting. The board gets about twenty posts a day and there is a high level of familiarity among members, who have obviously come to know each other quite well. The board has a high level of moderation, and often a moderator locks down or removes posts that do not fit the rules.

ArmyMomsToo: This group is a split off group from a larger message board of Army mothers. The mothers who started ArmyMomsToo disagreed with the open, publicly accessible, and often contentious ArmyMoms group. As a result, this group has a high level of moderation. The message board is inaccessible to the public, and each of the eight hundred members were approved by an individual founder and moderator. Posts are often shut down when they do not follow rules. There are about sixty messages posted per day, and members can subscribe to posts through email.

Semper Fi: More than ten thousand Marine Corps mothers belong to the largest group, Semper Fi. The message board is broken down into multiple sub-threads about the different aspects of service (enlistment, training, deployment), and sub-threads for "Gold Star Moms" and even "Marine Dads." With so many members, there are well over one hundred posts each day. The forum is highly controlled by a team of moderators who step in when rules are broken or when discussions become heated. Semper Fi also contains useful information for mothers learning about the Marine Corps—glossaries of terms, lists of care package items, mailing instructions, etc.

Moms of Marines (MOM): MOM's homepage includes images of the Marine Corps logo and the Twin Towers. The message board is small, with only three hundred members and only about twenty-five posts each day. Many of the members participate through email. Anyone can join, and although there is a moderator, there is no moderation of posts.

Marine Moms Online: Despite a small membership of only fifty-five mothers, this is an active message board with more than one hundred posts per day. There is very little moderation of posts, largely because of the high level of trust and familiarity among members. The homepage of the group includes pictures of members at a care package drive, and links to information about sending care packages to the troops.

Each of the groups has a mission statement and a set of rules for participation. For example, the group Moms of Marines articulates specific goals for supporting mothers and the troops on their homepage. The goals center on the connective power of the message boards— bringing mothers together around supporting, sharing, and connecting with one another:

1. *Supporting*: Provide emotional and spiritual support and encouragement to each other, support to our Marines and Recruits, and encourage troop support through community awareness projects
2. *Connecting*: Provide the website along with various online communications as a means for mothers of Marines and Recruits around the world to connect with one other
3. *Sharing*: Share news, stories, and communications related to our Marines and Recruits to help other mothers, family and friends feel more connected to their Marine or Recruit

The goals of "supporting," "connecting," and "sharing" illustrate the power of connection in how online groups define and understand their functions. The troops need "emotional and spiritual" support, while mothers need to connect with one another, and to share communications that make them feel more connected to the troops. What this support means (unconditional support for the war effort) is defined later on during group interactions.

The group Marine Moms Online, one of the longest-running groups, has the following story of how it began as a part of their mission statement:

> Marine Moms Online was first conceived in late Spring 1996 from the worry, fear, pride, and devotion of Jean, whose son Allen left home in February of that year to become a U.S. Marine. She desperately yearned to share the unequaled pride as well as the deep heartache of being a Marine's mom with others that would truly understand her feelings.

The Marine Moms Online mission emphasizes the feeling mothers have that no one else can understand their unique sense of "unequaled pride" and "deep heartache." This is typical of group mission statements. They all begin with the shared bond of military motherhood.

The group MOM has a similar mission statement. The group mission appears on the homepage alongside an illustration of combat boots with a heart around them.

> We are mothers first. And not just ordinary mothers, we are the elite Mothers of Marines! Our Mission is to help one another and support our Marines in their Mission. As Marine Moms we are filled with pride and we try to be just as brave as our sons!

The MOM mission statement draws parallels between the mission of the group and the mission of the Marines. They identify as not "just ordinary" mothers, but as "elite mothers." Sounding much like they see themselves as enlisted along with their children, MOM's mission statement is also to "try to be brave."

Support group mission statements also focus on connecting mothers through the shared goal of providing physical and emotional support for the troops. For example, Operation Mom's goals are supporting military personnel along with providing support for each other:

> It is important we support one another, assist one another, and meet the special needs all of us are having or soon will experience, no matter what branch of service our loved one is in.
>
> We also provide direct support to our military personnel who are currently deployed overseas through letters of encouragement, food packages, and other necessities that will remind our troops of how much they are supported and loved.
>
> Operation Mom includes mothers from all branches and appeals to mothers' compassion for all service members who are deployed, and focuses on what the needs mothers share during wartime.

As the group Marine Moms Online explains in their mission statement:

> We also provide direct support to our military personnel who are currently deployed overseas through letters of encouragement, food packages, and other necessities that will remind our troops of how much they are supported and loved. We remind them of our great appreciation for their contribution to each and every one of us on the home front.

This Marine mothers' mission statement positively frames the issue of support; the only way to value the troops as people is to value their service and contribution. Implicitly, speaking out against the war would devalue the contribution the troops are making to "each and every one of us on the home front."

Groups have home pages cluttered with images (combat boots and camouflage) and sayings about the military and motherhood. Army-Moms2 has an illustration of a t-shirt that reads "Proud Army Mom." The group Semper Fi has a banner that reads, "Sleep tight, America. My Marine has your back." PAM's website opens with a set of guidelines for understanding military mothers:

> Mom's Anxiety Levels:
>   Green—my child is home and all is right with the world
>   Yellow—my child is in Iraq, but there is not much going on there, so I'm o.k.
>   Orange—my child is in Iraq, and there is stuff going on, but I can still function
>   Red—my child is in Iraq, there is stuff going on, there is a commo blackout, things are really bad, I am worried sick, and if anyone talks to me I will either rip their head off or burst into tears

Playing on the Terror Alert Levels (the Homeland Security Advisory System) adopted in the United States after 9/11, the anxiety levels correspond to whether the mother's child is in any danger. The greater the danger, the greater the fear. And the greater the danger, the more emotional the mother is likely to be. Just like group mission statements, Mom's Anxiety Levels show that the home front is still gendered and worry is woman's work.

FINDING SUPPORT ONLINE

> If your shopping cart contains tuna fish, beef jerky, foot powder, Chapstick, playing cards, disposable shavers, car magazines, a prepaid phone card and small children's toys . . . you just might be the parent of a U.S. Marine who is spending a lot of his time patrolling the streets of Iraq.
>   —Excerpt from a post to a Marine mother's group

Mothers join message boards to find others who share their experiences of having a child in the military. Living day to day with the realities of war, as the quote above describes, makes mothers feel isolated from civilians who have no connection to the military. This becomes the foundation for mothers "closing ranks" in online support groups. Along with closing ranks around their experiences of war, mothers come to see themselves as a part of the military, even when they are technically civilians. Mothers describe having duties during war—to provide physical and emotional support, to be strong, etc.—in a way that makes them feel enlisted along with their children.

As part of closing ranks, online groups frequently include images and slogans such as "Army Mom, Army Strong," "My Son, My Hero," "The only thing stronger than a Marine is the Mom who raised him," or "Before there was Boot Camp there was Mom." These slogans create a sense of collective strength as mothers, and shared pride for their service members. It is not uncommon to see images of pink military boots, or pink hearts decorating the Army or Marine Corps logos. The toughness that mothers describe themselves as needing is to compensate for the vulnerability they feel having a child in a war zone. Together, mothers in online support groups describe themselves as trying to be strong and being tough—closing ranks to protect themselves from those who cannot understand and may say uninformed inconsiderate things about war.

Mothers join online support groups to find others who share their experiences of having a child enlist in the military, go through training, and deploy in a war zone. The need to join an online support group is particularly strong during this war, where the all-volunteer military (instead of a widespread draft) means the gap between those connected to the military and civilians is particularly wide.[10] Mothers are often encouraged by recruiters to find support groups and seek them out when they feel that no one else but another military mother can understand what they are experiencing. As one mother described in her first posting to a support website: "I don't think anyone can begin to know how it feels to send YOUR OWN CHILD to a war zone until you've experienced it."

Mothers' common bonds—that they are mothers, and mothers with children in dangerous situations—are especially visible when new mothers join the online discussions. As one mother online advises a new mother worried about her son who is being deployed soon,

> I think what you are feeling is very normal for moms. I feel like no one around you truly can understand how it feels to send your son off to war, where he could actually die.

When mothers join online groups they introduce themselves in a post. These posts typically describe their children's path to the military, their reaction to enlistment, and what they might be struggling with. Others reply with welcoming messages. For example, this post is the first by Loreen in the Proud Army Mom forum:

> I am mom to Paul, who told us last week of his intention to join the Army. He and his father have spoken to a recruiter and created a plan. He needs to take a couple of courses spring quarter at college and then sign up. I am happy Paul has chosen a direction for his life and proud that he wants to serve his country . . . but I am also nervous. He is our youngest. He has had trouble settling on what to do with his life. Now, he is doing exercises twice a day from the manual the recruiter gave him. I'm happy and sad. I don't have much knowledge about the Army and how things are done. My husband was in the Army but that was many years ago. I know things have changed. . . . Anyway, I am here to see what I can do to help him achieve his goal. Any tips, hints or advice will be gladly received! I also would like to support others as their children go through this process and into their career in the Army.

Reassuring one another that their fears and worries are not only normal, but are shared by others, is a key function of the groups. Mothers who live in places away from other military families (not near a military base) are more likely to seek out the groups for company. As Clara, a mother active in an online support group for Army mothers, described,

> My son's recruiter gave me information about the Blue Star moms but there wasn't a chapter in our state. I came to realize that just like labor—only moms that have a son in the military know what you are really going through and feeling.

Mothers come to online groups for validation of what they are experiencing, feeling as if no one can "truly understand" what it is like to be the mother of a service member. This common bond not only helps mothers through the emotions of recruitment and deployment, but sets the stage for shared understandings of support and politics that depoliticize their relationship to war. As one mother described her devotion to the message board Semper Fi, "They have been there for me and I will be there for them too. Smiles, tears and fears. Just no politics!"

Military mothers often talk in online message boards about being strong or tough in order to support each other and the troops. This brings different meaning to the Army's "Army Strong" slogan. For example, Rachel, the mother of a National Guard soldier, explained to others in a thread about the stress of deployment:

> Being a mother of the deployed soldier is the toughest job I have ever had. I try to be strong. I worry more than normal. I cry at the smallest things. Others look at me strangely because they don't understand why I am crying. How can I stay strong when no one else understands?

Crying in public further sets military mothers apart from the civilian world, as a marker of experiencing something no one else but another military mother can understand. In this thread, other mothers chime in with advice on how to stay strong along with their service members during wartime. As one mother describes in response,

> You have to be strong because no one else is going to be strong for you. Our sons won't admit it but all the troops look to us at home to be tough and support them. Think about it as your duty to be strong for them. Hoo-rah!

This advice reflects the shared idea that mothers have to be strong and tough during wartime, and that doing so is their duty.

Mothers also describe how they experience enlistment, training, and deployment along with their children. For example, Dana told others online that she felt as if she was going along with her child in the military—that mothers also become enlisted along with their children.

> Some people look at me like I'm nuts when I say that we—mothers and loved ones—go right along with our sons and daughters when

they go through the training and, I guess, when they get deployed too. It's like we're right there, right next to them, going through as much of it as we can given the physical limitations. It's a stab of pride and fear and anxiety and a kind of helplessness all rolled together.

Dana, like many other mothers, expresses mixed emotions—pride and fear—but for her she is experiencing military service along with her child. Military service is all-encompassing for military families, and as mothers who care about their children, they need to participate in the military in order to continue to provide that care.

But participants in online groups do not always get along. Despite rules and moderation, every group experiences friction. The group Operation Mom had a significant drop in participation when many deployed units returned home at the same time. The few remaining members noted this drop in participation, and the absence of members who had once been very active. In response to the absences, a mother posts:

> I have noticed something. For some once their child is back in the US they seem to drop off and quietly go away. For those of us that still have children deployed to Iraq, or Afghanistan it is hurtful. We were there when your child was deployed. When you were afraid. When you cried. When you got a phone call and were in heaven.
>
> Why have you gone away when we need the support, when our children are still in harm's way? Did you never really care? Those of us that have children currently deployed still walk every day with that secret fear. We still can't always breathe. We are afraid. We check our mail a few times a day hoping to hear from our child. We wait for phone calls.
>
> So you see, we are still going through what you have already gone through. However, we were there when you went through it. You are not there for us. That is so sad. We NEED you long after your time in Hell is over!!

As this mother explains, seeing people drop off when their child returns is "hurtful" for mothers who are still experiencing deployment ("our children are still in harm's way") and still need support. She describes the anxiety of having a child at war as "hell" and appeals to the shared experiences that mothers have—"we are still going through what you have already gone through."

The above post winds up being circulated through the group for several days, and receives so much support from members that eventually a moderator turns it into a "pinned post" that stays at the top of the group's message board permanently. In reply to the pinned post a participant writes,

> Some of you have asked me how and why I stay on this list. This is why—you all have been here for me and I will be here for you too. Smiles, tears, and fears. Just no politics!

Mothers are united by their maternal emotions. But as the last comment explains, these emotions are separate from politics, and must remain so. This perpetuates the gendered divide of war. Mothers hold down the home front while men fight. Women's home front role includes nurturing—"smiles, tears, and fears."

CONCLUSION: MATERNAL SUPPORT

When their children join the armed forces, mothers find themselves isolated from civilians, and part of a new military family. In dealing with the daily experiences of war, mothers seek out in-person or online groups. In these groups they share experiences that bring them together as mothers, and this emphasizes a gendered division during wartime. Mothers do the work of physically supplying the troops with what they need, while holding down the home front with the weight of moral worry and pride as mothers. While providing support to one another and the troops, they are collectively negotiating what that support means.

When mothers come together in online support groups, they do so for reasons that are gendered (i.e., related to their maternal connection to war). They take on a supportive role during wartime for one another and for their children, creating a model of supportive wartime motherhood. As depicted in recruitment materials, the supportive wartime mother is worried, but also proud. She is fearful for her child, but also supports his mission. She takes on the job of supporting the troops by providing care packages, and ensures that other military mothers also feel supportive. This ideal of supportive wartime motherhood structures mothers' relationship to militarism and war.[11]

Mothers spend a lot of time online talking about various kinds of support. Defining support is a way for mothers to understand their experiences and duties during wartime, but there are also ambiguities over what support means. It takes many kinds of support to wage war. The military needs material and political support from lawmakers, the public, and service members and their families. Service members need material support from the military, emotional (and material) support from their families, and moral support from politicians and citizens for the war they are fighting. Military families need similar kinds of support—emotional support, and material support to hold down the home front during deployment. Their maternal role, in the way Enloe talks about militarized motherhood, becomes a part of the military and mechanisms for making war. Militarizing maternal practices in this way also puts mothers in a gendered position during wartime. [12]

Yet, these mothers do not fit Enloe's ideal of the fully militarized mother. First, the militarized mother defines her citizenship through motherhood, and strives to be a "patriotic mother" who must sacrifice her son for war. This kind of motherhood is depicted in military advertising, and is present in some of the mission statement language on support websites. The second aspect of militarized motherhood is more visible in online support groups. Militarized mothers mobilize their own support activities such as sending soldiers care packages and letters, and caring for wounded children. The final aspect of militarized motherhood is when mothers perpetuate militarization. For example, when a mother acts as the public face of war for her child, asking others to support the troops, she is calling for support of war.

Enloe's concept is useful for seeing the ways that maternal practices can be mobilized in support of war, but is problematic in other ways. For example, mothers do have agency in how they respond to socialization into the military institution. Fully militarized motherhood largely emphasizes one-sided Department of Defense militarization. In her ideal, mothers have little say in how their mothering identity is used to support the war machine, since any of their efforts to support their children during their enlistment, by definition, would also support the war.

The model of the fully militarized mother does not take into account mothers who may initially be the targets of governments' mobilization efforts to garner war support, but then may begin to organize themselves on different terms, and may come to challenge the war policies of the government. As such, the concept of militarized motherhood also misses the ways in which mothers are both empowered and disempowered to participate in public politics as mothers of service members.

The experience of being the mother of a service member is complex and contradictory. But the kinds of support—for the troops and for mothers—described here are not controversial. As I explore in the next chapter, mothers also disagree on what support they should provide. For some mothers, supporting the troops means politically supporting the war. For many mothers, politics is unrelated to the care of their children and the troops.

4

"MY SON FIGHTS FOR YOUR FREEDOM"

The Politics of Support

I met Debbie late one night on the Semper Fi message board. The message board had a private chat option for members, and her name popped up around 2:30 a.m. She was one of the board's moderators; she asked me how my research was going. When I joked about how late she was up, she explained that this hour was typical for her. She usually spent her nights on the message board and news websites. She'd go to sleep around 4:00 a.m., sleeping for a few hours before going to work at 8:00 a.m. I asked her if it was board moderation work that kept her up late. She replied,

> It's the fear that keeps me awake. The worry. It's too loud in my head at night so I try to distract myself with online reading and busy work. As a mom, I've always been a worrier but this is harder. My son is facing something that he has to do alone. I can't fix it, I can't help him, I can't make it easier—and that is supposed to be a mother's job.

A forty-six-year-old widow, Debbie describes herself in her online profile as the "Devoted Mom of 2 children, and 1 Marine. Ooh-Rah!" By day, she is an administrative assistant at a local elementary school, but she describes her "real job" as moderating Semper Fi. She joined the community when her son enlisted in the Marines. She became so active in the large message board community that by the time Dave deployed, she was a moderator. She is one of twelve moderators for the board, and spends about four to five hours a day reading, responding to, and sometimes screening posts from members. Her other children, two daughters, are fifteen and seventeen, and Dave, the Marine, is twenty-three.

One of Debbie's jobs as moderator on Semper Fi is screening members' posts when they are "flagged" by other members to ensure that they follow the message board rules. Semper Fi rules state: "We DO NOT address or allow political issues and discussions. We are always faithful to the United States Marine Corps and Marines." As a member and moderator, Debbie takes the rules seriously, explaining,

> That one simple rule [no politics] made Semper Fi a safe space for me when I was a newbie who didn't know anything about the Corps. I knew I could come here and not deal with people questioning my son's decision, or questioning the war, or going over the same arguments about WMDs and whatever crap was on the news that day. As a moderator I try to remember what I felt like as a newbie. If I see politics in any posts, or see a conversation is heading down that dangerous path, I step in and shut it down. Well, usually, I don't shut it down unless it's really out of control. Usually I email the members involved and ask them to stop, and then we shut the thread down.

Debbie describes her moderation duties as making sure that members feel safe and supported. Political discussions or anything deemed controversial are considered unsafe because members might become upset. For Debbie, leaving politics out of the discussions mothers are having is not only better for mothers but also respectful to the troops.

> I was a kid during the Vietnam era. Those soldiers, sailors, Marines, pilots, nurses, doctors came home to a country that despised them for what they were called to do, many of whom had no choice because of the draft system in place at the time. We Americans let them down, did not acknowledge their sacrifice, their pain, or some of the wounds they suffered. I'm grateful this isn't the case today.

Debbie monitored discussions, reading hundreds of threads a day, to make sure that they never ventured into politics. By her estimates, around five discussions each week needed some kind of moderator intervention for being too political—"If a thread is supportive of our

Marines, it's OK, but if it starts questioning the war or the commander in chief then it's out of bounds and we're going to most likely step in and shut things down."

The message forum Debbie moderates, Semper Fi, is one of the largest and most strictly moderated message boards. Other message boards have less direct moderation, and political discussions go on for a while until they are finally shut down. In every message board, if moderators do not police "out of bounds" discussions, then members themselves police the discussions. Members do this by arguing with one another over the meanings of terms such as *support* and *politics*, or over the message board rules. Members also sometimes exercise control by completely ignoring discussion posts they perceive as inappropriately political.

This chapter looks at how mothers collectively make sense of the military's demands for unconditional support of war in their online discussion groups. Even though every group has rules (whether explicit or unspoken) against discussing "politics," mothers collectively define "politics" as speaking out against the war. Together, mothers assert that politics has no place in supporting other mothers, or in supporting the troops.

MOTHERHOOD AND POLITICS

While online groups describe themselves as providing validation and ways to support other mothers and the service members, they usually state somewhere in their description or rules that no political discussions are allowed. Their mission statements often posit politics as the antithesis to motherhood and maternal support during wartime. Moderators like Debbie make sure that what they perceive to be "too political" is shut down. Positioning politics against motherhood has implications for women's active citizenship and political participation.

Just as citizenship can be understood as gendered, political participation is also framed by ideas about gender. Women are usually associated with the home and nurturing, the private sphere. Men are associated with the public sphere, work and politics.[1] Thus, political authority—who has the authority to speak politically—is organized by gender and women,[2] through their association with the home, do not have the same political authority as men.

Maternal ideology also shapes women's political authority.[3] Just as activists like Cindy Sheehan find a public voice to talk about politics and war policy through their grief, maternal ideology can also keep women trapped in a gendered political role. Women can speak out with authority about issues associated with the home, children, caregiving, etc., but those political voices are only amplified through their role as mothers.[4]

Military mothers find themselves both empowered and disempowered by their maternal authority. On one hand, they may feel empowered to take political positions as mothers during wartime.[5] But on the other hand, if they take political stances on issues considered outside of their maternal knowledge, they can be marginalized and dissuaded from speaking.[6] When are mothers, through their maternal role during wartime, empowered to speak out? When are they disempowered, and silence their own political views?

This tension is at the heart of struggles in online groups over what's considered "too political." Carreon and Moghadam posit that the key intervening mechanism in whether political participation through maternal authority is empowering for women is the state's influence.[7] The state, or more specifically in this case, the military, can use maternal frames to encourage mothers to not question the state and to reinforce the patriarchy. Thus, when mothers in online message boards echo military ideologies that prescribe mothers to support the troops and the war, and to steer clear of politics, that is "maternalism-from-above."

Conversely, in "maternalism-from-below" mothers use maternalism in grassroots mobilizations, empowering themselves to become politically active. The outcome of "maternalism-from-below" is de facto feminist, whether or not the group calls themselves feminist. Carreon and Moghadam argue that the act of mobilizing as mothers empowers the group in a way that is feminist, whether or not they see themselves as feminist. In this chapter I consider how much maternal ideologies prescribed by the military prevent mothers from taking part in critical politics during wartime. I also examine how mothers collectively carry out "maternalism-from-above," socializing and limiting one another in a way that keeps them from politically questioning war.

MESSAGE BOARD RULES AND MODERATION

The amount of disagreement allowed in an online group depends, in part, on the rules and moderators in that group. Some forums have few rules and thus more open discussion. In these groups, mothers often police their own discussions, deferring to military authority, and arguing that political talk is harmful to the troops. Other forums have strict policies as to whether they allow antiwar or antimilitary (political) discussions at all.

Message board rules serve as a foundation for placing boundaries around what support and politics mean online. Each of the mothers' online groups has rules that focus on supporting each other and the service members, and often expressly state that the group is not "political." A Marine mothers' group slogan is typical: "Marine Moms Online is patriotic. Not political," and the description of the Operation Mom message board reads:

> We are proud of our sons and their commitment to keeping this country free. We do NOT get in the political end of it all. Our sons were called up to do what they were trained to do and it's their job. We support our troops unconditionally.

Another message board, Proud Army Moms, has the no-politics rule, but also adds others:

> No politics, no bashing of personnel, no identifying by last name of recruits or Marines, no links to websites that can't be verified or that can change (we only allow .mil links or Snopes.com), no spreading of rumors, but we do allow a call to prayer, and patriotism.

Operation Moms' mission statement is a bit more forthright with its association of troop support with war support. It states that "the troops need full support" and that as Americans we are united around "one great purpose: FREEDOM":

> We believe that the troops need full support from all Americans. Our military troops will face their enemies knowing we are praying for each and every one of them, and thinking of them often. We are united as Americans, one country, and for one great purpose: FREEDOM!

The Operation Moms' mission statement shows that while groups work to connect military mothers around their shared need of support for themselves and the troops, they also include phrases that suggest the troops' mission itself is an intrinsic part of that support. The Marine mothers group calls for appreciating their "contribution to each and every one of us on the home front" and the Operation Moms group describes the troops as facing the "enemies" of freedom, which is everyone's goal. These statements imply that fighting in war is fighting for the freedom of all Americans, and that no American could be against the goal of freedom (and thus could not be "against" the troops).

Some message boards relegate political discussions to boards such as the "controversy central: enter at your own risk" forum. The assumption with these "controversial" forums is that politics is going to generate controversy, so it needs to be separated from the rest of the discussion. Message boards with these sub-forums are controlled just as tightly as others—with rules for posting, moderators, etc., but there are few rules and moderators in the "controversy central" forum. Instead, nearly anything is OK to post and discuss, and moderators only step in when participants are disrespectful to one another. "Disrespectful," as one moderator explained, amounts to name-calling and shouting (writing in all capital letters). Otherwise, members talk about politics and elections, and share news stories about political leaders.

Despite the fact that these "controversial" sub-forums offer a nearly free space to hash out political differences and anti- and pro-war sentiments, they tend to be inactive compared with message boards that have no set space for controversial topics. For example, Military Moms Online "controversy central" contained only forty-one total discussion threads for the two years I monitored the board, and the majority of those were during the 2008 presidential campaign season. Other message boards, like Moms of Marines and Operation Mom, which had no sub-forums for controversial discussions (and no pre-posting moderation) had well over two hundred discussion threads that included controversial topics (like politics) per year. It is the message boards that have no set space for controversy that erupt into debates.

In addition to the common "no politics" rule, Proud Army Moms has rules against "bashing" service personnel, but does allow "prayer and patriotism." Given that under the militarized, enlisted motherhood, patriotism means unconditional support for the war, allowing patriotism

while not allowing politics defines politics as only one side of a controversy, questioning the war. This disjuncture between politics and support is also described in the rules for the Semper Fi online community:

> We DO NOT address or allow political issues and discussions. We
> DO allow freedom of spiritual proclamations, support and prayer.
> We DO believe in God, Family, Country and The United States
> Marine Corps. We are always faithful to the United States Marine
> Corps and Marines: Semper Fidelis!

These rules state clearly that "political issues and discussions" are
not allowed, but the idea of what support means, and what politics
means, is defined by the other rules. For example, while politics is not
allowed, "freedom of spiritual proclamations, support and prayer" are
allowed. Furthermore "believing in . . . Country and The United States
Marine Corps" could be interpreted as political, since unquestioning
nationalism is certainly a non-universal and debatable perspective and
the motto Semper Fidelis means "always faithful," and reiterates the
idea of believing in/having faith in the corps and the chain of command.
The kind of politics that is not allowed online is whatever could be
considered opposite to faith/prayer, belief in "the country" and the
corps, and to support (of the troops, corps, mission etc.). These message
board rules, and others, are frequently cited by mothers and moderators online to police the boundaries of discussions.

The rules are enforced through moderators. Depending on the
board, moderators are either the individual mothers, like Debbie, who
started the message board—they administer the board and serve as
moderators—or, moderators are chosen by other moderators from active message board participants. For instance, Rebecca explained, "I
remember posting so much in the area regarding our wounded. I
seemed to be drawn to them. One of the moderators hinted through
email that I should help out there and I jumped at the chance." Occasionally mothers volunteer to become moderators; "I appreciated the
support I received. I wrote the discussion admin and asked to become a
volunteer." In the case of the groups I studied, moderators were always
other military mothers. In larger message boards, moderators have to
go through training to learn how to use the technological features to
enforce the rules by PMing (private messaging) members, shutting
down discussions, banning participants, etc. One moderator who volun-

teers twenty-plus hours a week to the message board explained, "Our forum does not just allow anyone to volunteer and requires many hours of training before being 'sent out into the world.'"

In these forums, when military mothers are critical of the war effort, they are sanctioned for taking too "political" a stance, one that is considered the antithesis of support and potentially dangerous for service members. In all these spaces, mothers who might question the war learn to silence their own views in the name of supporting the troops. Following their militarized sense of duty to provide unconditional love and support, participants construct mothers' political participation as the opposite of support. Through their unofficial enlistment, the military situates them in a maternal role that removes them from the political decisions necessary in a democracy during wartime, even while they claim the special knowledge that emotional closeness to the front may offer.

These mission statements and posted rules are sure to discourage some mothers from joining altogether. During this period, there were no online support groups for expressly antiwar mothers. Mothers who join these groups either agreed with the notion that politics has no place in a supportive space, or they were willing to overlook those rules in order to join the community. While some mothers were surely discouraged from joining and are not part of this book, the mothers who do join and are interviewed here represent far more diversity of opinions about war than the mission statements and online discussions suggest.

CO-ENLISTED COMMUNITIES

In these message boards military mothers consider themselves a part of the military and war effort and take on some of the rules meant for military personnel. Many message boards describe military directives as rules for participation and rules for mothers' own conduct during wartime. As Renee, a moderator for Proud Army Moms, explained, military rules like DoD Directive 1344.10 apply to military mothers, and that means that political discussions should be kept to "close family and friends."

> We know the rules the military uses apply to us, no political involvement when in uniform or as a representative of the military, but OK as a private citizen. I try to follow that rule, no outright discussion with people I don't know, but OK with close family and friends.

DoD Directive 1344.10 states that active duty service members are not allowed to publicly participate in the political process while in uniform—to identify with or support one political candidate or party over another as a service member.[8] This directive, of which service members are typically reminded during election campaigns, separates the election of politicians from military service and the military chain of command. Service members and their families are encouraged to vote in elections, but not to participate in public politics in any way, particularly while in uniform where they might be seen therefore representing the military. Mothers, considering themselves co-enlistees, no longer identify as civilians so they believe that just like service members, they are not allowed to participate publicly in political activities.

The message boards and the rules they follow work to "close ranks" to military outsiders. This follows mothers' general feeling of not being understood by those not connected to war. Because Renee feels that she is more a part of the military than a civilian, she and other mothers actively believe they have no civic responsibilities to participate in public political debates, particularly with anyone outside the military institution. Their responsibility during war is to support the troops.

SUPPORTING THE TROOPS, SUPPORTING THE WAR

As chapter 3 showed, the overt goals of the message boards are (1) for mothers to provide support for each other and (2) to support the troops. But there is another implicit goal online: to encourage mothers to support the war itself by silencing dissent. This is accomplished through making mothers feel co-enlisted in the war, and through conflating support for the troops with support for the war itself.

The current unequal distribution of war costs has led to public debates about what it means in practice to "support the troops."[9] Although the American public as a whole struggles with conflicting notions of what is meant by "supporting" the troops, the war, their families' interests, and the national interest, these issues are even more acute for military families. As Debbie explained in the opening of the chapter, the idea that one has to support the war in order to support the troops has origins in the Vietnam War protests of the 1960s and 1970s. Mothers often refer to this as "avoiding another Vietnam" which essentially means unconditionally supporting the war itself.

While mothers generally agree on how to support one another, and how to support the troops physically and emotionally, other definitions of support are much more controversial. One distinction that comes up frequently is whether there is a difference between "supporting the troops" and "supporting the war."

As the rules for each message board state, political engagement is not supportive to the troops. When mothers talk about this, they invert the feminist phrase "the personal is political" to argue that the personal (their maternal relationship to war) is not political. In fact, participating in politics jeopardizes mothers' personal connection to war.

For instance, Marie, the mother of a soldier, was particularly active in an ongoing discussion about whether it was supportive to criticize the reasons for war. Some online participants tried to discuss whether the presence of weapons of mass destruction (WMDs) in Iraq was a lie that President Bush used to justify war. A few mothers were active in the discussion until it was shut down by a moderator. Marie explained afterward her own reasons for not wanting the conversation to continue: "It's personal for military mothers. It's our children out there; it's our children being criticized. I'm a mom and I can't support and criticize at the same time." Marie's explanation highlights the role of the personal—motherhood—in silencing political conversations about war. Support is maternal and is provided through mothers' personal connection to war.

The unconditional support mothers urge each other to provide makes criticism of war difficult. When women do participate in politics, they often do so as women and are called on to contribute discussions of issues close to home—childcare, health care, and education. One way women can claim authority to speak about political issues is through their role as mothers. But, as mothers, women may also abdicate their political authority by stressing their personal (and not political) connection to war. The rules for participation and the discussions among military mothers in online forums show the rules of engagement in the democratic process by showing when and how women both claim and reject political authority.

Associating women with home front support that centers on care work (caring for each other and the troops) casts women in a politically inactive role during war. This reasserts men's association with both war and with the political process of making decisions about war. In a political process shaped by gender, military mothers like these are on the margins of politics during wartime.

POLICING CRITICAL POLITICS

Despite all the rules and moderation, politics comes up often in every message board I studied. The only kinds of political discussion met with argument and hostility are when the war itself is questioned. Politics is allowed as long as it is in support of the reasons for war and the commander in chief who started the wars (President George W. Bush), or supports the perception that positive progress is being made during the wars. The boundaries of what counts as "politics" is actually more about not allowing critical politics—political discussions that criticize the war, the commander in chief, or the troops in any way.

One such discussion began when a popular email article was circulated on the Semper Fi message board. A member posted a link to an article and photo, showing the newly elected President Obama not saluting the flag during the national anthem, and describing him as not saying the Pledge of Allegiance. While the board had largely avoided political controversy during the election (Semper Fi has very strict moderation and no sub-board for controversial topics), the posting of this article and photo gave mothers an opportunity to voice their opinions on the new president. One mother, Patty, responded to the article saying:

> I don't have a lot of faith in Obama. I really don't care about the man's skin color but his name WOW!! For me, it's too much like the enemy. But Obama is our President and I will do my best to respect and support him. And he should say the Pledge of Allegiance and respect our marines!

Patty's views on the president's name sounding "too much like the enemy" causes quite a stir in the message board. One mother posts back that a person's name "doesn't mean anything" and describes how she has friends with "Arabic sounding" names who are not connected to the enemy. Another mother describes feeling "hurt and disgusted" that the president does not respect her son who is currently deployed to Iraq. Another mother, whose username is only "BradsMom" says that she is sure President Obama salutes the flag, and she posts a picture of him at another event doing exactly that. Soon after BradsMom's post, another mother tries to calm everyone down by reminding mothers of how stressful the war is:

> As this war heats up things can get even more stressful on this site. We are not know-it-alls but, trust me . . . no one should dare tread the path of saying they know what they are talking about. Mr. Obama "DOES NOT SAY THE PLEDGE OF ALLEGIANCE" refused to put his hand on his heart. Check it out on "snopes." I for one am not a big fan of a President that disrespects the flag.

What is interesting about this particular post is that the mother describes fact checking, and posting alternative information as "no one should dare tread the path of saying they know what they are talking about" as mothers are "not know-it-alls." However, she looks up the original article on Snopes.com and finds confirmation of the fact that Obama did not salute the flag or say the pledge. The conversation continues when another mother, only known as "MarineMom54" posts:

> I see that this group is now turning into a political forum. Well. I am sure that the moms who have lost sons or daughters over there, or who have sons or daughters over there would appreciate support rather than your opinions on President Obama. Snopes also shows pictures of Obama putting his hand over his heart for the Pledge! I am sick of this new president being smashed by uninformed opinionated know-it-alls.

MarineMom54 sees the ongoing conversation as a sign the website has turned into "a political forum." She reminds mothers that what they are online for is to provide one another, and the troops, with support instead of "opinions." Political opinions are not supportive.

Finally, the controversial post is shut down by a moderator, but not before a mother who has lost her son in Iraq joins in the discussion. She invokes her privileged identity among mothers as a "GOLD STAR

MOM" and claims that she has "MORAL authority" just as the press has granted Cindy Sheehan:

> I just want to say as a GOLD STAR MOM, maybe what we don't need is someone thinking they know what we need? And thinking that everyone else is ignorant about Obama. I am not so sure of Obama. It is looking like other countries are doing exactly what they please right now and he is just smiling and trying to make friends with dictators. Makes me wonder if he will man up or turn and run? If I have to choose between what Obama tells us or the Generals who have been involved with the fight against terror since 2001, sorry Obama just doesn't know jack! And since the press conferred MORAL authority on Cindy Sheehan to say whatever she wanted because Casey died in Iraq, I think I have just as much moral authority too!

This Gold Star mother addresses MarineMom54's post, but asserts that maybe mothers do need to express opinions about the new president, "we don't need someone thinking they know what we need." Claiming her moral authority as the mother of a Marine killed in action, this mother goes on to express her opinion about the president—that she "wonders if he will man up or turn and run?" and that he "doesn't know jack" about the war. While the moderator ends the discussion right after this post, this particular mother is able to describe how she feels about Obama, while arguing that when others express their feelings (by sticking up for the president) it is not what mothers need.

This mother's explanation of her problems with Obama also illustrates how war (and politics) are seen as men's territory, where a certain kind of tough masculinity (not smiling or making friends) is valued. This conversation, which started with a circulated article and photo, shows how mothers work together to further some definitions of support online, but also how that power is limited through different mothers making claims to online authority (either authority to find information, or authority as a certain type of mother).

Another discussion on ArmyMoms2 veered into political territory before moderators stepped in. The post began when a mother posted a link to a *U.S. News and World Report* article questioning whether the United States should have gone to war in Iraq. The opinion piece argued that in hindsight, a more diplomatic solution should have been tried first. The mother who posted it wrote with the post, "This is something to think about. Maybe more diplomacy should be tried before putting our kids in harm's way."

ArmyMoms2 is a highly moderated board and typically moderators jump in to shut down controversial posts within seconds. This post, however, stayed online for about an hour, long enough for a few other mothers to chime in. One mother replied,

> There is no way diplomacy would've worked. Look at the mess there right now! No one could've talked there [sic] way out of that! Don't ya [sic] think politicians thought about going the diplomatic route first?

Another mother, JennieB, answered,

> Whether or not they thought about it doesn't even matter. We're at war now. Our troops have a mission to do. They don't need us here at home arguing over whether or not they should be there! We have to do better than that for them! Focus on the mission for our soldiers' sake!

JennieB's post suggests that political questions do not matter once a war is going on and troops are deployed. Like other similar conversations online, she reminds mothers to focus on the mission. The original poster, Gab67, responds, "I just think it's useful to read about diplomacy because we could avoid war in the future." JennieB responds quickly, "No, it's not useful because we're at war now!" Another mother joins the conversation before it is finally deleted by moderators:

> I have no idea why we are talking about this! We are at WAR! Our soldiers are in the sandbox! They don't need us—their mothers—talking about whether we should have had more talks first. I trust Bush did what was right and I trust that politicians knew they had exhausted diplomacy first. That's their job! We're at WAR now and our job is to take care of our soldiers. Let's be their mothers, not politicians!

This last mother makes it clear that not only is it inappropriate to talk about politics during wartime; it is not the role of mothers to talk about politics. Mothers, she explains, have another "job" and that job is to be mothers—to care for soldiers. Mothers' domain during wartime is the home front and family, and political decisions about war and diplomacy should be left to others—to men.

In a democracy, the assumption is often that everyone has equal permission to speak publicly and express their opinions about political issues. However, some people have much more political authority to speak publicly than others. Variations in political authority have to do, in part, with the gendered ways that we think about politics and political authority. Women, for instance, do not have the same kind of political authority that men have. Moreover, as motherhood is a gendered identity and experience, mothers' relationship to politics is often contradictory. On one hand, mothers are sometimes granted political authority and are privileged to speak out publicly about political issues because they are mothers. Maternal authority often comes from the association of mothers with the realm of the personal and private—the home, families, care work, and nurturing. However, mothers' political positions may also be marginalized if they raise issues that are *outside* of the range of what is considered women's domain—for instance, issues surrounding the public/political domain, which is usually associated with men. Mothers of service members provide a way to understand how women engage with the process of gaining permission through a gendered identity (motherhood) to be public political citizens.

In sum, this process of collective depoliticization has three steps. All three steps build on the association of motherhood with the home and private life.[10] The first occurs when mothers become a part of the military institution. As part I described, mothers start to consider themselves a non-civilian part of the military family even when they are technically civilians as soon as their children enlist. The second mechanism is how the term *support* is defined online. Supporting the troops means supporting their mission and the war. The third mechanism is how the term *political* is defined. For mothers who consider themselves enlisted in the military along with their children, politics is associated with civilians and is not related to the military or carrying out a war. Mothers who consider themselves to still be civilians, on the other hand, see politics as necessary for getting the service members the care they need when they return from deployment.

CONCLUSION

The mothers of service members examined here negotiate their person-al/private concern for their children, and the public/political issue of war. Collectively these mothers define "support" and "politics." Support is defined as (private) maternal duty, and critical (public) politics is incompatible with providing that support. Politics is defined as outside of the gendered (personal) sphere of motherhood, and separate from the masculine military institution and leadership. Even mothers who may hold their own critical antiwar views learn to silence their views about war online. Mothers are encouraged by their peers and by message board rules to be supportive and proud, and to not take critical stances questioning war. Together, mothers teach each other the ideal of a good motherhood during wartime. To be patriotic "good mothers," they must subordinate their opinions as citizens and support the military during times of war.

In all these spaces, mothers who might question the war learn to silence their own views in the name of supporting the troops. In these forums mothers could openly discuss politics when it was in support of the pro-war position. Critical views of war or the military were not allowed. In doing this collectively, mothers took on a militarized position, where they must offer unconditional war support. This is an example of the "maternalism-from-above" Carreon and Moghadam theorize.[11] When they take on this militarized role, their motherhood is coopted for the war effort. By encouraging one another to be "good mothers" during wartime, they are contributing to the structure of support the military needs to wage war. Their collective ideas for what a "good mother" is during wartime is framed by the military and militarism.

In doing this collectively, it appears as if mothers are self-organizing and practicing "maternalism-from-below." Following Carreon and Moghadam's model, this "maternalism-from-below" would make maternal support groups feminist. But these support groups are not feminist. They dissuade mothers from active political participation and tie their maternal support for their children to intrinsically supporting the war. The appearance of "maternalism-from-below"—the fact that the groups are run by mothers—only reinforces the perception that these groups are supportive spaces autonomous from militarized discourse, when in fact they are shaped by that discourse. While Carreon and Moghadam consider these separate processes of mobilization, the mothers here show how both the "below" and "above" processes can be used simultaneously to discourage political participation. This reinforces gender inequality during war. For these mothers of service members online, motherhood becomes a depoliticized identity, discouraging any questioning of war policy or participation in politics during wartime.

Part III

Post-Deployment Health Care

5

RETURNING HOME

The Invisible Burden of Caregiving

> I didn't know what to expect when Charlie got home. I didn't know what he would be like. I know it sounds silly but I was so nervous I would say something wrong or ask him something wrong. I never was nervous with him before. We always talked easy about everything. He was in Special Forces, you know, so I knew there was going to be a lot he could not talk about.
>
> —Dawn

When Dawn first contacted me, her son, Charlie, had been home for three weeks. At forty-eight, Dawn is a longtime employee at a furniture outlet who never finished college. She describes herself as "too old to be on my feet all day selling" but enjoys her coworkers and her job. She's married to a city bus driver, Paul, who hopes to retire soon. Charlie is their only child. At twenty-three years old, Charlie was living with his parents again after deployment, taking his time deciding what kind of college to attend with his veteran's benefits.

> Paul told me to just not ask Charlie lots of questions. See, he remembers when his uncle got home from Vietnam and didn't want to talk about the war. His uncle never talked about the war. But he did tell Paul how he was treated when he returned home from that war. I never got to meet him, but Paul said he always told them about how he was spit on by protesters. He was called baby killer and murderer. He was drafted but the people who called him a baby killer burned

their draft cards. He was very angry. I guess he instilled in Paul the importance of making vets feel thanked and welcomed, even when the war wasn't winnable, you know, when they get home.

Paul's uncle's returning home from Vietnam is a narrative that reverberates through mothers' stories of their children coming home from the wars in Iraq and Afghanistan. Mothers describe this poor treatment of Vietnam War troops when they returned home as a warning—a reason to make sure that their children do not experience the same.

When Charlie came home from his eighteen-month deployment, Dawn described how there was no ceremony or fanfare for his unit. There were no WWII–style ticker tape parades in the streets. As Green Berets, their exact return date and time was unknown. Paul and Dawn drove six hours and stayed in a motel for three days so they would be nearby when Charlie's unit arrived. When Charlie's flight touched down on the Army base at 11:00 p.m., there were only a dozen family members there. "I was so sad for those boys. They looked so worn. Most of their parents and wives couldn't be there. The trip was too far. The BC [base commander] was there to shake their hands. That was it."

Dawn's description of Charlie's return home is typical. Some service members return home to bands, balloons, banners, and dozens of families. Most return home in the middle of the night to nearly empty airstrips on bases far away from their homes and families. Military families describe the celebratory videos and photos of returning troops as "reunion porn." Those kinds of reunions make for good news, and go viral when they are shared online, but they are not the norm. Instead, the military warns family members that reunions after long deployments can be awkward. Service members will be tired, jet lagged, and emotionally drained.[1] Dawn describes Charlie's return as "anticlimactic" and "unsettling." She found him to be "different."

We spent another night and then Charlie wanted to go home the next day. There was optional reintegration workshop, but he didn't want to attend. Like most of his buddies, he basically wanted a good meal and a quiet night of sleep in his own bed. He was quiet most of the drive home. Asked us questions about people at home. He seemed the same, but different. Tired. Far off. I figured that would sort itself out after a few days home. I mean, he was physically fine. I was so grateful he came home in one piece!

But Charlie's "far off" demeanor did not "sort itself out." Dawn made his favorite meals. He watched a lot of television, and slept sometimes twelve hours straight. He showed no interest in catching up with old friends, or even going out to run errands around town. After a few weeks, Dawn was worried. She did not know who to turn to in the VA or in his unit for help, so she asked other military mothers in her online forum—ArmyMoms2—what to do. The advice she received included everything from encouraging him to get together with old friends to getting him immediate counseling at the nearest VA Center. Much to Dawn's dismay, neither of these options were things Charlie showed any interest in, and the nearest VA Center was over an hour away. Like so many military mothers and family members, Dawn found herself online, trying to find out how she herself could help her son.

No matter how prepared they are by Family Readiness Programs (which usually only target spouses and dependents), deployments are stressful for families. Marines are deployed for seven months at a time, and Army soldiers like Charlie for more than twice that. While deployed, service members become incredibly used to their routines and used to living with a constant sense of danger. Even service members without physical wounds come home with emotional issues such as anxiety, depression, and PTSD. PTSD is common, although underdiagnosing means that the exact numbers of those who suffer PTSD are unknown. The military counts roughly 200,000 service members post-9/11 with diagnosed PTSD, but with 2.5 million service members in Iraq and Afghanistan, the number is believed to be much higher. RAND estimates that roughly 20 percent of service members suffer from PTSD.[2] Only 23 percent of those seek mental health care.[3]

This chapter is about the work mothers do to take care of their physically and emotionally injured children after deployment. Dawn is one of an estimated 5.5 million military caregivers in the United States.[4] While Dawn was grateful that Charlie came home in one piece, other mothers are not as lucky. This chapter describes mothers who have taken on caring for seriously wounded service members, even quitting their jobs in order to provide round-the-clock care. This is the invisible, unpaid, work of war. For some mothers, whose stories are told in the next chapter, this invisible care work leads to criticizing the military institution and the war, in a way they did not feel free to do before.

"NEVER AGAIN"

In 2009, PBS released the documentary *The Way We Get By* about an organization of "troop greeters" in Bangor, Maine. The documentary describes a group of older veterans and military family members in a remote part of Maine where many returning troops first touch down on US soil. The group is motivated by the necessity to ensure that the troops feel welcomed when they return from war. To do this, the Maine Troop Greeters meet every flight of returning soldiers at Bangor International Airport. The organization of volunteers ensures that every service member is greeted with American flags, band music, handshakes, cheers and applause, and even hugs. The website for the Maine Troop Greeters describes their mission as "expressing the nation's gratitude and appreciation to the troops." The need to show troops appreciation is very much a concern for mothers like Dawn.

Karen is part of another smaller group of troop greeters in Jacksonville, North Carolina. The group is mostly made up of military mothers who all know one another from their children's deployment. Living near a Marine Corps base, the mothers supported each other through four years of multiple deployments. While their children were deployed, they organized care packages and holiday cards and gifts for the troops. Then, as their service members began returning from war, they decided it was important that they not come home to an empty airport.

> I remember hearing about how service members were treated during Vietnam. Not only did they see protests going on at home while they were deployed, they got disrespected by protesters and hippies when they returned. Our service members deserve so much more than that! Here they are making sacrifices that very few are willing to make, and they get spit on? Or ignored? A few of us [mothers] talked and decided we did not want our sons coming home with any sense that they are not appreciated. There have been protests. Not as many as during Vietnam. The last thing we want is protesters greeting them. Or maybe worse would be no one there for them at all.

Even though historians like Lembcke argue that there is no evidence that Vietnam troops were actually spit on, the collective memory of spitting on troops is alive and well in military memories about Vietnam.[5] Mothers either described hearing directly from a family member that they were mistreated by Vietnam War protestors, or had heard about mistreatment from others in the military. The image of an unappreciative country, in the face of such immense sacrifice, drives mothers to ensure troops feel thanked and welcomed when they return home.

Susan, another mother who regularly greets returning troops at the nearby airport, explained,

> Ed (my older brother) was in the Vietnam War. He saw first-hand the hideous welcoming home of our troops. So when our son signed up for the Marines, something welled up in me and it wasn't pride! I was worried that what happened to Ed would never happen to him and his friends. So yes, now we Moms are part of the veteran's experience of returning home. That is not gonna happen to my son or anyone else who serves our country, if I can help it. "Never Again!"

Susan and a small group of mothers join family members between midnight and 3:00 a.m. to welcome troops home. They sing, pass out homemade cookies, and often send every service member home with a "goodie bag" of treats and thank-you notes from local school children. Susan told me, "They are often overcome with emotion. A female soldier I remember broke down crying and said she wasn't expecting this."

Tracey told me that she regretted how many of the troops came home to little or no welcoming. She described the post-deployment experience as incredibly isolating for service members. Her son, Donald, has suffered from PTSD since his return home. After months of depression and outbursts of anger, Tracey was able to convince him to join a group for young veterans at a local counseling center. It was there that he started talking about his experiences in Afghanistan, and the stresses of battle and seeing friends wounded and killed. Tracey compared Donald's experience to that of her Uncle Mike during Vietnam.

> He came home needing some support, needing someone to talk to. It was a terrible war. Instead of consolation, cruel words were hurled at him from protesters at the airport. They didn't care about who he was, or what he had done. They just knew he was returning from Vietnam. He actually hid out in a bathroom stall to avoid protesters. He stayed there for hours, finally leaving the airport when it was safe. He was shell-shocked. Maybe they don't call it that anymore but they

didn't know about PTSD back then. After that he removed himself from everyone around him. He was quiet and reclusive and became quite a shut-in. No one could reach him. He was never the same. My mother always wondered if her brother would have had a chance had his veteran's care been better.

With PTSD now recognized, and more veteran's services offering counseling after deployment, Tracey was able to insist that Donald get the help her uncle did not have. A year after his deployment, Donald actually joined Tracey in welcoming another unit home. He wanted to make sure the troops felt supported and welcomed.

Surprisingly, returning service members rarely receive any kind of reentry counseling. Service members are given a Post-Deployment Health Assessment (PDHA) form to fill out within thirty days of reentry.[6] The form is a self-assessment and includes one half-page (out of three pages) on mental health concerns. Starting in 2008, the military made a follow-up meeting with a health care provider for evaluation mandatory. In 2008–2009, 10 percent of returning service members needed a screening after completing the form for PTSD, and 49 percent of those were diagnosed with PTSD.[7]

Reentry programs are optional, and if units take part in reentry counseling it is at their own initiative. Families—spouses, especially, and parents—are given materials to prepare them for what to expect from their returned service member. Websites describe a rollercoaster of emotions—short "honeymoons" after deployment, and then the possibility for anxiety, sleep problems, and anger issues. Pamphlets and websites, however, do not fully prepare families for the serious issues they may have to navigate with and for their loved ones.

VA HEALTH CARE: QUICKER AND SICKER

Family support is critical to patients' successful rehabilitation. Especially in a prolonged recovery, it is family members who make therapy appointments and ensure they are kept, drive the service member to these appointments, pick up medications and make sure they are taken, provide a wide range of personal care, become the impassioned advocates, take care of the kids, pay the bills and negotiate with the benefits offices, find suitable housing for a family that includes a person with a disability, provide emotional support, and, in short, find they have a full-time job—or more—for which they never prepared. When family members give up jobs to become caregivers, income can drop precipitously.

—*DoD Economic Impact on Caregivers of the Seriously Wounded,*
Ill, and Injured

Veterans of the post-9/11 wars are the fastest growing group of veterans. During each year of the wars in Iraq and Afghanistan, approximately 720 new veterans need constant daily care from physical injuries (not including PTSD and other mental disorders). As of 2017, 32,226 service members have been wounded in action in Iraq,[8] and 20,083 in Afghanistan. In total 970,000 temporary or permanent disability claims have been filed since the start of the wars.[9] Thirty percent of all post-9/11 veterans have received service-related disability.

The official wounded in action (WIA) designation leaves out a lot of war injuries. WIA does not include "mild" traumatic brain injuries, hearing loss, breathing disorders, vision problems, PTSD, anxiety, or depression. The Pentagon's Defense and Veterans Brain Injury Center counted over 230,000 mild to severe TBIs from 2001 to 2011.[10] The use of multiple deployments has put measurable strain on the troops. Of those who have been deployed three to four times, 27 percent are diagnosed with depression, anxiety, and PTSD, compared to 12 percent of those deployed only once. Suicide is also a serious issue for post-9/11 veterans. There are forty-five suicides per 100,000 veterans eighteen to twenty-nine years old.[11] That is more than twice the civilian population of the same age (20.4/100,000).

The DoD knows that family care work is critical, acknowledging that service members are much less likely to make recoveries without a familial support system.[12] Taking care of veterans requires a network of coordinated work from the Office of Veterans Affairs, the Veterans Health Administration, the Social Security Disability Administration, countless sub-offices, Veterans Service Officers (VSOs), and of course, veterans' family members. VA benefits are known for being difficult to understand, difficult to file for, and difficult to navigate.[13] Even websites offering to "make sense" of benefits for veterans (especially injured veterans) and their families offer labyrinths of links to different VA subpages.[14]

Where a wife may step in for married service members, 58 percent of new post-9/11 service members are under thirty-four, and 65 percent of them are either not married or divorced.[15] Just as other care work is gendered female, this burden is one that rests on the shoulders of mothers and wives. According to the Department of Defense, 57 percent of Primary Support Persons (PSPs) are mothers, and 83 percent of these mothers have unmarried service members under thirty years old. The care work mothers provide—whether it's at a hospital, full time at-home care, or transportation to and from appointments—is full-time work for about 25 percent of PSPs.[16]

The need for nonmedical caregivers in the military follows the civilian trend of offloading care work to families. The medical industry has been shifting the burden of care to families for decades.[17] Patients leave hospitals "quicker and sicker," staying fewer days after surgeries and receiving little in the way of discharge instructions.[18] More post-surgery care, physical therapy, infusion treatments, and end-of-life care that would have once been done in a hospital or outpatient setting have been offloaded onto families who are trained to do everything from daily care (lifting, bathing, dressing), to wound care, to administering IV medications at home. Just as with civilian health care, military family members are doing the work that would have been done by paid, trained, medical professionals.[19]

Care work is a physical and emotional burden for caregivers, many of whom may deal with physical ailments of their own, in addition to anxiety and depression.[20] Only about 50 percent of caregivers of veterans ask for help when meeting with a VA health care professional, so clinicians have a difficult time evaluating the kind of assistance patients and their caregivers need. There are programs ancillary to the military that offer help to military caregivers (wellness, mental health, advocacy, financial, helping hands, etc.). But most programs are geared toward older populations (i.e., pre-9/11 veterans, or vets sixty and over), and are reserved for caregivers who are immediate family members (i.e., wives and not mothers).[21]

MOTHERS' CAREGIVING BURDEN

The experience of learning that her child is injured is one that a mother remembers in detail. Cindy is a forty-seven-year-old divorced mother who lives on an island near Seattle. A dedicated teacher, she's spent her life teaching year-round, even summer school. She left her job when Jayson was injured.

> No military mother wants to get the phone call I got. I know it could have been worse. It could have been a knock on the door instead of a phone call. . . . I am grateful, don't misunderstand me. To answer the phone and hear "Ma'am, I am sorry to tell you but your son Jayson was critically injured on patrol last night." I just sat down and just couldn't think. I was listening to this calm voice telling me when and where Jayson would get stateside. I can't believe I remembered the details. I asked him if Jayson would live, and he answered that he could not make that kind of promise.

What Cindy describes afterward is a long ordeal of telling her other children—Jayson's siblings—what happened, and calling her own mother to make arrangements for the younger children to stay with her. She booked a flight across the country to Bethesda, Maryland, charging the tickets on her one and only credit card. She said,

> I was so calm. I just wanted to do whatever was necessary to lay my eyes on my son again. I wanted him near me. I wanted to see him, and comfort him. I would've left that afternoon if it were possible.

Cindy's mother contacted a few of the mothers of service members she knew, and found out through them what hotels in Bethesda were the most accommodating for long-term stays. One of the mothers Cindy knew from online met her flight in Bethesda and drove her to the hospital.

> Shocked is probably the best way to describe what I felt when I saw him. Shocked and heartbroken. He was such a beautiful boy, in shape, always took good care of his body. Instead he was fractured and broken. He had a skull fracture, broken jaw, his pelvis was broken. His right arm was broken and several tendons severed. He had internal injuries, bleeding and acute renal failure. He was running a

fever and had infections. Eventually he went septic and we almost lost him.

Soon Cindy's world was taken over with the details of Jayson's many surgeries. He lost both of his legs and use of his right arm. He was in the hospital 265 days, in the ICU for sixty-four days, and had nineteen surgeries. Cindy explained,

> He had something like twenty-four different medical teams. More doctors than I could keep straight. It was almost easier when he was in ICU because I had time to coordinate his care. Once he left ICU and started PT, I was booking and coordinating multiple appointments every day. That was a full-time job!

Cindy left her teaching position, and missed teaching summer school for two summers. Her mother struggled to take care of her bills and her children, while Cindy struggled to afford the hotel and expenses. When Jayson was discharged from the hospital, he moved into an apartment near the VA because he would need a year of rehab. Cindy chose to stay for that year as well, to help Jayson adjust.

While the VA provides health care for veterans, that health care is not free, and any round-the-clock medical and physical therapy care often costs extra. And if the injury is not considered a "wounded in action" injury (injured on base, or while off duty), it may not be covered at all once the service member is discharged. Copays and medication costs add up quickly with a serious injury with multiple months of physical therapy. Anne, whose son Bill spent most of his time on a base in Iraq and developed asthma, found herself unable to cover the cost of Bill's respiratory therapy once he was discharged from the Army.

> He would have had to stay on active duty and potentially be deployed again just to receive health care coverage. He developed severe asthma from months of living on base in Iraq. I'm grateful he wasn't actually in much danger, but he didn't receive hazard pay, so he's been out of work and money. It's been hard trying to help him get control of his asthma and find a job. There's no help from the VA for him to do those things. They discharged him, and he's on his own.

The financial costs of care work for families are difficult to measure; they vary based on family circumstances. Families that live further away from major VA hospitals such Walter Reed in Washington, DC must pay travel costs to be with their injured loved one. Often families like Cindy's rearrange their lives—moving to a hotel near the hospital, having another family member cover childcare at home, taking time off from work, or leaving (or losing) their employment.

The time spent coordinating care in a complex medical system is impossible to measure. Another mother, Nancy, whose son Ryan suffered from a TBI from a fall during combat, explained,

> I spend hours on the phone with the VA and the DoD coordinating Ryan's care. I keep track of his appointments, schedule transportation to and from hospitals and rehab centers. He sees every kind of doctor and PT imaginable. Honestly, if he didn't have me doing these things, I don't know what he would do. What do guys do who don't have mothers and wives to do this stuff? It would be impossible. He gets frustrated when the doctors forget what meds he's on, let alone answering all the repetitive questions I answer at every appointment.

Nancy arranged to work part-time remotely while she stayed with her son at Walter Reed. The small insurance office she works for was able to set her up with a phone and computer so she could work anywhere. Many caregivers lose their jobs or go on complete leave with no pay when taking care of a wounded service member. As a result, 33 percent of post-9/11 caregivers lack health insurance for themselves as they navigate the VA health care system.[22] Of the fifteen mothers I interviewed, Nancy was the only one who was able to keep her job and at least a part-time paycheck while staying at the hospital providing care for her son. Additionally, 50 percent of caregivers report sleep disturbances and 33 percent report physical strain.[23]

The military refers to mothers like Nancy as nonmedical attendants (NMAs). In order to be compensated for their time, NMAs must file paperwork documenting the care work they provide in order to receive $60 per diem. The paperwork must be refiled monthly. Funds of $150 per day are also available for lodging expenses, but must be approved through a separate process ahead of time and completed monthly. As Nancy described, this is enough to supplement her part-time work, but for lots of women who lose their jobs or leave their jobs, it is not enough to live on. That $60 per day does not cover flights, living expenses, meals, and transportation, and definitely does not cover costs of leaving home (such as childcare). On average, NMAs report losing $60,000 in yearly income.[24] On average, injured service members need nineteen months of care.

The time commitment in caring for an injured vet is apparent in Cindy's and Nancy's stories. Caring for anyone with an illness or injury is time consuming. Caregivers for military veterans do everything from making phone calls and filing paperwork, to driving to doctors' appointments and providing emotional support. Twenty-five percent of caregivers provide care forty hours a week, and 60 percent were the sole caregiver (with no regular nursing assistance).[25] In 2007, 21 percent of injured veterans needed a family member to leave a job in order to provide some level of health care.

Leaving their jobs, and sometimes moving across the country, removes mothers from their daily support systems. The isolation that military mother caregivers describe is much like the isolation experienced by civilian caregivers.[26] Without a support system, and with limited access to nurses and home health care aides, social isolation can lead to higher rates of depression, sleep problems, and other poor health outcomes for caregivers. For military mothers, caregiving isolation is compounded by their alienation from civilians not familiar with the impact of war. As Cindy explains,

> No one understands what this is like. A friend of mine compared it to her son's car accident last year. No! It's not the same thing! I never spoke to her again. . . . Our house needs renovations to accommodate his disabilities, and no one is helping to pay for that. My mother and sister are trying to get donations for renovations. We need a new bathroom, wider doors, a ramp. . . . When they call contractors, some of them are surprised the war is still going on! Can you imagine!

Jayson's injuries only make Cindy feel more alienated from her civilian friends and family. She echoes other mothers who realize that no one else knows what it's like to have a child deployed or injured in a war. Moving across the country and focusing on her son's care made Cindy geographically isolated from friends and family. She lost every support system she had, and instead found herself navigating the maze of veteran's health care, making calls, and filling out paperwork.

I missed my kids horribly. I hate to say that because Jayson needed to be my priority. They understood that and they visited once. It was too expensive for us to travel back and forth for visits. I missed Alexa's sophomore and junior years of high school. She was dating and I wasn't there to meet boyfriends and help with homework. I met some great people—other mothers—who I keep in touch with even now years later. But while I was in Maryland, I was really alone. It was one of the loneliest times in my life.

Cindy's story is common. As the mother of a young, unmarried Marine, she took full responsibility for his care when he was injured. The military acknowledges mothers' care work, but does little to support it. A *Washington Post* article describes crowded conditions at Walter Reed Army Medical Center:

The squad leader who lost one leg and the use of his other in a grenade attack, said his recovery was made more difficult by a Marine liaison officer who had never seen combat but dogged him about having his mother in his room on post. The rules allowed her to be there, but the officer said she was taking up valuable bed space.

"When you join the Marine Corps, they tell you, you can forget about your mama. 'You have no mama. We are your mama,'" Groves said. "That training works in combat. It doesn't work when you are wounded."[27]

As this squad leader quote explains, mothers have a contradictory place in the military. Full grown men—Marines—don't need their mothers. But when service members are injured, mothers are key.

Mothers describe their invisible caregiving work in two ways. First, they see it as an extension of their mothering duties, part of their maternal instinct.[28] Cindy, for example, just wanted to comfort her son, to be able to see him. Jenni, whose son Rich suffered a TBI from an improvised explosive device (IED) explosion, described her "maternal instinct" to take care of her son when he was injured.

I have never left a kid of mine alone in a hospital. I stayed with each of them every time they were hospitalized, night and day until I could take them home. I had to watch over their care, with my maternal instincts, to make sure they were receiving the proper amount of attention.

It's not that the military requires Jenni to watch over his care, it's that she sees it as her duty, as his mother. This is similar to how supporting the troops—not just their child—is described as "natural" for mothers.

> When Rich finally returned home after three deployments to Iraq, I didn't stop caring for the other deployed soldiers and Marines. All those who are deployed are my "kids" and they need to know the people at home support them. I can never express enough gratitude to them. I can help Rich out with his PTSD appointments and meetings, and I can still send care packages until they all come home.

The other way mothers describe their care work of mentally or physically injured service members is as their military duty. As other military mothers talk about being strong for their children, these mothers take on mottos of "Army Mom Strong" and "If you think Marines are tough, you haven't met their mothers" and put that strength into their injured children. They become their children's cheerleaders, encouraging them to fight to recover from their injuries. Jillian, for example, talked about how she dealt with her own emotions helping her son Eddie, a double amputee.

> When Eddie was in the hospital I had to be strong and act like I was in control of my emotions. I had to be so strong. I couldn't show my struggle, when my son didn't know at first how much recovery was ahead of him. I talked with so many doctors trying to figure out if they had a good plan for his care and weren't dropping the ball on him. He deserves the best with all he's sacrificed!

Mothers like Jillian talk about the care their children *deserve* because of the sacrifice they have made for their country. They evoke the idea that they—as mothers—are also a part of the military that must support the warriors after war, and that their job is to coordinate care within the VA.

Like Cindy's son, Jillian's son needed multiple operations and a year of physical therapy. Eddie's fiancé, Laura, was in college full-time and could not risk her scholarship by taking time off from school. The VA hospital nearby was able to get Jillian a room next to her son during his surgeries, and they had an apartment for her to share with him on the hospital campus when he needed physical therapy. Laura came to visit on weekends and school breaks to help out. Like Cindy, Jillian quit her job to care for Eddie. Her husband, Frank, worked, so they were in the fortunate position to only need to tighten their budget during Eddie's recovery. Like other mothers, Jillian also described the isolation of helping her son during his recovery.

> The hardest thing for me was being away from Frank. He always worked long hours, so I would only see him weekends and evenings. Being a few hours away, we only saw each other once a month or so. And my friends didn't understand. They thought the military should take care of anything. I would tell them, "he needs his mother to help him heal!" They didn't understand that medical care isn't everything. Eddie needed me.

Tessa, the mother of two service members, one still deployed and one home and injured in an IED explosion, described how she had to be "Soldier Mom" during Joe's recovery.

> It's only me helping him. His brother is still in Afghanistan, and his girlfriend can't leave her job and their child. So he's got me by his bedside pushing him to get off his butt and take those first steps. I'm "Soldier Mom" right now. And I don't feel like a soldier. His amputation (below ankle) is terrifying for me. I have a hard time looking at it. But, I've got to be strong for both of us. Soldier Mom.

Tessa echoes message boards where mothers reiterate how mothers are enlisted along with their service members. They are "soldiers" along with their service members. Mothers adopt the language of being a part of the war effort, but here they are enlisted as caregiving warriors. This casts mothers, again, as playing an important role in the war, but a highly gendered one. In women, care work is often devalued, underpaid, and invisible. Mothers of soldiers go from doing invisible support work during deployment to doing life-saving necessary caregiving labor after their children return home.

CONCLUSION

While the Veterans Administration takes care of most medical needs, it is military family members—most often wives and mothers—who step in to provide the care not covered by the VA. Veterans come home with injuries of different severities, some recognized combat injuries, others either undiagnosed (such as PTSD), or not categorized as combat injuries and thus not receiving full health care coverage. Service members need physical and mental recovery support when they return from war, and with an overworked Veterans Administration, mothers are picking up much of the slack.

Here, again, mothers step in to provide the necessary support for veterans, describing it as their maternal duty. Mothers make drastic life changes in order to provide this support—some moving across the country and many giving up their own jobs to supply round-the-clock care. This care work is uncompensated and largely invisible, and yet a critical part of what makes war possible. Cynthia Enloe would see this work as part of fully militarized motherhood. In full militarization, motherhood (caregiving) has been coopted by the military for the state during wartime.[29] But mothers also rightly see their care work as stemming from their own love of their children and their children's immediate and serious needs.

Mother caregivers take on a burden that is invisible and they do so from an isolated position (away from family and friends) without a lot of support. Like other civilian caregivers, they suffer physically, emotionally, and financially from what is largely volunteer labor. Even VA compensation for NMAs does not begin to cover lost wages, missing family and friends, and the emotional and physical work of caregiving.

Caregiving—nurturing and taking care of the home and family—is one way in which women's citizenship is defined.[30] Care work usually keeps women from participating as engaged citizens in politics. They are busy at home, with no time for political engagement. Aileen, for example, became a "news junkie" while her daughter was deployed, reading and following everything she could about the war, but now her war focus was intensely personal.

> When Sarah's unit finally returned home, it was the second greatest feeling of my life to hug her tight, only behind the first time I held her when she was born. I was so lucky she came home to me in one piece physically. But as soon as she came home, something weird happened. I lost all my tightly focused interest in the war. I turned off all my email alerts and stopped going to my war news websites. I stopped posting in the mothers' group I was a part of. It was as if

Sarah—who represented my personal stake in the war—came home safe, and needed my attention. A few weeks after her deployment she started having symptoms of PTSD and getting her diagnosed and help has consumed my life. I've kept up with some news from friends' children who returned home, but I rarely watch the news any more. My focus is on Sarah.

As Aileen describes, her daughter Sarah was her personal connection to war. She kept up with news about the war because her daughter was deployed and all the news was a "personal stake." Once she was home, however, Aileen turned the war off to focus on her daughter and "going on with life." With her daughter's diagnosis of PTSD, what was once her focus on the war became a focus only on helping Sarah. Any political interests she had in following the war were not relevant to her anymore because she no longer had that personal connection to politics.

Mothers like Aileen are not necessarily disengaged citizens, however. Herd and Meyer argue that even through the act of caregiving, women are participating in civic society.[31] As caregivers, women are contributing volunteer labor to the larger cause of helping those in need. Indeed, as we will see in the next chapter, some women, through their work as caregivers and mothers, become more engaged in politics. Mothers' gendered role during wartime simultaneously offers a way to "tune out" from politics in order to focus on caregiving, and a way to become politically active when necessary.

6

THE FEW, THE PROUD, THE FORGOTTEN

The mothers in this chapter become politically active when they perceive that the Veterans Administration is not meeting their side of the bargain of war. When their children are recruited, mothers are promised that the military will take care of them by providing the best training, technology, and support during deployment—and that when they return, injured mentally and/or physically, the VA will make sure they get the health care they need. Mothers who previously never questioned the military speak from their own maternal experience to demand better care for their children and the troops.

Laurie, for example, was one of the first mothers to criticize veterans' health care in the online message groups. I met Laurie online in 2008 while monitoring the GoArmyMoms message forum. Her son Daryl had just returned from deployment, and she posted asking mothers what the signs of PTSD were.

> My son is back home, but he's having a difficult time sleeping. He's up all night playing video games, and then falls asleep early in the morning and sleeps all day. He's only been home two weeks and I don't want this to become a lifestyle for him. He was always the kind of boy who had plans and places to be, or at least he'd be busy in the morning working out. I know he needs a rest after deployment, but I don't know how typical it is for him to be like this. He barely eats. He doesn't talk much to us. He hasn't seen any of his friends. I called his squad leader and he said just to let him rest for a while. Well, is this resting? Is it normal? Is it something I need to worry about?

The response to Laurie's post was overwhelming. Dozens of mothers chimed in to encourage her to get help for her son. One mother wrote,

> You can't be too careful these days with PTSD. My grandmother used to call it shell shock but now we know better. PTSD can lead to anger outbursts, self-harm, and can lead to suicide. I think a lot of the troops suffer from it, and don't get help and that needs to change!

A few mothers posted a link to counseling services for the VA. Laurie called the VA's mental health hotline, and was given the number of a local clinic that provided PTSD counseling. She described,

> They gave me a number of a local counseling center. Well that's all fine and good, but local still means thirty minutes away. And none of that means Daryl is actually going to go. If I tell him to go, he definitely won't go. The only way I could see him getting help is if one of his buddies made him go. Or if his squad leader required it. He's still sleeping! He'll sleep for eighteen hours at a time. This is not living!

Another online mother, Julie, jumped in to the message board conversation, criticizing the VA response to PTSD. Usually posts perceived to be too critical of the military were closed or deleted by a moderator. This post was not. Instead, the mothers responded to Julie, agreeing that veteran's care was inadequate.

> It is not right that the counseling center can't see him for a month! He sounds like he needs help NOW. Why can't the VA get him immediate counseling? Don't they know about the dangers of suicide among our troops? They are really dropping the ball!! Every single service member should receive counseling after they return home!

In all the message boards I studied, even the most heavily moderated allowed posts criticizing post-deployment health care for the troops. After this post asking for all service members to receive counseling, other mothers chimed in with ideas for helping service members with PTSD. One mother blamed PTSD and high suicide rates directly on the VA, and others blamed squad and platoon leaders.

A friend of mine called her son's platoon leader because she was worried about her son. He laughed it off, saying that some stress after deployment was typical, let him adjust, let him rest, give him time, and all that stuff. He had no suggestions and couldn't offer any way to help. And her son was angry and paranoid! He needed help! The platoon leader just blew it off. They should all be trained in how to recognize and deal with PTSD!

Other mothers added their own horror stories about trying to deal with veterans' PTSD. One mother described a friend of her son's who committed suicide after developing a post-deployment drinking problem. Another mother pointed out that female veterans often have PTSD, and that her own daughter struggled with terrible anxiety after three consecutive deployments. Each mother described inaction on the part of the VA. When Laurie posted again, she was more concerned about her son's behavior than before.

You all have me more on edge about Daryl's behavior. Maybe he is depressed. He's sleeping too much and I don't want it to get worse. I put in a call to the platoon leader a week ago and heard nothing back. I called the VA again, asking for a different local counseling center, but everything they have is located too far for us. The only option would be to pay for something local out of pocket. I wouldn't mind doing that, but Daryl won't go! He's a soldier through-and-through and he's tough. He doesn't think he needs any help at all.

When I checked in with Laurie four years later, Daryl was doing much better. A friend from his platoon visited him during "the worst of it" and as Laurie described,

Basically his friend told him to snap out of it! So he went to apply for jobs, and found a mechanic job he was happy with. I told him he couldn't live with me for free. So he went to work every day and made good friends. He still has insomnia, but his GP gave him some mild sleeping pills for it. He seems to be doing OK.

Laurie went from believing in supporting the troops by supporting the war to questioning the VA's handling of PTSD for the troops. While her son was deployed, Laurie was very active doing supportive work in a local Blue Star Mothers group. The mothers regularly stood in front of the local grocery stores, collecting items for care packages, and handing out yellow "support the troops" ribbons. Her posts on the message board during this time were always supportive of the troops, and of other mothers. But as she explained years later, "something happened" when her son returned home.

> He was different and I couldn't help him. I couldn't reach him. No one could help. The mothers online were supportive but they didn't have helpful suggestions. I felt suddenly so angry at the military. I'd call the VA, get put on hold, and then get handed off to someone who would just give me a phone number. Now I guess there's a mental health website with resources, but that didn't exist four years ago. No counseling when my son's unit returned after two long deployments. No support for them at all. They took care of him when he was training. They took care of him when he was deployed. And all of a sudden, they didn't care. I felt betrayed. I decided to spread awareness about PTSD because I saw the VA wasn't doing their job.

Laurie's sense of betrayal is one described by numerous mothers of service members. After trusting the military to properly train their children for war, and then seeing them off to multiple deployments, mothers describe feeling as if the military abandons veterans. The women in this chapter have children dealing with injuries that are not as visible as typical combat injuries such as amputations and paralysis. Instead, their children have more invisible wounds such as PTSD and TBI. The military knew how to find recruits, but not how to help them after their deployments when their injuries are atypical. As one mother said online, "Once they're stateside they're done with them. They don't need them anymore."

This chapter is about mothers like Laurie who feel that the military is not doing what they ought to for veterans returning from war. When their children return home from war with physical and mental injuries, they expect the veteran's health care system to be there, helping each step of the way. When the VA is not there to help the struggles of returning service members, mothers describe losing faith in the military they once trusted to train and care for their children. Some blame the military for misleading them during recruitment. Others blame the VA for poor care. Some mothers argue that those who do not understand the military—civilian politicians—are underfunding veterans' care.

Mothers like Laurie who advocate for their sons' care after deployment end up going through a process of politicization. Mothers who would never question the war or political decisions in order to make sure the troops are supported find themselves publicly and politically demanding that changes be made to what they see as an inadequate health care system. Feeling betrayed by the system they had learned to trust, they use their maternal authority to get help where they see the military is lacking—specifically with treating PTSD and preventing suicide among veterans.

These mothers are an example of how caregiving and motherhood can stimulate engaged citizenship.[1] As we have seen in previous chapters, defining citizenship for women through their role as mothers can limit their political engagement. Mothers like Barbara in chapter 1 learn from other mothers to quiet their own questions about war in order to show full support for the troops. As experts in the home and family, mothers are seen as having moral authority to speak about these issues. Mobilizing engaged citizenship through the role of motherhood, though, can limit women to only being able to speak out on issues related to the family and home. Groups of mothers initially organizing around a gendered identity such as motherhood might not consider their work as political initially, but come to understand their activities as political after engaging with political institutions.[2]

But women's voices can also be devalued when they speak on issues such as work, politics, and war, that are seen as outside their perceived areas of knowledge. However, women's relationship to political engagement and citizenship is not that easily limited, as the mothers in this chapter show. Herd and Meyer argue that caregiving work itself counts as civic engagement.[3] Based on Putnam's definition of civic engagement as "civic activity must be voluntary and altruistic in nature, while simultaneously nurturing reciprocity, social ties, and social trust" (p. 674), caregiving counts. Even when they are not participating directly in politics, they are doing unpaid labor that contributes to the social good. Lister and Skocpol argue that motherhood can be an inroad into fully engaged citizenship.[4] Acting as caregivers, a role that is often unvalued and invisible, can bring women together as caregivers to work for legislative change. Their initial political engagement might stem from their roles as wives and mothers, but expand beyond those limitations to include full engagement in politics.[5]

A SENSE OF BETRAYAL

> I get angry that these kids were good enough to fight for us, but they aren't good enough to take care of. That's not what I wanted or expected when I sent my son to the Army. I didn't want him to come home this way.
>
> —Susan

Mothers who never criticized the military during their children's deployment openly criticized the military over issues of health care. While message boards usually do not allow any questioning of war or the reasons for war, discussions that question the quality of care provided to injured service members are allowed. Some mothers even become political activists, lobbying politicians and the military for better veterans' care. Mothers describe a sense of betrayal that the institution they trusted is not doing its job. Susan went on to tell me,

> I did everything I could do to support Sandra while she was deployed. I sent care packages to her unit. I volunteered with a group of wives and mothers to take donations at the mall and educate people about the war. Now, when Sandra is home and injured, they're not holding up their end of the bargain. I gave my support, and now Sandra needs theirs!

As Susan describes above, the treatment the troops receive is a reflection of how appreciated they are. They are appreciated during deployment, when they are needed to fight. But after deployment, they come home to a broken health care system and long waiting times for critical medical attention. Just as mothers' wartime role becomes one of maternal support when their children are deployed, mothers find their war roles changing again when their children return. As Susan described,

> I expected more when Sandra came home. I expected more fanfare to welcome her squad back. I expected they'd go through a few days of "debriefing" or something like that to help with their adjustment. And then maybe they'd leave with some resources where they could turn to if they had trouble. Hers was a convoy unit and they saw a lot of action. She had nightmares. I asked her what they told her to do, she said "nothing." Nothing! Nothing for my child who sacrificed

years of her life for her country! I decided I had to do something about it.

Susan reached out to other mothers from her daughter's squad, and organized an informational meeting with a counselor who could talk with them about PTSD. Many of the mothers recognized PTSD signs during the meeting but did not know where in the military to turn to for help.

> I was outraged. We had to bring in a civilian to teach us about PTSD! We should know about it! Our children should know about it so they can help each other and help themselves! I know the military is doing a little more now. Pamphlets and a hotline, or something, but for so many it's too little too late. Much too little.

Susan's experiences with the VA's treatment of PTSD is unfortunately common. According to an extensive three part report by psychologists, the PDHA form that all service members must complete to be screened for PTSD is untested and has not been evaluated for effectiveness since 2013.[6] VA mental health care is comprised of some 226 community-based programs that serve veterans.[7] But the requirements to qualify for each vary, and programs are not geographically accessible to everyone. The untested, uncoordinated, and largely inaccessible prevention, identification, and treatment of PTSD made psychologists conclude that "veterans and their families appear possibly more likely to be harmed than helped by the US military's policies and procedures."[8]

Mothers end up providing critical assistance to veterans, filling in for everything from identifying PTSD in their children to finding treatment. Their cognizance of how little the VA is doing to help their children changes their relationship to politics. Instead of defining support for their children as unwavering support for the war and institutions that make war, they redefine it as criticizing the institutions that are not providing the assistance they should. Just like their supportive wartime role, their new relationship to war and politics stems from their maternal role of caregiver. Their children need immediate care that the military is not providing. Out of that maternal action, mothers find themselves empowered to question the military and the war. Susan, for example, did research online and started complaining loudly to the VA, and then to local politicians, about the lack of PTSD care.

I could not find the right forms to fill out to file for travel support for Sandy to receive counseling. I was online, and on the phone with a VA operator, and neither of us could find the right form. Every VA website is a mess of forms of acronyms no one could ever understand. They need to just get rid of it all and start from scratch! After writing a letter of complaint to the VA, I called my senator and demanded the senate address changing the VA system. Streamline it or something. Senators should know our kids aren't getting the help they need.

PTSD is just one of the wartime injuries for which mothers find it hard to get help. Other injuries, not easily identifiable as combat injuries, are also difficult to get treatment for. Tracey's son, for example, has struggled with ongoing neuropathy and numbness in his right hand since a car crash in Iraq. Steven needed a specific, specialized kind of physical therapy so that he could work again. When Tracey made the appointments, she received a message telling her that the appointments were with a PT for the wrong unit. His physical therapy appointments were canceled, and rescheduling was delayed for six months. Tracey could not afford out-of-pocket therapy during that time.

He went downhill with every delay. His spirit was crushed. He tried exercising on his own to strengthen the arm, but it made it worse. He wanted to work, but couldn't even get the treatment he needed. The military did little (NOTHING) to make sure Steve was taken care of.

Finally, after many phone calls to local facilities, Tracey was able to get Steven transferred to an inpatient rehab facility in a nearby city. At that point his arm was not functional, so he qualified for care and constant therapy under the supervision of a good neurologist. But even as he was getting the PT he needed, Tracey had to keep filing papers to show that Steve needed the treatment.

He needed to be there. He was practically paralyzed. They kept asking me [on the phone] what wound he had, what his injury was, and I was trying to explain the neurological symptoms. And the person on the other end was never a medical person! They don't even have medical people taking medical information, making medical decisions. Nonmedical military officers should not be making medical decisions!

Tracey started a support group for mothers and wives at the VA center near her. They began distributing information about how to navigate the VA system and how to advocate for their service members. They made a list of "demands" to the VA center, advocating for each patient to have a medical contact person who coordinates their care. They were told there simply were too many wounded and not enough VA medical personnel to do that. Tracey and some of the other family caregivers started writing their congressional representatives.

> I had to look up who my congressmen were. I had no idea who they were. I followed only war news. I found their office addresses and wrote the first political letters I have ever written in my life. I've never cared about politics before, but I wanted these guys to know what our service members were going through. I don't know what they could do, but as a mother, I wanted to be the one to tell them.

As a mother, Tracey found that she had a voice that politicians might listen to, but she ended up discouraged about getting anything accomplished. "One congressman wrote back to me, thanking me for my family's sacrifice. But he did nothing to improve vet's care. He can bet I'm not going to shut up about this!"

INVISIBLE WOUNDS, INVISIBLE CARE

> My son Rich came home with memories of stepping over the dead bodies of his friends. He remembers carrying dead friends through streets, while being shot at. He's gone to countless memorial services. He's deeply depressed and when people don't understand what he's been through, he comes across as angry. He removes himself from anyone who doesn't get it.
>
> —Jamie

As Jamie explains above, some wounds of war are invisible or misunderstood by civilians. Mothers who are dealing with the military and VA system in order to care for their children already feel isolated from their civilian counterparts. Some mothers blame the dysfunctions of the VA system on civilians and nonmilitary politicians, whom they see as isolated from the experiences of war. As Debra explained,

> People have no clue what our soldiers have experienced and what sacrifices they've made. They have little compassion for veterans. If anything, veterans are invisible to the public. Unless they behave strangely, then they must have PTSD, or abusers of alcohol or drugs. Unless they have missing limbs, they're invisible. Even when they can't hang out with family and friends like they could before.

Mothers who felt that civilians were ignoring the war and troops take their activism for the troops to a new level when they are advocating for better health care for the troops. Debra wrote letters to the editor, and to her congressional representatives, about how wounds that are less visible than the "missing limbs" get less attention from civilians and from the VA. With so much of VA PTSD care relying on community mental health facilities, the invisibility of these war-related injuries makes getting help more difficult.

Jamie, whose son Rich experienced severe PTSD, kept in touch with two other mothers from her son's unit, but lived in a nonmilitary town and knew no one else in the service. She was an active member of two online message boards during her son's deployment and described much of those interactions as "We were like cheerleaders online for our guys. Ooh-Rah! Go Leathernecks!" For Jamie, like so many other mothers, that cheerleading helped get her through deployment. "We had a strong sense of 'we're all in this together' and that we were proud of our Marines. It helped me get through."

Jamie described herself as an active person in her small community, volunteering at a local shelter and playing racquetball at the local Y. But after her son Rich came back, and was discharged after his third deployment, she found herself not wanting to leave him home alone. She stopped most of her activities to focus on him, and she began to suspect that he was struggling from PTSD. Her friends did not understand.

> He went from a funny, loving kid, to an angry and hurting man. He has no friends left, and now he's cutting himself off from us—his family. We are watching him self-destruct, and the more we try to love him, the more he retreats from us. I find myself afraid to leave him alone. So I stay home all the time. I check in on him every thirty minutes or so. I make sure he eats something. Friends don't get it. He's an adult, you know. A Marine. But, until we get some help, I'm the only thing he's got.

After lobbying the VA for mental health care support for Rich, Jamie was able to find a counselor who could talk with Rich on the phone about his PTSD. No one in her nearby area was prepared or qualified to deal with combat trauma–related PTSD. Once he began counseling, he started taking antianxiety medication and that helped his mood swings and made it possible for him to sleep regularly.

Wanting to do more, Jamie applied for a veterans' grant to have a picnic day in town for military families and civilians. She went to a city council meeting and got the town involved in the planning. Along with her son's unit, she planned a ceremony of appreciation for veterans at the picnic. The regional United Service Organization (USO) sent in a team of counselors to talk to veterans at the picnic about PTSD and suicide. Over two hundred people and thirty veterans showed up that day, many from other units Jamie had not met yet. She considered the day a success.

> I used to plan events for work, but it's been years since I did anything like this. I had grant money and had to get a caterer, band, activities, everything together. The USO was wonderful. They brought counselors to talk to vets and their families about PTSD. We had WWII vets talk with the crowd about shell shock and battle fatigue. We had flags everywhere, and sparklers at night. It was a party. I don't know if it made a difference, but it brought people together.

For Jamie, part of her job as a mother included educating civilians about war and now about veterans' struggles. All the families in attendance, however, were military families. She explained, "I think we're really off the radar of nonmilitary families. They don't have to think about this. They probably thought the event didn't apply to them." Even if she could not reach out to civilians, she wanted the veterans themselves to feel appreciated and supported. The day was a celebration, but she described feeling angry and disappointed that the military was not a part of it.

> I did invite the squad and platoon leaders. No one responded. I was kind of hoping that the military would step up and say "yes, we'll bring some brass, and have the VA send some counselors over to talk about veterans' mental health." They didn't even respond. I was so angry. The Marines discharged him and now he gets nothing from

them! What happened to "the few, the proud?" As a mother, I am so disappointed. Our Marines deserve so much more than this.

Jamie's disappointment in the military is a sharp contrast to the cheerleader of the Marines she described herself as during deployment. Instead of rallying around cries of Ooh-rah, she's angry that the Marines have forgotten their own, and that the VA is not adequately helping with the PTSD so many veterans have.

ANTI-SUICIDE ADVOCACY

Nobody wants to show weaknesses. You want to be perceived as perfection.

—Carol

The first thing Carol says about her son Dan is that he's "a statistic." Dan, an Army sniper, committed suicide in 2008, after three consecutive deployments to Iraq. Dan is part of the alarming statistic of veteran suicides. Eighteen veterans commit suicide each day in the United States.[9] Moreover, 37 percent of post-9/11 service members knew one veteran who later committed suicide.[10] She emphasizes his place in that statistic in order to drive home the problems of untreated PTSD and suicide among service members.

Not only do twenty-two veterans kill themselves each day, but about 40 percent of our current servicemen [sic] know someone who served post-9/11 who killed themselves. These kids are dealing with a lot of trauma and a lot of death. It's not just at war, but here at home.

Dan joined the military in 2005 after two years in college. He trained as an Army sniper and was sent to Iraq as soon as BCT was over. Carol was initially very supportive of the war effort,

I'm not a joiner. But I did help out in a couple care package drives during Dan's first deployment. It helped to talk with other moms. It helped that we could rally together around how tough and strong our sons are—that we're proud they're part of the greatest Army in the world. But I'm not a joiner, so I didn't really reach out to many other mothers.

In 2007, during Dan's service and at the height of the wars in Iraq and Afghanistan, the Army extended deployments to fifteen months. Multiple deployments were more common, and her son was deployed for a third time. She started to notice the strain on him.

> I think it was after the first deployment I started to really notice a difference in Dan. He was never a normal teenager who went out partying. He was much more into computers and computer games. More quiet than most of his friends, but never quiet with us. When he came back from his first deployment he was more, I guess, you'd call it, reserved. More guarded? I didn't think too much about it because I knew his job in Iraq was so hard.

During Dan's second deployment, his friend was injured with a traumatic brain injury. He was discharged, and Carol noticed Dan became less communicative. "He stopped calling home. Well, he would call every couple weeks, but he always sounded distracted and far away. Again, we thought it was the intensity of the mission he was on." When Dan returned from his third deployment, he filled out all the forms and received an honorary discharge and a clean bill of health. Never having lived on his own, he moved back in with his parents.

> He was discharged with no counseling. No information about PTSD. For all we could see, he came home to us in good health. Rick and I noticed how quiet he was from the beginning. He didn't want to talk about anything. He saw an Army friend of his, from the same unit, once or twice in a nearby hospital. Jerome [his friend] was peppered with shrapnel during a raid. He was having a difficult time recovering. Dan visited him a couple times, but that was it. He watched a lot of TV and had insomnia. Rick talked with him, but he didn't open up. He told us everything was fine.

A few years after Dan took his own life, Carol described that she "will never heal from his death, but I have some perspective on the VA." She started to understand that the military did not provide the necessary screening for PTSD, and that once Dan was discharged as healthy, he was really on his own with no monitoring from the VA.

> What went wrong? I kept thinking of who could have picked up on Dan's PTSD and how severe it was. Could we have known? I thought

for a while we should've known . . . but we aren't trained professionals. He needed a professional. He needed someone to check in a
month after, a few months after deployment. He was in a war zone
and saw things no one else could understand. The VA needed to do
more than just say he was OK!

Carol became active in the National Alliance to End Veteran Suicide, an organization aiming to raise awareness, educate, and support
veterans. She organized workshops in her community for Operation:
Veteran Freedom, getting groups of veterans together to talk about the
trauma of war. Carol described these groups as a chance for "warriors to
talk with each other openly when usually they wall off all us non-warri-
ors." She explained,

I always felt like all the troops were my guys, but now I feel that even
more. I want our guys to feel like getting help is OK. The military
trains them to think they're invincible. That you're the one to defend
the country, and you have to be strong for your buddies and for the
mission. It's an intense culture. Then they leave the military and all
that structure and support is gone. And the military doesn't help
them. I'm not embarrassed to tell people my son killed himself. I'm
embarrassed our military didn't help him.

Even mothers who have not lost children to suicide become anti-
suicide advocates, particularly if they've seen suicide impact their service member's unit. Beth, another mother who was active in pro-war
groups during her son's deployment, echoes Carol's assessment that the
loss of military structure and support is hard on troops when they come
home.

They get used to military life. They have buddies around them who
are going through the same things. They have their own way of
talking, processing, being angry. They literally keep each other alive.
They come home and all that is gone. All that support is gone. No
counseling, no group therapy. No one even calls to see how they are!

When Beth's son's unit returned from their last tour to Afghanistan,
Beth expected some kind of "exit counseling" or support system to help
the unit deal with PTSD. She knew her son's unit dealt with a lot of
injuries and death, and had difficult, often secret missions that meant a

lot of pressure. Beth's son, Rob, started running again and dealing with his insomnia and anxiety by training for a marathon. But his best friend, Alex, suffered from debilitating PTSD, and eventually committed suicide.

> It was hard. Alex's mother was someone I made care packages with. We stood across from antiwar protests and waved American flags. Both of us joked about the number of "Mom of Marine" sweatshirts we owned. After Alex killed himself, Joan shut down. When she did reach out to me, her sadness was anger. She was furious that the units Alex and Rob were in did nothing for their PTSD.

Beth suggested to Joan that she funnel her grief and anger into energy for anti-suicide activism, but Joan was not interested. Beth took on the cause herself.

> I started contacting other mothers in the unit and together we wrote letters to newspapers, letters to our senators, and letters to the local VA hospital. We demanded more attention be paid to treating PTSD and preventing suicide. We wrote "AS MOTHERS" telling the stories of our servicemen and their friends. We staged sit-ins outside VA hospitals, handing out suicide information. We still waved our flags. It was patriotic. It is patriotic to take care of the troops!

Another mother, Barbara, described herself as a "patriotic lifelong Republican" who was "disgusted with the lack of PTSD care" for veterans. Barbara's son Chase came home from three deployments with severe PTSD. She set out to find him help, expecting the VA to provide whatever they could:

> I really thought I could go online, find a phone number, and get Chase help. No problem, right? I was wrong. Well, I did call the VA mental health line, but I was referred to a website of recommended community programs, and another website of mental health coverage forms I could print and fill out. I've been dealing with government paperwork my whole career and I couldn't even understand those darn forms!

Barbara's background in social work meant she could recognize Chase's PTSD symptoms, and knew how to navigate a bureaucracy, but she still could not get the VA to help Chase. She found him counseling in a nearby city and filled out a few forms to see if that counseling could be paid for. But she was also "pissed."

> Yes, I'm pissed. I'm one pissed Mama! You don't ask people to serve in a war and then leave them when they need help. I called my reps. I called those Republican senators I've been voting for years. One is even on the Armed Services Committee! I gave them a mom's earful about how our military just discharges people without adequate mental health screening, and then the VA leaves them with no health care!

With her background in social work, she ended up talking with many veterans herself about their experiences. She teamed up with a local counseling group to offer group sessions for veterans.

> These vets are trying to straddle two worlds. They feel safe because they are at home and no longer getting shot at, but in their minds, they still think they're in a war zone. They still respond as if they're in danger all the time. They aren't trained for this transition. It's deplorable that our veterans aren't given what they need to come home and be safe and healthy.

Like so many mothers faced with PTSD, high suicide rates, and little help from the VA, Barbara, Carol, and Beth became outspoken advocates for awareness and treatment. They describe speaking out "as mothers," using their experience and close positioning to war in order to speak with authority about these issues. Once believing that the only way to support the troops was to support the war and military, these mothers are now supporting the troops by demanding better care for them. The maternal instinct that once kept them supporting the troops and the war now questions the military.

> We must never forget those who are serving just as we must support all who have served. We need to remember those who paid the ultimate price and support their families whenever possible, as well as our wounded warriors. Just because your family member came home and is no longer active, doesn't mean the war is over. It just means you can now help someone else's son or daughter or mother or father, etc.

What initially kept mothers from being politically active—their personal connection to war—has made these mothers politically active. They busied themselves contacting senators, organizing events, and writing lists of demands. Beth likened this generation of veterans to the "Greatest Generation" (WWII veterans), deserving of the same respect.

> Like the "Greatest Generation" this is truly the "Strongest Generation" having sustained multiple deployments and surviving cataclysmic injuries. The war might not have been as morally justified as WWII but we must make sure they are Never Forgotten.

Here, Beth asserts a difference between WWII and the wars in Iraq and Afghanistan. She refers to WWII as "morally justified" while questioning the premise for the current wars. Despite lingering doubts about the premise for war they served in, Beth argues these veterans should also not be forgotten.

CONCLUSION

When mothers give up their children to the state for war, they enter a bargain with the state. The state, through the military, provides expert training and technology to ensure the safety of their service members, no matter how dangerous war is. During recruitment and deployment, mothers are enlisted along with their children to provide maternal support for the troops, and to make sure the troops know they are loved and supported at home. For some, providing this support means not being critical of the military or the war itself. But when service members arrive home with mental and physical wounds, mothers pick up the caregiving slack, providing care where the VA does not. When the state fails veterans—by not treating PTSD and not providing anti-suicide education—mothers turn their maternal authority to political advocacy. They use their voices to criticize the lack of mental health care and demand change from military and political leaders.

Mothers allow criticism of the health care system for returning service members, especially when it comes from a mother involved in the care of her injured child. Even for mothers who argue that the only way to support the troops is to not question the war, veterans' health care is an issue that they will be outspoken and actively political about. Mothers who are engaged in changing veterans' health care blame either the public or the military for the inadequate system. Mothers who blame the civilian population argue that health care is underfunded because civilians know very little about the sacrifices made during wartime. However, many mothers criticize the military itself for the lack of adequate care.

These mothers describe a strong sense of betrayal toward the military. Some become politically active, advocating for VA improvements, awareness of invisible injuries such as TBI, and treatment of PTSD, and are especially concerned with the high suicide rate among veterans. The same sense of maternal duty that the military uses to silence their engagement during deployment now drives their political activism. When they talk about improving veterans' care, they invoke similar maternal ideas of support; but rather than using this "co-enlistment" to justify not questioning the war, they now argue that it is their duty to advocate politically for the care their children deserve.

CONCLUSION

Is Maternal Citizenship Full Citizenship?

As I write this, we are nearly two decades into the protracted War on Terrorism. After the post-9/11 invasion of Afghanistan, and the long, drawn-out debate before entering the war in Iraq in 2003, most Americans did not expect to be at war this long. We still have troops stationed in Iraq and Afghanistan, and we still have military families worrying and taking on support work that is invisible to civilians who are largely unaware of the continuing wars. During past wars with mandatory drafts (WWII and Vietnam) at least 10 percent of the population knew someone in the military. During WWII, even Americans who did not know service members were involved in the war effort, planting victory gardens and buying war bonds. Now, with less than 2 percent of Americans connected to war, that is not the case today.

The war in Afghanistan entered the news briefly in 2017 when President Trump suggested increasing the number of deployed troops to try ending a war many are beginning to see as unwinnable.[1] After nearly two decades, the War on Terrorism has now shaped a generation of service members, two presidential elections, and our national policy agenda.[2] But despite the tremendous impact on our country, only military families shoulder the war burden. And as the wars continue in one form or another, mothers like the ones in this book continue grappling with issues of support and the severe consequences of war for military families.

> I am so grateful for this group. I don't think I could survive deploy-
> ment without you all. No one understands the stress of having a child
> deployed in a war zone. No one sees the worry in our faces when
> we're standing in line at the store and they're chatting about the
> President or WMDs or whatever the news of the day is. No one else
> understands how personal this war is. This war is my child. I'll do
> whatever it takes to support him.
>
> —MikesMom64

A large part of this book is about the stories that are invisible during
wartime. As MikesMom64 explains in an online Army support group,
there is a lot that goes into war that civilians do not see. Civilians do not
see the worry on mothers' faces when they go about their days casually
discussing news about the war. After many years, most Americans are
unaware of the ongoing wars. This book is about mothers like Joanne in
chapter 3, who sought out an online support group when her son Rob
joined the military and she felt that her civilian friends could not understand what she was going through. Mothers like Debbie in chapter 4,
the mother of a Marine, who stays up all hours of the night ensuring
that the message board she moderates is a space safe from posts that are
critical of the war. Mothers like Cindy in chapter 5, who left her job to
provide round-the-clock care for her injured son, Jayson.

Mothers do invisible work at each stage of the war—getting over
their own fears during recruitment, cheering their children through
basic training, sending care packages and cards overseas, waving flags
when troops come home, caring for the wounded, and worrying about
PTSD symptoms. These mothers silence their own criticisms of the war
and the military during deployments in order to make sure the troops
have home front support and "avoid another Vietnam." And when the
VA lets mothers down when their service members come home injured,
mothers take on public criticism of veterans' health care. Embracing
political engagement for the sake of their children, mothers write letters to senators and organize protests, demanding the VA do more to
treat PTSD and prevent suicide.

Not only is this burden largely invisible to the nonmilitary population; it is an unequal burden, one that families—and particularly wom-
en—from lower socioeconomic and racial minority statuses bear. Military recruitment advertising has long targeted specific groups for enlistment, and has used strategic messages to encourage enlistment.[3] For

example, drawing on the vulnerable racial and socioeconomic position black single mothers occupy, the military sells itself as an avenue for successful citizenship for those typically viewed as failed citizens. The military offers a route to successful parenting and citizenship, but reliance on inequalities to do so leaves the route to citizenship incomplete. The consequence of enlisting unequally means that a small portion of the population already struggling with inequality is doing the work of supporting the war and supporting the troops—and potentially silencing their own antiwar voices.

MOTHERS' EXPERIENCES OF WAR

The military is not only in the business of making war. As the mothers in this book show, the military's reach extends beyond the war front, and far into the family lives and relationships on the home front. Military service is not confined to the individual service member or their immediate family (children and wives). With younger enlistees, and later ages until marriage, the "military family" also includes extended family (i.e., parents) who have specific duties during recruitment, training, and deployment. Given that mothers have moral authority to expose the familial consequences of war, the military needs the backing of mothers to recruit and to run a successful war.[4]

In order to make war successful, the military needs supportive families. Despite gender changes in the military, such as allowing women in combat positions, military families are largely assumed to be female (wives, mothers, and girlfriends). Even as more women join the military, war remains a gendered experience.[5] Warriors and battle, technology, and defense of the homeland are still linked with masculinity, while nurturing, care, and the homeland are linked with femininity.[6]

Women's support of the troops during wartime is gendered in that the military understands that mothers are the gatekeepers to military service. Targeting mothers specifically for recruitment draws mothers into the military institution and translates for them what their relationship with their children means in this new context—the "good mother" during wartime. With their approval of recruitment, mothers can provide emotional and physical support to their enlisted children. During deployment, mothers are encouraged to be supportive and proud, and to not take political stances that question war. By making them feel enlisted along with their children, the military empowers mothers to support each other and the troops as a whole—as a part of the larger military family. This support is critical for waging a successful war. As the keepers of the home front, mothers in particular are encouraged by the military to ensure that the public will support the troops and the war. In this way, the military takes advantage of mothers' public moral authority as mothers to drum up support. Such unconditional support is construed as patriotic. This shores up Cynthia Enloe's contention that "the only way for women to enter patriotism is as a mother or wife."[7]

The variety of mothers' experiences of war are a central part of this book. Mothers like Cindy Sheehan using their maternal authority, as an "inherently peaceful mother" to speak out against war garner media attention. Mothers mobilizing support for the troops and the war by raising funds and supplies for care packages also become visible in the public sphere through their rallying for the war. And mothers criticize the military and VA publicly when their children come home from war and do not get the care they deserve. In Enloe's model of the "fully militarized mother," the work all of these mothers do for their loved ones is always co-opted by the state to support war itself.

But little attention is paid to mothers who do not fit these two extremes, or the mothers who move between being supportive in some ways, or not supporting war in other ways. With these two extreme images of motherhood during wartime, it is easy to assume that if mothers are not publicly antiwar, and are supporting the troops, they must be pro-war. In fact, mothers have both public and private ideas about the policies surrounding war. Mothers cope with their children's recruitment and deployment by silencing their own public criticisms, in order to support the troops. Mothers police one another's questions about the reasons for war in order to keep a supportive environment. And mothers who encounter poor care when their children return with physical and psychological injuries are quick to mobilize to political action to improve the VA health care system.

Mothers' experiences of war depend, in part, upon their relationship to the military, and the stage of deployment their children are going through. If mothers see themselves as a part of the military institution along with their enlisted children, they are more likely to adopt the idea that the only way to support the troops is to also support the war by being noncritical of the military and military political leaders. Critical views of the war and the military are silenced in online discussions in order to keep the space supportive for mothers. Mothers learn to keep their own antiwar views to themselves during deployment in order to support their children and the troops. This self-silencing of criticism in order to be supportive illustrates one of the mechanisms that makes war possible. When mothers—who have the potential power of maternal authority against war—silence that authority, then there is less threat to the overall war effort.

DEFINING THE GOOD WARTIME MOTHER

Understanding the positionality of mothers during wartime means examining the discursive mechanisms available to define the boundaries of mothers' experience during war. Take, for example, the overarching narrative of what "good motherhood" means during wartime. Military literature describes a mother experiencing anxiety, then becoming proud, and finally becoming unconditionally supportive of her child and war. This narrative carries through the Department of Defense recruitment, training, and deployment materials. Boundaries are placed around who and what a "good wartime mother" is through definitions of *patriotism*, *support*, and *pride*. The definitions of these terms are modeled to mothers, and then picked up by mothers in online forums. When disagreements occur online, they are discursive struggles over what it means to *support*, and whether it is OK to question the commander in chief. Mothers with alternative views are able to participate in limited ways in some forums (the ones with the lowest moderation levels) but are shut out from participating when they overstep the boundaries of discussion. These same issues extend to more recent social networks such as Facebook, which offers closed groups with moderation power.

The online technology of message boards facilitates the process of women limiting or claiming their political authority by providing mechanisms for individuals to police and censor what is said online. The Internet is not as empowering for individuals in a democracy as some have imagined it is. Yes, the Internet brings the war closer to home by making it easy for military families to communicate with their loved ones who are serving, and providing spaces for military families to support one another. But it also offers new ways for constraining wartime experiences. Mothers are able to shape and limit ideas about what support means during wartime vis-à-vis this new technology. However, message boards do provide some chance for mothers to argue over the meanings of terms like *support* that are "empty and overflowing,"[8] and even when these discussions are shut down, it is nevertheless some form of public debate.

Motherhood itself is an ideology that has strong social significance, and is used by states, social movements, nationalist projects, and militaries to build support and organize women's relationship to the cause.[9] Maternal images (such as the grieving mother) have a kind of moral weight and "currency" that makes them particularly powerful for taking public political stances.[10] Mothers can be a powerful state ally when they voice their support of war.[11] On WWI and WWII posters mothers urged civilians to contribute to the war effort—"Don't travel. Won't you give my boy a chance to get home?" pleads a woman on a WWII poster.[12] Mothers can draw on the same moral authority to urge support of the war effort to keep their children safe, arguing that the only way to support the troops is to support their mission.

But mothers are a potential liability for the military if they speak out against the war. Cindy Sheehan, whose son was killed in Iraq, energized the American antiwar movement when she demanded to speak with then President Bush about ending the war. As a grieving mother, Sheehan had authority as a mother to speak against the war.[13] The image of the mother grieving for her child killed in action is a powerful one, and it has been successfully harnessed by movements throughout history to protest war. By constructing a narrative during recruitment that leads mothers to believe that supporting the war effort is the same as supporting their children, the military aims to control mothers and prevent their use of this culturally resonant image for antiwar purposes. This is a critical part of home front war support for the military—preventing mothers from criticizing war.

MOTHERHOOD AND GENDERED CITIZENSHIP

Full citizenship requires active participation in political processes. The mothers in this book show that gender continues to shape women's empowerment or disempowerment to participate in public political discourse during times of war. During recruitment when mothers are construed as a part of the military through caring for all service members, mothers are disempowered to speak out against the war. They learn to default to their service members', politicians', and military's decisions about war. Questioning the reasons for war becomes linked with jeopardizing the safety of the troops. Speaking out against the war (being political or critical) is considered dangerous to the troops—hurting their morale and thus jeopardizing their mission—and is considered political. As a part of the military institution, mothers consider politics as separate from war, and irrelevant to the troops. Mothers are discouraged from questioning war; doing so might endanger their children who are serving. This pits wartime support (patriotism) against engaged citizenship.

Some mothers, like antiwar mother Cindy Sheehan, and pro-war political mothers like some interviewed in this book, do claim their maternal authority to speak publicly *as mothers*. But the political authority women are able to claim as mothers makes it impossible for women to be fully engaged citizens, or to influence debates about public issues such as war. When women's power comes from a gendered identity like motherhood, it will fundamentally undermine women's equality as citizens. Engaging in the public sphere as mothers limits women's political authority to only those experiences that are relevant to motherhood (the home and nurturing) and ultimately makes them less than full citizens. Their political voices can be ignored or dismissed on the grounds that women have little or no expertise outside of care work and nurturing.[14] In the end, men have a valued voice in war (either as citizens or warriors) and women, speaking outside their supposed areas of expertise, do not.

Whether mothers are empowered or disempowered to be critical of war depends on how maternal ideologies are used and who uses them. The mothers here also suggest that there is more to how states mobilize maternal images than Carreon and Moghadam's typology of "maternalism from above" and "maternalism from below."[15] According to this typology, maternal frames mobilized by the state for their needs is "maternalism from above." The state can use maternal frames to encourage mothers not to question the state in a way that reinforces patriarchy. Or the state can use maternal frames to empower women to challenge the public/private gendered divide of politics and mobilize against inequality. In "maternalism from below" mothers use maternalism in grassroots mobilizations and in doing so, empower themselves to become more politically active. According to this theory, the outcome is always feminist, whether or not the group considers themselves feminist.

The mothers in this book engage in "maternalism from above" collectively in online forums. They echo the state's idea of a "good mother" during wartime by encouraging one another to unconditionally support the troops and refrain from public political criticism about the war. This "maternalism from above" happens collectively among mothers, and therefore has the appearance of community action—of "maternalism from below." But, as "maternalism from above" imposes state-sanctioned ideas of "good motherhood" on mothers, "maternalism from below" for them becomes disempowering, and not feminist. "From below" they evoke state-driven militaristic ideas to discourage each other from participating in the political process during wartime.

In this way, the mothers here show that the process of limiting debate is not only a top-down process of "maternalism from above." The power to suppress ideas by defining words such as *support* is collective. In online forums, mothers can control (through rules and moderation) what kinds of support are allowed, and what kind of political discussion is allowed. When ideologies such as patriotism and "support the troops" are mobilized, the diversity of experiences and points of view from mothers that do not fit with the dominant discourse are silenced.

The mothers here suggest that we need a new model of engaged citizenship that includes the work mothers do on behalf of their enlisted children. Women engaging politically through their gendered identity of motherhood does not lead to second-class citizenship. Not only does caregiving itself constitute "civic engagement"; caregiving leads mothers to become involved in public political criticism.[16] Only when the military fails to live up to their end of the support agreement do mothers find their own public voice to question military and political policy.

Mothers who once silenced their opposition to war find themselves empowered politically to get their children the medical and mental health care they need after deployment. Here, mothers go through a process of empowerment. They become active in politics, reaching out to the VA, DoD, and congressional representatives. Through their caregiving work, mothers become engaged citizens, finding their voices to question not only VA policies, but the political policies that led to war in the first place. When women enter citizenship through motherhood, their political activism on behalf of their children should not be devalued.

EASING THE BURDEN: POLICY IMPLICATIONS

Mothers' wartime support work illuminates new modes of political participation and civic engagement. With the all-volunteer force, the US population fighting in wars is a smaller segment of the citizenry, and their family members are more isolated than ever before from nonmilitary citizens. Without the entire country mobilized for war, military families close ranks to do the majority of support work during each stage of deployment. The military relies on them to provide moral support during recruitment, moral and material support during deployment, and caregiving support when they return home. Multiple deployments, cuts to military budgets, and an overburdened VA health care system means that the burden on these families is tremendous.

At each stage of the recruitment, enlistment, and post-deployment process there is opportunity to improve the experience for service members and their families. During recruitment, families need to hear multiple viewpoints about the pros and cons of military service. JROTC programs need to be clear about what enlistment and deployments entail. Instead of focusing on individuals most likely to enlist (typically minority individuals from lower socioeconomic backgrounds), the military can expand career training and college funding options to draw a wider variety of young people to service. Recruiting from a larger portion of the population will make the war more of a shared burden, instead of further dividing it along race and class lines.

During deployment, families need more emotional and material support to deal with the daily stress of war. The definition of family needs to be expanded to include parents, who are still heavily involved in the lives of young adults who are not yet married. Family Readiness programs need to include parents of unmarried service members, and include training and support on issues such as deployment stress and preparation for homecoming. Allowing parents access to these resources will help connect them to the military and support them during deployment.

But these are only general guidelines. The mothers in this book have some suggestions that come from their perspectives and focus on their experiences of war. Their suggestions for change may seem simple or obvious, but many echo the conclusions of countless military and civilian studies and reports of the same issues.[17] And despite official reports, not much has changed. Perhaps listening to these mothers in the trenches of supporting and caring for our troops will lead to change. We need to "ask mothers," as Lenora, whose son Ryan was diagnosed with a severe brain injury after deployment explained.

> My son didn't ask for this. He enlisted to help his country. I knew it was a risk, and I was against him enlisting at first because of that. I never expected his injuries to be so severe. He came home looking fine. Friends and family were overjoyed he was in one piece. Then the VA bungled his care. They couldn't get the tests right, couldn't get the diagnosis right, couldn't understand why we needed clinics close to home. Then they couldn't understand why I was asking for money to take care of him. I had to leave my job! I couldn't find the right paperwork and filled out the wrong form, delaying processing for months. Really, if they just sat us mothers down and asked us how they could help us and our kids, they'd be doing better. They'd get an earful for sure! They should just scrap every part of the VA system and start from scratch! Ask us how to run it! But nobody asks mothers. We know what's needed, but no one pays attention.

1. Extend the official definition of "family" to include parents, especially when a service member is unmarried, or has a spouse who is not able to be a caregiver (is also in the military, or in college, etc.).
2. Exit counseling and in-person mental health evaluations must be mandatory for all service members (combat and noncombat) and occur at regular intervals for a year after deployment.

3. A system of support for veterans immediately after deployment where mental health professionals check in on veterans and their families at regular intervals for signs of PTSD and potential suicide.

4. Streamline the VA health system for caregivers (as one mother suggested this, she laughed and said it would be like "herding cats"). Evaluate all forms and resources for redundancies, and streamline the process of applying for coverage and documenting injuries and illnesses.

5. Expand VA coverage to include noncombat injuries such as hearing impairments and neurological disorders, as well as PTSD in noncombat service members.

6. Assign each injured service member a professional case manager with a reasonable case load. This individual would be able to oversee hospital stays, surgeries, and treatments and help caregivers navigate paperwork and resources.

7. Ensure that mental health facilities covered by the VA are accessible in all geographic regions, or provide travel and housing for service members who must travel for such care. When the VA runs mental health facilities, make sure that counselors are familiar with and trained in dealing with PTSD.

8. Provide financial support for families to be with their injured service members when they arrive stateside (airfare and hotel).

9. Improve PTSD diagnostic criteria to align with recent psychological research, and abandon old military definitions of mental disorders. Include noncombat service members in PTSD evaluations.

10. Provide easy-to-apply-for, long-term support (housing, childcare, living stipend) for family members who serve as primary caregivers to injured service members.

With an ongoing war, and new deployments of troops, these changes are urgent for military families. As the extensive three-part psychiatric PTSD report concluded, "veterans and their families appear possibly more likely to be harmed than helped by the US military's policies and procedures."[18] Our veterans may be safe at home, but their lives are literally at stake. After nearly two decades of war, the problems of deployment support and veterans' care are not going away.

Finally, if our country is going to fight a war, all Americans (military families and civilians) need to be involved in making political decisions about war. We need the voices of those who are directly impacted by the war and aftermath of deployment to lead conversations about how to improve things such as deployment support and post-deployment health care. Women (wives and mothers), as the majority of caregivers, have a unique perspective of the care needed to heal from the consequences of war.

APPENDIX
Methodology

In this appendix I explain the details of the methods used for this research. First, I describe the content analysis I conducted of Department of Defense recruitment and support documents. Then, I lay out my methodology for conducting interviews with mothers, detailing my sampling and interviewing methods. Here I include demographic details for interviewees. Third, I describe the online ethnography I conducted of military mothers' message forums. Finally, I discuss my research process as a military "outsider."

I. CONTENT ANALYSIS OF DEPARTMENT OF DEFENSE DOCUMENTS

Chapters 1 and 2 are based on a content analysis of how the Department of Defense targets mothers of US service members in recruitment material. The materials analyzed came from DoD-produced recruitment websites and publications from September 2006 to September 2009. DoD documents (both print and electronic) are crucial tools for military families to navigate the complex bureaucracy of the military. I met with a recruiter from each branch of the armed services and learned what materials they provide to mothers during the recruitment process, and what resources they point them toward when their children go through training and deployment. The recruiters I interviewed provide print material to mothers and direct them toward the branches' websites for further information. Three of the recruiters of the five with whom I spoke also directed mothers to online support groups for parents (typically mothers) of that branch. This practice reinforces the importance of online groups as a resource for mothers.

Sample and Sampling Strategy

While there are many publications for families on military websites, I concentrated on documents aimed primarily at mothers of service members. These online and offline documents fit into two categories: (1) military recruitment documents, and (2) informational documents from DoD organizations.

(1) Recruitment materials that target mothers are available on each military branch's website and are available at military recruitment offices. Recruitment websites include information on military opportunities and benefits and describe the processes of training, deployment, and veterans' benefits/care. Each branch of the military has its own recruitment website, and the DoD runs a general recruitment website for all branches (e.g., TodaysMilitary.com). These websites use a variety of media—including pictures, quotes, and stories from parents, FAQ pages, and videos of actual recruits and their parents talking about different aspects of joining. I identified additional material for analysis by following suggested links on these sites to other sites' specific information on training and deployment support.

(2) Informational documents analyzed for this book include literature from a selection of the many DoD sub-organizations that are closely involved with service members and their families. These organizations focus on providing home front and deployment support for all members of military families, and assist family members with health concerns they may have for their returning recruits. Some focus on health issues for soldiers, such as the Force Health Protection and Readiness Office (FHPRO) and the Army Behavioral Health Organization, while others focus on military family and soldier "well-being," such as the United Service Organizations (USO), the NMFA (National Military Family Association), and the Marine Corps Community Services and Deployment Support Organization. Some organizations publish

newsletters for military families such as the *Army Well-Being Newsletter* and *FLO Notes* (Family Liaison Office) that often include stories about the activities and experiences of mothers of service members, as well as tips and information on how to survive the deployment of a loved one.

To sample DoD documents, I strategically selected documents that (a) covered the range of subject matter in each category (i.e., recruitment videos, and deployment guides), (b) represent each branch of the military as well as the DoD generally, and (c) are prominently displayed on and linked to from military websites. I discarded documents that did not specifically address mothers, and that repeated information also provided elsewhere (e.g., a checklist of what not to bring to training, or a step-by-step description of the recruitment process). While it is difficult in the online context to count exactly how many "pieces" of information there were (websites have multiple pages, videos, with rotating boxes of quotes and information, etc.), I coded 258 phrases in total over the different sources.

Coding and Analysis

First I collected three years of online recruitment and deployment materials by downloading content from websites and online newsletters. I began the coding process by putting each page into NVivo and coding each piece of material by branch, type (recruitment, deployment, training, information), and the website it came from or was associated with. I coded each example (examples are the quotes and stories from parents/ mothers portrayed online) for the gender of the parent (mother or father), the gender of the child, whether he or she was a single parent, and the observable racial background (which could only be determined when pictures were present).

Second, I used the grounded theory method of "open coding" and then "focused coding" on a random subset of ten texts to identify the major themes present.[1] In open coding, "the goal is to remain open to all possible theoretical directions"; this allowed me to identify themes in the data that I did not anticipate, such as the themes of a recruit growing up within the military or a mother's emotional support during training.[2] Based on my open coding, I developed a focused coding scheme to "synthesize and explain larger segments of data" by selecting the most salient themes found in the open coding process.[3]

Using a narrative approach, I focus on how the story of recruitment (recruitment, training, deployment) models the ideal military mother. Mothers are not telling their own unedited stories; the military institution tells their stories. I coded whole stories to understand how individual pieces fit into the larger context of the story.[4] Narrative analysis is valuable for capturing how stories change.[5] While all recruitment stories show mothers shifting from apprehension to acceptance and support, those targeting black mothers emphasized assumed racial and class difference.

Changes over time: After the recruitment advertising for every branch underwent a massive overall in late 2005, recruitment websites have remained relatively static in design and content over the period since 2006. I downloaded each website roughly once a month and noted any changes. New content (particularly new example stories, pictures, and videos) were added a few times a year to GoArmy.com and Todays-Military.com. The Marine Corps website seems to rotate through the same group of fifteen stories every few months. For the purposes of this analysis, I counted all the example stories on each site displayed during the two-plus-year period, even if they were not all present at the same time. TodaysMilitary.com, for example, rotated through thirty-four example stories over the two-year period, and the Go Army Parents website rotated through thirty-one different stories over the same period. There were no significant changes in the themes used over the period of analysis.

2. INTERVIEWS WITH MOTHERS

I interviewed fifty mothers who participated in online message boards, and later twenty mothers who were taking care of injured service members post-deployment. I used interviews as a supplement to the online ethnography, asking mothers to reflect on their interactions online and to articulate their views of the message forums as collective spaces. I interviewed mothers to learn their individual stories about when their children enlisted, trained, and deployed, and to hear their individual views on what military motherhood, support, and politics meant. Individual interviews with mothers provided a way for them to share their private views with me—views that they would never share in the online space. I chose mothers of service members who participate in online support groups, as opposed to mothers who do not, in order to understand the mothers who join support groups online and to gain insight into how different their views may be outside of the group.

Interview Sampling Procedures

I used purposive sampling to find a variety of participants on each message board. I aimed for roughly ten participants per message board to reach theoretical saturation in terms of different ideological orientations toward military motherhood.[6] I selected persons to interview from watching online interactions, choosing strategically from each message board to cover a range of attitudes about war, branches of the military, etc. During my observation of online interactions, I paid particular attention to the types of participants on each message board, noting the kinds of discussions they were involved in, and the kinds of stances they took when defining "support" and "politics." I included both individuals who took particularly strong stances online and individuals who emphasized the "supportive" and "noncontroversial" nature of the groups. I aimed for ten individuals from each message board who represented the various perspectives present in the discussions. For example, if there were more participants who took part in controversial discussions online, I asked more of these "controversial participants" to take part in interviews. If there were a high number of members who taught new participants what was allowed online, I sampled more of these members for interviews.

Once I identified individuals to interview, I contacted them through their provided email address or private messaging. I contacted 128 individuals for interviews. I sent potential interviewees a link to a website with information about my research and inquired as to whether they were interested in being a part of the study. I received positive replies from sixty-nine individuals, and fifty-five individuals finished the course of interviews. The fourteen who ended up not participating usually dropped out after the first or second set of questions. After three unanswered reminder emails, I stopped contacting them. My final response rate was 43 percent. I discussed issues of consent, and provided an online page where they could electronically consent, before beginning the email interviews. My response rate for moderators was much higher (67 percent or eight out of twelve), which I argue reflects the fact that moderators tend to be more invested in the message board community.

One of the limitations in recruiting from online message boards is that "lurkers" are by definition invisible and thus would not be selected for interviews. Individuals may lurk for long periods, only posting occasionally, if at all. Five of the message boards in my sample show the number of members online, and the number of non-logged in "guests" online. I used these numbers as some indication of how many lurkers there were on each site. On message boards with high numbers of lurkers (notably Marine Moms Online and Operation Mom), I asked the moderators to post a message on the board inviting "lurkers" to contact me for interviews. I added four mothers to my interview sample this way.

My interview sampling strategy shifted several times during the data collection process. Because it was hard to find antiwar mothers in online groups, I had to work harder to find enough antiwar mothers and self-silencing mothers to make sure I had a variety of mothers in my interview sample. To do this, I paid particular attention to group members who avoided participating in discussions that ended up becoming controversial, or stopped participating in discussions when political issues arose. I watched some of these conversations from each website to add antiwar mothers to my sample. I also needed the perspective of mothers who had lost children in the war, whom the military calls Gold Star mothers. Gold Star mothers proved especially difficult to find and to recruit for interviews. Often Gold Star mothers' message boards are completely inaccessible to outsiders. The two Gold Star mothers I interviewed participated in online discussions but volunteered for interviews through emails/messages they saw from group moderators.

In interviews, I asked mothers about their experiences of having a child in the military, from when their children first decided to enlist through the recruitment and training process. I asked them about how they related to the public (to those not connected to the military) and what kind of public, political activities they had participated in as mothers of service members. Questions also covered the stress of deployment on them and their families, how they kept in touch with their children during deployment, and their opinions on other mothers of service members who take different stances on the war. I also asked them to describe their experiences participating in online support groups. I asked moderators an additional set of questions about their moderation experiences and the message board rules.

Four years after interviewing mothers from online message boards, I reached out to the mothers I had interviewed previously for follow-up interviews. At this point I also asked mothers if they, or another mother they knew, had a service member injured in the war. Through this method, I identified twelve mothers to interview. Wanting more mothers, and more diversity in the mostly white sample, I contacted two local VA clinics for recommendations of mothers who were caregivers for service members. Through these clinics, I identified and interviewed eight more mothers—four black and four Hispanic.

Demographic Profile of Interviewees

Distribution of Interviewed Mothers by Household Income

Income	N	%
0–$25,000	7	10.0
$25,001–$50,000	24	34.3
$50,001–$75,000	30	42.9
$75,000–$100,000	7	10.0
$100,000+	2	2.9
Total	**70**	

Distribution of Gender of Children in the Military

Gender	N	%
Female	7	9.3
Male	68	90.7
Total	**75***	

* Five mothers in this study have two children in the military.

Distribution of Mothers' Military Family Backgrounds

Military Background?	N	%
Yes	32	45.7
No	38	54.2
Total	**70**	

Distribution of Mothers by Race

Race	N	%
White	50	71.4
Black	12	17.2
Hispanic/Latina	8	11.4
American Indian	0	—
Asian/Pacific Islander	0	—
Total	70	

Distribution of Interviewed Mothers by Military Branch

Branch	N	%
Army	30	42.9
Marines	31	44.3
National Guard	8	11.4
Navy	1	1.4
Total	70	

Coding and Analysis

As with the DoD documents, I followed the process of open and focused coding for interview data. I started by open coding a smaller set of preliminary message board and interview data, strategically chosen to represent the range of military mothers I had seen so far in the data. Then, I moved to focused coding by synthesizing and selecting themes for analysis. I used the same resulting coding scheme for the interviews and for the online ethnography (I describe online ethnography data and sampling procedures in the next section). While my final list of focused codes is far beyond the scope of what I utilize in this book, it provides roads to future projects on issues such as veterans' health care, war as gendered protection of the homeland, and military conceptions of who the "enemy" is during wartime. I analyzed the data in NVivo using content analysis procedures—coding and sorting the data into themes and categories, attributes, and coding nodes based on my coding scheme.[7]

The Benefits and Drawbacks of Email Interviewing

There are pros and cons to conducting interviews through email, but in this case, I believe the benefits outweighed any drawbacks. In general, my findings reflect the findings of others who have done online research that email interviews provide data rich in unique ways.[8]

I anticipated that some of the interview practices of asking follow-up and probing questions (particularly nonverbal probes) would be difficult through email. Because of this, I tried to organize and word my questions in a way that encouraged respondents to elaborate on their answers. When I received answers to a set of questions from a respondent, I answered back with follow-up "clarification probes" and "sequence probes" as quickly as I could, and found that I could receive well-thought-out elaborations that way.[9] Interview through email, however, does not allow the interviewer (or interviewee) to respond to the body language, pauses, laughter, etc. of the respondent, so I am sure I missed follow-up and probing opportunities from my lack of those nontextual cues. However, as other researchers have pointed out, individuals often feel more comfortable expressing their thoughts through writing (email), and by giving the respondent the time to think of answers, rewrite answers, and come back to their responses before emailing me back, the data achieved from email interviews can be rich in different ways.[10] I found this to be true; many respondents sent me long, detailed, and self-reflexive responses to questions.

Early in my data-gathering process, I made significant changes to interview protocols. I started with four sets of interview questions, but narrowed them down to three sets after receiving a low follow-up rate in the first batch of interviews. And after initially receiving a low response rate to the first set of interview questions I sent out, I reordered the questions so that the first set prompted mothers to talk about their children and their experiences of their children's enlistment and deployment. With these questions, I worked to "show empathy" in order to make the interviewees feel comfortable sharing with me.[11] I also brought in a few general questions about their political involvement early on, and saved the potentially controversial, or "threatening" questions about political activities, and their thoughts on the war for later in the second and third sets of questions.[12] I also made sure the second and third sets of questions contained opportunities for mothers to tell detailed stories about their children's return, etc. This increased response rates, and I started to get much more regular and detailed responses.

I also made changes to the wording of some of my questions based on the first few interview responses I received. I discovered quite a few assumptions about military mothers in what I initially thought were my own carefully worded questions. For instance, initially I asked mothers "Could you tell me about a time you encountered another mother (either online or in person) who was against the war?" but the question assumed that I was interviewing mothers who all supported the war. Part of my assumption came from what I initially saw online—that these online mothers all seemed to support the war (it was not until I started interviews that I learned there were many quiet antiwar mothers in the same message boards). After running into an antiwar mother in an interview, I changed the question to "Could you tell me about a time you encountered another mother of a soldier (either online or in person) who felt differently about the war than you do?" In addition, I initially did not anticipate interviewing mothers of service members killed in action. These mothers were also present in message boards, although to a lesser extent. When I realized that I needed their perspectives for my analysis, I rewrote the interview questions for them, making sure that they were sensitive to their loss.

Email also made it easy for respondents to communicate with me informally and keep in touch with me long after their interviews. For instance, on more than a dozen occasions, respondents would email me with their own clarifications to their answers, or would supplement their answers with a story/illustration of what they were talking about, without being prompted for a follow-up. While this is often the case with face-to-face interviews, the fact that interviewees were already comfortable communicating online made it easy for them to send more information through emails when they thought of it (e.g., in the middle of the night). Over half of my respondents have kept in touch with me since their interviews were formally completed. They emailed me to let me know when their child returned from deployment (and in some cases called me to tell me the exciting news), or to tell me that they will be deployed again. Mothers with their own blogs, or who do their own writing (poetry, journaling) have sent me copies of things they have written that they thought captured part of being the mother of a service member. This has been not only invaluable for my research, but personally enriching. I feel differently now when I see the mother of a service member—either wearing a t-shirt or button in a store, or driving in a bumper-stickered car—I feel that I know them and appreciate their experience in a way I never would have before beginning this study.

A Note on Emotions and Interviewing

Ethnographers have often noted the importance of addressing the emotion and emotion-work that goes into conducting research.[13] The reading I did on the military and on mothers of service members did not prepare me for how openly emotional their responses would be, or that I would have my own emotional reactions to their experiences. Take, for instance, this excerpt from my research journal from my first weeks of conducting email interviews:

> I am just now realizing that the people I interview actually have loved ones in VERY dangerous situations. The people I interview talk with me about their children, who very well might die today. I knew this on some level before, but now it is VERY apparent to me, and I hope that I am being sensitive to this during my interviews. They aren't just participating in a study—they are talking about something that is intensely emotional and personal for them every single day.
>
> To do: Tone down my own exclamation points and enthusiasm.

Years later, I am surprised with how candid I was in my journal, and I am also surprised that I barely remember feeling this way. After reading these women's stories repeatedly for years, I have grown accustomed to my emotional reactions to certain things mothers tell me—for instance, when one respondent emailed me in the middle of the night to tell me she had woken up shaking and crying after having a nightmare that her son was killed. I had a difficult time getting her raw emotion out of my head, and a hard time sleeping myself that night. Similarly, when a participant called me a year after finishing with formal interviews to tell me her daughter had arrived home safe from Iraq and express how happy and relieved she was, I was elated, and went back over what she wrote in her interviews to compare her deployment experiences to her experiences of homecoming.

3. ONLINE ETHNOGRAPHY OF MILITARY MOTHERS' SUPPORT GROUPS

For chapters 3 and 4, I conducted an online ethnography of how mothers come together in online forums to provide their children and one another with support focused on the mothers' interaction with each other and on the technological context that gave the interactions their specific form. I chose to do an online ethnography because the online communication in Internet forums is a useful place to see how democracy, gender, and discourse are linked.[14] The military has long used the Internet to connect service members with their families, to build strong military family networks. The Internet is also a space that is used increasingly for support groups, social movement mobilization, and the distribution of news and information during wartime.[15]

I chose online groups, and not other online spaces (such as weblogs or Facebook groups) because message boards are unique for the threaded conversations that occur between individuals. Online groups provide a way to see interactions between mothers and especially their struggles over the meanings of terms such as *politics* and *support*. Message boards also each have different rules, structures, and moderation levels that enable and limit certain kinds of discussion. Comparing how discussions are enabled and limited on each message board is key for understanding how mothers use metaphors like *support* and *patriotism* to control one another's discourse. While message boards are great places to see discursive interactions, studying online groups meant that I missed the physical interactions (facial expressions and body language) between mothers that would happen during in-person meetings. This drawback, however, also provides unique insight into the nonphysical (discursive) ways that mothers may ignore one another and silence certain perspectives during discussions.

My methodological approach to online ethnography is an adaptation of Smith's approach to understanding texts and her method of institutional ethnography. In an institutional ethnography, the researcher works outward from the local, everyday world to "excavate" how the everyday lives of individuals are organized through texts.[16] According to Smith, "the idea is to map the institutional aspects of the ruling relations so that people can expand their own knowledge of their everyday worlds by being able to see how what they are doing is coordinated with others' doings elsewhere and elsewhen."[17] It is the combination of taking into account both the experiences of individuals, and how those experiences are mediated beyond individuals' views that makes this method useful for seeing the typically unseen technological texts that mediate the online world. For this research, I do not take up the complete practice of doing an institutional ethnography. Instead, I use some of the principles that are useful to analyzing texts and power on the Internet. The following is Smith's step-by-step guide for doing institutional ethnography that I have remodeled for this study:[18]

1. Begin with the actual activities and experiences of individuals online. Understanding the online world as an actual experience for participants, that is organized and mediated in much the same way as the offline world, centers the individuals who are in the process of creating, reading, and activating online texts. What technological connections does the user employ? How is the information (photos, posts, links) they share with and organize with others distributed? For instance, when looking at how someone presents themselves online, consider what choices they have to make in that technological context, as well as what kind of information is required from them, and by whom (the message board rules, their Internet service provider, online moderators, etc.). The goal here is to uncover disjunctures between how technology structures the connections and distribution of information online, and how participants employ the technology. I examine how technology may limit in some ways the actions and interactions individuals have online.

2. Understand where the "field" of research begins and ends for participants. How many websites are used, and how? What kinds of Internet technologies are employed (message boards, links to personal blogs, etc.)? At this level, I consider the technological organization of the place where experiences and interactions occur. This entails examining how the coordination works by focusing on the active texts involved, particularly the technological

texts such as hyperlinks to other websites and threaded discussions. At this point, the dynamic, ongoing coordination of the
Internet as constantly changing needs to be considered. As texts
only have meaning in the context where they have action, looking
at where and when the action occurs is key. For example, when
analyzing information provided on a message board, I consider
what links/references individuals use to back up their information, what links readers follow, and why. I consider what specific
text-based technologies individuals employ when online—who
engages in distributing and categorizing of what information in
online message boards.

3. I interview participants about their online activities, as well as
   their perceptions, expectations, and knowledges of the online
   world. Participation in the online world is also key for getting at
   how the Internet is used, and for identifying online rules and
   boundaries. I examine how people use online spaces differently,
   and how and why individuals engage in active organizing of information for others.

4. I follow the online texts through their connections to examine
   how individuals' activities and ideas online are coordinated, and
   what larger institutions (such as the military's own websites) are
   involved in this coordination. Considering texts as a mediator of
   the social world provides a way to account for both individual
   power in organizing and interpreting the social world, and the
   larger networks of institutional and technological power that
   shape and constrain the social world for individuals. I examine
   material and technological places that mediate the social space.
   Getting at this means following the texts online outward to see
   how individual online experiences are coordinated through different locations and across different times.

Message Board Sampling Procedures

My initial goal in sampling message boards was to end up with eight to
ten message boards from a variety of different branches (with at least
one from each branch, and one mixed-branch board), and representing
a variety of variations in public accessibility and restrictiveness. I sampled online communities that (a) were aimed primarily at mothers of

service members currently deployed; (b) describe themselves as "support" sites, both in terms of providing support for each other and in terms of supporting the troops; and (c) have an active online message board/forum space where participants interact with each other. During my preliminary analysis, I identified thirty-seven message boards that fit these criteria, with memberships ranging from roughly fifty to more than ten thousand members who are active daily.

From the thirty-seven message boards that I identified, I began by excluding the message boards that were the least active and had fewer than forty participants. I excluded nine groups with infrequent postings that would not yield enough data, and I excluded six groups with very few participants because they were most likely extensions of military mothers' groups that also meet in person. Of the remaining twenty-two message boards, sixteen were open for the public to browse (registration was necessary for posting), and eight had message boards that could be accessed only by members.

I began by initiating contact with the moderators of message boards in batches, with the goal of gaining access to eight message boards—representing a wide variety of military branches and boards with different degrees of accessibility represented. In my initial contact with message board moderators, I introduced myself and my research, providing them with a link to my research website. I explained to the moderator that my intentions were not to participate, but to observe message board interactions, and to contact specific members about interviewing them privately. I explained that my observations of the group would do nothing to break the groups' or participants' anonymity and that any personal details about members on the website would be kept private. I told moderators that I wanted message board participants to be aware of my presence (through a "sticky" or through an email to all from the moderator) and I encouraged moderators to consult with their group members before granting permission.

From these I selected nine message boards for analysis (my resulting sample was only eight message boards—one went offline before I began my research). The message boards I selected are among the most active daily, and include some that are open to the public and some open to members only. The message boards represent a variety of branches of the military (two are for all military branches and seven are for specific branches) and this reflects the fact that Marine Corps and

Army message boards dominate the Internet (twenty-five out of thirty-seven total message boards are specifically for Army and Marine Corps mothers). The message board geared specifically toward National Guard and reserve mothers was also the only such board for this branch that I could find online. I selected the final eight message boards based on a combination of my own goal of having a theoretically representative sample, and how much success I had in contacting moderators and gaining permission to observe the groups. Additionally, eight of my interviews were with mothers who served as moderators in a group, and they provided additional insight into the groups' goals and their own processes of moderation.

In addition to the message boards that were a part of my online ethnography, I strategically selected two websites for expressly antiwar mothers for comparison of discourses and themes (since the primary message boards I studied appeared to have few antiwar mothers). Only one of the two groups had a message board, and that was all but inactive. Instead of following discussions, I gained permission from group leaders to read and analyze the groups' public writings and press releases. Although this material could have warranted its own study, I used it as a kind of qualitative hypothesis test to make sure I was getting the full variety of mothers' views on politics, war, and troop support. The content in these websites confirmed that I was getting a wide spectrum of mothers' views on war, and that the antiwar mothers who were a part of discussions in my primary sample were much like other antiwar mothers in the ways they understood and argued against war.

I monitored two and a half years (June 2006–January 2009) of online message board discussions. This included eight message boards, all branches, and mixed branch boards, with over seven thousand discussion threads in total and memberships ranging from fifty to three thousand participants. It is impossible to know the total number of discussion threads because each single board counts what a "thread" is differently and displays the threads differently depending upon the technology used. For some boards, posts include replies to former posts, or are displayed as one continuous conversation.

I "lurked" online. I did not want to interfere with discussions, so I chose not to participate, but instead observed interactions and privately contacted specific members about interviewing them. Following the ethical traditions of online ethnographers, even though I was a lurker, I tried not to use "cyberstealth."[19] I treated online discussions as private, no matter how technically public they were, and I felt strongly that I had an ethical obligation to protect the members of these online communities.[20]

Thus, I aimed to be an overt lurker, and made sure that message board participants were provided with an explanation of my presence and a way to contact me if they did not want their part of the discussions included. Due to high expectation of privacy in the closed message boards, the moderators created a static page visible to all participants that described my project and provided contact information. For the publicly accessible message boards, there was no way to notify every participant over the two and a half years of the study, so I worked with the moderators to provide ongoing information to their participants in a way that made them comfortable with my research. I explained that my observations of the group would do nothing to break the groups' or participants' anonymity.

Message Board Coding and Analysis

I followed these steps in coding and analyzing message board data:

1. As explained in the previous section on coding interview data, message board data were included during the process of open and focused coding.
2. In order to analyze the more than seven thousand discussion threads in my sample, I used keywords from the final coding scheme to identify discussions for complete coding. The keywords I chose were particularly salient in how mothers defined support and politics in their discussions, in how they policed one another's views online, and in how they understood (and justified to others) their children's military service. For example, mothers often evoked patriotism when talking about feeling proud of the troops, or when discussing antiwar protestors. When shutting down discussions perceived to be "too political," mothers often evoke the terms *opinion* and *personal belief* in order to dismiss others' views.

   At both the piece level and the narrative level, I coded themes such as worry (safety, education, job prospects), motherhood (emotional, irrational), pride (in decision, in achievements), family situations (absence of father, behavioral problems), positive individual growth (achievement, adulthood), national service (duty, patriotism), support from the military (safety, a family, father figure), support from mothers (for children's decision, for the war, for emotional or physical needs of the troops).

3. I searched all the discussions for these keywords, and then used the focused coding scheme to code entire threads that went with that particular discussion. These threads of discussions sometimes spanned one day and sometimes spanned months.

4. In order to ensure that I was not missing other salient themes and discussions, I chronologically coded every tenth discussion thread in each message board. In this coding, I included the entire discussion thread over the course of the discussion (sometimes up to three months). By following the entirety of a discussion thread, I was able to get at the trajectory of discussions. After doing this, I feel confident that the discussions I coded based on keywords were representative of the boards as a whole. This technique also ensured that I did not waste time coding repetitive discussions distributing information (such as mailing instructions for care packages) or personal nonmilitary-related issues that mothers shared about their own lives with the group.

5. I also coded each message board's posted rules, descriptions, mission statements, and other informational pages.

6. I also mapped the technological structure of each message board. I noted the organization of the discussion space and what technology was being used to facilitate the discussions and moderations of the message boards (for example, could members privately email each other, could they receive discussion posts through their own email accounts, did moderators need to approve every post before it went live?).

7. I used the data on the rules, structure, and moderator presence on each message board to determine its moderation level. I considered a message board to have a "low" moderation level if participants could post without initial moderation screening, and if moderators rarely stepped in to monitor and shut down discussions. Message boards with "medium" moderation level had a trial period for new members (where their posts would need to

be approved by a moderator) and moderators were more active stepping in to stop specific discussions from happening. Message boards with a "high" level of moderation were boards where every new discussion thread had to be approved by a moderator before going live. After that initial screening, if any discussion posts stepped out of the bounds of the forums' rules, they were shut down by moderators immediately. Of my eight boards, three had low moderation, two had medium levels of moderation, and three were high in moderation.

Conducting Research as an "Outsider"

Although there is much to critique about the polarity of the "insider/outsider" paradigm in ethnographic research, I began a project feeling like an "outsider"—an unlikely candidate to study mothers and the military.[21] I am not a mother, nor am I a member of the military, and I have no immediate family members serving in the armed forces. My outsider status made me initially apprehensive about gaining access to both message boards and individual participants. Why would they want to talk to me? I decided that the only way to deal with my outsider status was to address it directly when contacting message board administrators and potential respondents.

Even when I received replies of interest despite my stated outsider status, I continued to worry about being seen as too much of an outsider by those respondents. However, I soon found that I was able to harness my lack of motherly and military experience to ask moderators and participants for clarification about conversations and rules online, the worries and emotions involved in being a parent, and about the workings of the military institution. As Naples argues, my "outsiderness became a resource through which I was able to acquire an insider's perspective."[22] Indeed, even the fact that I had marked myself as an "outsider" and anticipated mothers seeing me as an "outsider" illustrated for me throughout my research how "being a military mother" is construed and understood. I came to see my outsider perspective as an invaluable part of my research, because mothers took it upon themselves to explain as clearly as possible to me what it meant for them to be what I was not—a mother and the mother of a service member.

At various points, my "outsider" status was incredibly apparent to me and offered opportunities to learn the insider view I was missing. For example, in the first few batches of interview questions that I sent out to mothers, I naively referred to all service members as "soldiers." It took the first Marine mother all of five minutes after I sent her the questions to email me back and correct me by explaining differences in the branches (from the perspective of a Marine mother, who, of course, believes Marines are the best). This was instructional for me for a few reasons. On a practical level, I immediately went through and rewrote a new set of questions for each branch—making sure to distinguish between BCT for the Army and boot camp for Marines. The Marine mother's correction also showed me how little I knew, despite all my research, about the military. This sent me in search of basic guides to the military—such as *A Civilian's Guide to the U.S. Military* and *Married to the Military: A Survival Guide for Military Wives, Girlfriends, and Women in Uniform*.[23] These, along with the Internet, became my go-to guides for looking at acronyms and other military terms used in interviews and message boards. Finally, the Marine mother's correction made me pay attention to hierarchies within the military—Army vs. Marine Corps, deployed vs. nondeployed, reserves vs. active duty, and "regular" Army vs. National Guard.

NOTES

INTRODUCTION

1. George H. Roeder Jr., *The Censored War: American Visual Experience during World War Two* (New Haven, CT: Yale University Press, 1995).

2. "CNN Poll: Afghanistan War Arguably Most Unpopular in U.S. History," accessed August 23, 2017, http://politicalticker.blogs.cnn.com/2013/12/30/cnn-poll-afghanistan-war-most-unpopular-in-u-s-history.

3. Dominic Tierney, "Forgetting Afghanistan," *Atlantic*, June 24, 2015, https://www.theatlantic.com/international/archive/2015/06/afghanistan-war-memory/396701.

4. Lisa Leitz, *Fighting for Peace: Veterans and Military Families in the Anti–Iraq War Movement* (Minneapolis: University of Minnesota Press, 2014); Karen Slattery and Ana C. Garner, "News Coverage of U.S. Mothers of Soldiers during the Vietnam War," *Journalism Practice* 9, no. 2 (March 4, 2015): 265–78, https://doi.org/10.1080/17512786.2014.924735.

5. Richard Sisk, "US Doubles Number of Advisers in Iraq as Forces Push into Mosul," Military.com, accessed August 30, 2017, http://www.military.com/daily-news/2017/01/04/us-doubles-number-advisers-in-iraq-forces-push-mosul.html.

6. Cynthia Cockburn, "Gender Relations as Causal in Militarization and War," *International Feminist Journal of Politics* 12, no. 2 (2010): 139–57; Cynthia Cockburn, "War and Security, Women and Gender: An Overview of the Issues," *Gender & Development* 21, no. 3 (November 1, 2013): 433–52, https://doi.org/10.1080/13552074.2013.846632.

7. Elisabeth Bumiller and Thom Shanker, "Pentagon Set to Lift Ban on Women in Combat Roles," *New York Times*, January 23, 2013, https://www.

nytimes.com/2013/01/24/us/pentagon-says-it-is-lifting-ban-on-women-in-combat.html.

8. Orna Sasson-Levy, "Contradictory Consequences of Mandatory Conscription: The Case of Women Secretaries in the Israeli Military," *Gender & Society* 21, no. 4 (August 1, 2007): 481–507, https://doi.org/10.1177/0891243207303538.

9. Arlie Russell Hochschild, *The Managed Heart: Commercialization of Human Feeling, Twentieth Anniversary Edition, With a New Afterword* (Berkeley: University of California Press, 2003).

10. Sara Ruddick, *Maternal Thinking: Toward a Politics of Peace* (Boston: Beacon, 1995); Sara Ruddick, "Rethinking Maternal Politics," in *The Politics of Motherhood: Activist Voices from Left to Right*, ed. Alexis Jetter, Annelise Orleck, and Diana Taylor (Hanover: University Press of New England [for] Dartmouth College, 1997).

11. Cynthia Enloe, *Maneuvers: The International Politics of Militarizing Women's Lives* (Austin, TX: Women's International News Gathering Service, 2000).

12. Marguerite Guzman Bouvard, *Revolutionizing Motherhood: The Mothers of the Plaza de Mayo* (Wilmington, DE: Scholarly Resources, 1994); Lorraine Bayard de Volo, "Mobilizing Mothers for War: Cross-National Framing Strategies in Nicaragua's Contra War," *Gender & Society* 18, no. 6 (2004): 715–34; Lorraine Bayard de Volo, *Mothers of Heroes and Martyrs: Gender Identity Politics in Nicaragua, 1979–1999* (Baltimore: Johns Hopkins University Press, 2001).

13. Jerry Lembcke, *The Spitting Image: Myth, Memory, and the Legacy of Vietnam* (New York: New York University Press, 1998).

14. Nancy Chodorow, *The Reproduction of Mothering: Psychoanalysis and the Sociology of Gender* (Berkeley: University of California Press, 1978); Evelyn Nakano Glenn, "Social Constructions of Mothering: A Thematic Overview," in *Mothering: Ideology, Experience, and Agency*, ed. Evelyn Nakano Glenn, Grace Chang, and Linda Rennie Forcey (New York: Routledge, 1994); Ruddick, *Maternal Thinking*.

15. R. L. Einwohner, Jocelyn A. Hollander, and Toska Olson, "Engendering Social Movements: Cultural Images and Movement Dynamics," *Gender & Society* 14, no. 5 (2000): 679–99.

16. Enloe, *Maneuvers*.

17. E. Ann Kaplan, *Motherhood and Representation: The Mother in Popular Culture and Melodrama* (New York: Routledge, 1992).

18. Enloe, *Maneuvers*; Kaplan, *Motherhood and Representation*.

19. C. J. Aducci et al., "The Recipe for Being a Good Military Wife: How Military Wives Managed OIF/OEF Deployment," *Journal of Feminist Family*

Therapy 23, no. 3–4 (July 1, 2011): 231–49; Jennifer Davis, David B. Ward, and Cheryl Storm, "The Unsilencing of Military Wives: Wartime Deployment Experiences and Citizen Responsibility," *Journal of Marital and Family Therapy* 37, no. 1 (January 1, 2011): 51–63; Laurie Lee Weinstein and Christie C. White, *Wives and Warriors: Women and the Military in the United States and Canada* (Westport, CT: Bergin & Garvey, 1997); Suzanne Wood, Jacquelyn Scarville, and Katherine S. Gravino, "Waiting Wives: Separation and Reunion among Army Wives," *Armed Forces & Society* 21, no. 2 (January 1995): 217–36.

20. Joshua S. Goldstein, *War and Gender: How Gender Shapes the War System and Vice Versa* (Cambridge, UK: Cambridge University Press, 2001); Jean Bethke Elshtain, *Women and War* (New York: Basic, 1987).

21. David R. Segal, *Recruiting for Uncle Sam* (Lawrence: University of Kansas, 1989); Bernard Rostker, *I Want You!: The Evolution of the All-Volunteer Force* (RAND, 2006).

22. Aline Quester and Robert Shuford, *Population Representation in the Military Services: Fiscal Year 2015 Summary Report* (Washington, DC: Center for Naval Analyses, 2017).

23. Frank F. Furstenberg, "On a New Schedule: Transitions to Adulthood and Family Change," *Future Child* 20, no. 1 (2010): 67–87; Frank F. Furstenberg, "The Sociology of Adolescence and Youth in the 1990s: A Critical Commentary." *Journal of Marriage and Family* 62, no. 4 (2004): 896–910.

24. Quester and Shuford, *Population Representation in the Military Services*.

25. Furstenberg, "On a New Schedule."

26. Hochschild, *The Managed Heart*.

27. Cynthia Enloe, *The Morning After: Sexual Politics at the End of the Cold War* (Berkeley: University of California Press, 1993).

28. "Social Media Fact Sheet," Pew Research Center, January 12, 2017, http://www.pewinternet.org/fact-sheet/social-media.

29. Segal, *Recruiting for Uncle Sam*.

30. "What Americans Don't Understand About Their Own Military." *Defense One*, May 6, 2015, http://www.defenseone.com/ideas/2015/05/what-americans-dont-understand-about-their-own-military/112042.

31. Beth J. Asch, Paul Heaton, and Bogdan Savych, "Recruiting Minorities: What Explains Recent Trends in the Army and Navy?" (RAND: National Defense Research Institute, 2009), http://www.rand.org/content/dam/rand/pubs/monographs/2009/RAND_MG861.pdf; Klaus Phillips, *War! What Is It Good For?: Black Freedom Struggles and the U.S. Military from World War II to Iraq* (Chapel Hill: University of North Carolina Press, 2012).

32. Mady Wechsler Segal, Meridith Hill Thanner, and David R. Segal, "His-panic and African American Men and Women in the U.S. Military: Trends in Representation," *Race, Gender, and Class* 14, no. 3–4 (2007): 48–64; Betty Maxfield, "Blacks in the U.S. Army," Office of Army Demographics, 2010; James Burk and Evelyn Espinoza, "Race Relations Within the US Military," *Annual Review of Sociology* 38 (2012): 401–22.

33. "U.S. Census Bureau QuickFacts Selected: United States," https://www.census.gov/quickfacts/fact/table/US/PST045216.

34. Maxfield, "Blacks in the U.S. Army."

35. Maxfield, "Blacks in the U.S. Army."

1. THE BARGAIN

1. Peter A. Padilla and Mary R. Laner, "Trends in Military Influences on Army Recruitment Themes: 1954-1990," *Journal of Political and Military Sociology* 30, no. 1 (2002): 113–33.

2. Maryann Rowland, "The Changing Face of the U.S. Military: A Textual Analysis of U.S. Army and U.S. Navy Recruiting and Advertisements from Pre-9/11 to Six Years into the Iraq War," master's thesis, University of Central Florida, 2006.

3. Rowland, "Changing Face of the U.S. Military."

4. Wendy M. Christensen, "Recruiting through Mothers: You Made Them Strong, We'll Make Them Army Strong," *Critical Military Studies* 2, no. 3 (September 1, 2016): 193–209, https://doi.org/10.1080/23337486.2016.1162975.

5. Rowland, "Changing Face of the U.S. Military."

6. Carl Hulse and Marjorie Connelly, "Poll Shows a Shift in Opinion on Iraq War," *New York Times*, August 23, 2006, https://www.nytimes.com/2006/08/23/washington/23poll.html.

7. David Kiley, "McCann-Erickson Wins Army Ad Biz. Good News For IPG," *Bloomberg*, December 7, 2005.

8. Richard Bowyer, "Recruiting 21st Century Army Warriors: A Task Requiring National Attention," USAWC Strategy Research Project, 2007; Douglas Yeung and Brian Gifford, "Potential Recruits Seek Information Online for Military Enlistment Decision Making: A Research Note," *Armed Forces & Society* 37, no. 3 (April 2010): 534–49.

9. Stuart Elliott, "Army's New Battle Cry Aims at Potential Recruits," *New York Times*, November 9, 2006, http://www.nytimes.com/2006/11/09/business/media/09adco.html; Stuart Elliott, "Army Tries a Reality Style for Recruit-

ment," *New York Times*, May 21, 2013, http://www.nytimes.com/2013/05/22/business/media/army-tries-a-reality-style-for-recruitment.html.

10. Bowyer, "Recruiting 21st Century Army Warriors."

11. Ryan Kelty, Meredith A. Kleykamp, and David R. Segal, "The Military and the Transition to Adulthood," *Armed Forces & Society* 20, no. 1 (2010).

12. *Population Representation in the Military Services* (Arlington, VA: CNA), accessed October 28, 2017, https://www.cna.org/research/pop-rep.

13. Frank F. Furstenberg, "The Sociology of Adolescence and Youth in the 1990s: A Critical Commentary," *Journal of Marriage and Family* 62, no. 4 (2004): 896–910; Frank F. Furstenberg, "On a New Schedule: Transitions to Adulthood and Family Change," *Future Child* 20, no. 1 (2010): 67–87; Richard A. Settersten and Barbara Ray, "What's Going on with Young People Today? The Long and Twisting Path to Adulthood," *Future of Children* 20, no. 1 (January 2010): 19–41.

14. Settersten and Ray, "What's Going on with Young People Today?"

15. Furstenberg, " Sociology of Adolescence and Youth"; Furstenberg, "On a New Schedule."

16. Damien Cave, "Growing Problem for Military Recruiters: Parents," *New York Times*, June 3, 2005.

17. Cave, "Growing Problem for Military Recruiters."

18. Bowyer, "Recruiting 21st Century Army Warriors."

19. R. W. Connell, "Arms and the Man: Using the New Research on Masculinity to Understand Violence and Promote Peace in the World," in *Male Roles, Masculinities and Violence: A Culture of Peace Perspective*, ed. Ingeborg Breines, R. W. Connell, and Ingrid Eide (Vendome: Presses Universitaires de France, 2000), 21–33; Paul Higate and John Hopton, "War, Militarism, and Masculinities," in *Handbook of Studies on Men and Masculinities*, ed. Michael S. Kimmel, Jeff R. Hearn, and Raewyn W. Connell (Thousand Oaks, CA: Sage, 2005), 432–47.

20. Meredith A. Kleykamp, "College, Jobs or the Military? Enlistment During Times of War," *Social Science Quarterly* 87, no. 2 (2006): 272–90; Jennifer Hickes Lundquist, "Ethnic and Gender Satisfaction in the Military: The Effect of a Meritocratic Institution," *American Sociological Review* 73, no. 3 (2008).

21. Mady Wechsler Segal, "Women's Military Roles Cross-Nationally: Past, Present, and Future," *Gender & Society* 9, no. 6 (1995); Kelty, Kleykamp, and Segal, "Military and the Transition to Adulthood."

22. Segal, "Women's Military Roles Cross-Nationally"; Kelty, Kleykamp, and Segal, "Military and the Transition to Adulthood."

23. Marc Cutright, "From Helicopter Parent to Valued Partner: Shaping the Parental Relationship for Student Success," *New Directions in Higher Education* 144 (2008): 38–48; Katherine Lynk Wartman and Marjorie Savage,

"Parental Involvement in Higher Education: Understanding the Relationship among Students, Parents, and the Institution," *ASHE Higher Education Report*, 2008.

2. BE ALL THAT YOU CAN BE

1. Paul R. Sackett and Anne S. Mavor, "Evaluating Military Advertising and Recruiting: Theory and Methodology," National Research Council, March 29, 2004; Betty Maxfield, "Blacks in the U.S. Army," Office of Army Demographics, 2010.

2. "U.S. Census Bureau QuickFacts Selected: United States," accessed October 28, 2017, https://www.census.gov/quickfacts/fact/table/US/PST045216.

3. Maxfield, "Blacks in the U.S. Army."

4. David R. Segal, *Recruiting for Uncle Sam* (Lawrence: University of Kansas Press, 1989); Meredith A. Kleykamp, "College, Jobs or the Military? Enlistment During Times of War," *Social Science Quarterly* 87, no. 2 (2006): 272–90; Bernard Rostker, *I Want You!: The Evolution of the All-Volunteer Force* (RAND, 2006).

5. "Demographic Trends and Economic Well-Being," Pew Research Center, June 27, 2016, http://www.pewsocialtrends.org/2016/06/27/1-demographic-trends-and-economic-well-being.

6. Amy Lutz, "Who Joins the Military?: A Look at Race, Class, and Immigration Status," *Journal of Political and Military Sociology* 36, no. 2 (January 1, 2008): 167–88.

7. Ryan Moffett, "The Transformation of the Demographic Differential Between the U.S. Military and the U.S. Population," master's thesis, University of California–Berkeley, 2009.

8. Lutz, "Who Joins the Military?"

9. Lolita C. Baldor, "Lower Standards Help Army Recruit More," *Washington Post*, October 10, 2006, http://www.washingtonpost.com/wp-dyn/content/article/2006/10/10/AR2006101000131.html.

10. ACLU, *Soldiers of Misfortune: Abusive U.S. Military Recruitment and Failure to Protect Child Soldiers* (American Civil Liberties Union, 2008).

11. Ryan Kelty, Meredith A. Kleykamp, and David R. Segal, "The Military and the Transition to Adulthood," *Armed Forces & Society* 20, no. 1 (2010).

12. "From Representation to Inclusion: Diversity Leadership for the 21st-Century Military," Military Leadership Diversity Commission, 2011.

13. Lutz, "Who Joins the Military?"

14. David R. Segal and Mady Wechsler Segal, "America's Military Population," *Population Bulletin* 59, no. 4 (2004); Hannah Fischer, *A Guide to U.S.*

Military Casualty Statistics: Operation Inherent Resolve, Operation New Dawn, Operation Iraqi Freedom, and Operation Enduring Freedom (Washington, DC: Library of Congress Congressional Research Service, 2014).

15. Wendy M. Christensen, "The Black Citizen-Subject: Black Single Mothers in US Military Recruitment Material," *Ethnic and Racial Studies* 39, no. 14 (November 13, 2016): 2508–26, https://doi.org/10.1080/01419870.2016.1160139.

16. Charles C. Moskos and John S. Butler, *All That We Can Be: Black Leadership and Racial Integration the Army Way* (New York: Basic, 1996); Daniel Woolever, "A Strategic Systems Model for Effective Recruiting," USAWC Strategy Research Project, 2003; Rostker, *I Want You!*; Klaus Phillips, *War! What Is It Good For?: Black Freedom Struggles and the U.S. Military from World War II to Iraq* (Chapel Hill: University of North Carolina Press, 2012).

17. Moskos and Butler, *All That We Can Be.*

18. Joyce P. Kaufman and Kristen P. Williams, *Women, the State, and War: A Comparative Perspective on Citizenship and Nationalism* (Lanham, MD: Lexington, 2007); Nira Yuval-Davis, *Gender & Nation* (London: Sage, 1997).

19. T. H. Marshall, *Citizenship and Social Class: And Other Essays* (Cambridge, UK: University Press, 1950).

20. Evelyn Nakano Glenn, *Unequal Freedom: How Race and Gender Shaped American Citizenship and Labor* (Cambridge, MA: Harvard University Press, 2002).

21. Herman Gray, *Watching Race: Television and the Struggle for Blackness* (Minneapolis: University of Minnesota Press, 2004).

22. Linda Gordon, *Pitied but Not Entitled: Single Mothers and the History of Welfare 1890–1935*, reprint edition (Cambridge, MA: Harvard University Press, 1998).

23. Michelle Alexander, *The New Jim Crow: Mass Incarceration in the Age of Colorblindness* (New York: New Press), 2012.

24. Patricia Hill Collins, *Black Feminist Thought: Knowledge, Consciousness, and the Politics of Empowerment* (London: Harper Collins Academics, 1990); Jill Quadagno, *The Color of Welfare: How Racism Undermined the War on Poverty* (New York: Oxford University Press, 1996).

25. Hector Amaya, "Dying American or the Violence of Citizenship: Latinos in Iraq," *Latino Studies* 5, no. 1 (2007): 3–24, https://doi.org/10.1057/palgrave.lst.8600240; Phillips, *War! What Is It Good For?*

26. Jacqueline Jones, *Labor of Love, Labor of Sorrow: Black Women, Work, and the Family, from Slavery to the Present* (New York: Basic, 2009); Evelyn Nakano Glenn, "Constructing Citizenship Exclusion, Subordination, and Resistance," *American Sociological Review* 76, no. 1 (February 1, 2011): 1–24.

27. Howard Winant, *The New Politics of Race: Globalism, Difference, Justice* (Minneapolis: University of Minnesota Press, 2004); Alexander, *New Jim Crow*.

28. Sackett and Mavor, "Evaluating Military Advertising and Recruiting."

29. Beth J. Asch, Paul Heaton, and Bogdan Savych, "Recruiting Minorities: What Explains Recent Trends in the Army and Navy?" (RAND: National Defense Research Institute, 2009), http://www.rand.org/content/dam/rand/pubs/monographs/2009/RAND_MG861.pdf.

30. Lutz, "Who Joins the Military?"; Asch, Heaton, and Savych, "Recruiting Minorities"; Maxfield, "Blacks in the U.S. Army."

31. Maxfield, "Blacks in the U.S. Army."

32. Asch, Heaton, and Savych, "Recruiting Minorities."

33. Kleykamp, "College, Jobs or the Military?"; ACLU, *Soldiers of Misfortune*.

34. Mady Wechsler Segal, Meridith Hill Thanner, and David R. Segal, "Hispanic and African American Men and Women in the U.S. Military: Trends in Representation," *Race, Gender, and Class* 14, no. 3–4 (2007): 48–64.

35. Segal, Thanner, and Segal, "Hispanic and African American Men and Women in the U.S. Military"; James Burk and Evelyn Espinoza, "Race Relations Within the US Military," *Annual Review of Sociology* 38 (2012): 401–22.

36. Moskos and Butler, *All That We Can Be*; Rostker, *I Want You!*

37. Woolever, "Strategic Systems Model."

38. Moskos and Butler, *All That We Can Be*.

39. Kleykamp, "College, Jobs or the Military?"

40. Glenn, *Unequal Freedom*.

41. Kleykamp, "College, Jobs or the Military?"

42. "From Representation to Inclusion."

43. Alexander, *New Jim Crow*.

44. Alexander, *New Jim Crow*.

45. Alexander, *New Jim Crow*; Loïc J. D. Wacquant, "From Slavery to Mass Incarceration: Rethinking the 'Race Question' in the US," *New Left Review* 13 (2002).

46. Suzanne M. Bianchi and Melissa A. Milkie, "Work and Family Research in the First Decade of the 21st Century," *Journal of Marriage and Family* 72, no. 3 (June 2010): 705–25.

47. Suzanne M. Bianchi, John P. Robinson, and Melissa A. Milkie, *Changing Rhythms of American Family Life* (New York: Russell Sage, 2006).

48. Alexander, *New Jim Crow*; Patricia Hill Collins, "It's All In the Family: Intersections of Gender, Race, and Nation," *Hypatia* 13, no. 3 (1998): 62–82.

49. Alexander, *New Jim Crow*, 49.

50. Collins, *Black Feminist Thought*.

51. Collins, *Black Feminist Thought*, 79.

52. Collins, *Black Feminist Thought*, 79.

53. Alexander, *New Jim Crow*.

3. "HALF MY HEART IS IN IRAQ"

1. Leora N. Rosen and Doris B. Durand, "Coping with the Unique Demands of Military Family Life," in *The Military Family: A Practice Guide for Human Service Providers*, ed. James A. Martin, Leora N. Rosen, and Linette R. Sparacino (Westport, CT: Praeger, 2000), 55–72; Leora N. Rosen, Doris B. Durand, and James A. Martin, "Wartime Stress and Family Adaptation," in *The Military Family: A Practice Guide for Human Service Providers*, ed. James A. Martin, Leora N. Rosen, and Linette R. Sparacino (Westport, CT: Praeger, 2000), 123–38.

2. Mady Wechsler Segal, "The Military and the Family as Greedy Institutions," *Armed Forces & Society* 13 (1986): 9–38; Morten G. Ender et al., "Greedy Media: Army Families, Embedded Reporting, and War in Iraq," *Sociological Focus* 40, no. 1 (2007).

3. Cynthia Enloe, *The Morning After: Sexual Politics at the End of the Cold War*. Berkeley: University of California Press, 1993.

4. Sondra Albano, "Military Recognition of Family Concerns: Revolutionary War to 1993." *Armed Forces & Society* 20, no. 2 (1994): 283; Mady Wechsler Segal, "Women's Military Roles Cross-Nationally: Past, Present, and Future," *Gender & Society* 9, no. 6 (1995).

5. Segal, "Women's Military Roles."

6. Blue Star Mothers of America, Inc., https://www.bluestarmothers.org.

7. Nira Yuval-Davis, *Gender & Nation* (London: Sage, 1997).

8. Stephen Earl Bennett and Richard S. Flickinger, "Americans' Knowledge of U.S. Military Deaths in Iraq, April 2004 to April 2008," *Armed Forces & Society* 35, no. 3 (2009): 587–604.

9. Scott Sigmund Gartner, "The Multiple Effects of Casualties on Public Support for War: An Experimental Approach," *American Political Science Review* 102, no. 01 (February 2008): 95–106, https://doi.org/10.1017/S0003055408080027; Scott Sigmund Gartner, "Ties to the Dead: Connections to Iraq War and 9/11 Casualties and Disapproval of the President," *American Sociological Review* 73, no. 4 (August 2008): 690–95, https://doi.org/10.1177/000312240807300408.

10. Yagil Levy, "A Revised Model of Civilian Control of the Military: The Interaction between the Republican Exchange and the Control Exchange," *Armed Forces & Society* 38, no. 4 (October 1, 2012): 529–56, https://doi.org/

10.1177/0095327X12439384; Lisa Leitz, *Fighting for Peace: Veterans and Military Families in the Anti–Iraq War Movement* (Minneapolis: University of Minnesota Press, 2014).

11. Tina Managhan, *Gender, Agency and War: The Maternalized Body in US Foreign Policy* (New York: Routledge, 2012).

12. Enloe, *The Morning After*.

4. "MY SON FIGHTS FOR YOUR FREEDOM"

1. Carole Pateman, *The Disorder of Women: Democracy, Feminism and Political Theory* (Cambridge, UK: Polity, 1989).

2. Joan Wallach Scott, "Some Reflections on Gender and Politics," in *Revisioning Gender*, ed. Myra Marx Ferree, Judith Lorber, and Beth B. Hess (New York: Rowman & Littlefield, 2000); Lisa D. Brush, *Gender and Governance* (Walnut Creek, CA: AltaMira, 2003).

3. Ruth Lister, *Citizenship: Feminist Perspectives* (New York: New York University Press, 2003).

4. Lorraine Bayard de Volo, *Mothers of Heroes and Martyrs: Gender Identity Politics in Nicaragua, 1979-1999* (Baltimore: Johns Hopkins University Press, 2001); Ann Marie Nicolosi, "Cindy Sheehan and the Politics of Motherhood: Politicized Maternity in the Twentieth and Twenty-First Centuries," *Genders* 58 (September 22, 2013).

5. de Volo, *Mothers of Heroes and Martyrs*; Nicolosi, "Cindy Sheehan and the Politics of Motherhood."

6. Pateman, *Disorder of Women*; Nira Yuval-Davis, *Gender & Nation* (London: Sage, 1997).

7. Michelle E. Carreon and Valentine M. Moghadam, "'Resistance Is Fertile': Revisiting Maternalist Frames across Cases of Women's Mobilization," *Women's Studies International Forum* 51 (July 2015): 19–30, https://doi.org/10.1016/j.wsif.2015.04.002.

8. Department of Defense Directive 1344.10 (amended February 19, 2008), *Political Activities by Members of the Armed Forces*, http://www.esd.whs.mil/DD; John Loran Kiel, "When Soldiers Speak Out: A Survey of Provisions Limiting Freedom of Speech in the Military," *Parameters* 37, no. 3 (September 22, 2007): 69.

9. Patrick G. Coy, Lynne M. Woehrle, and Gregory M. Maney, "Discursive Legacies: The U.S. Peace Movement and 'Support the Troops,'" *Social Problems* 55, no. 2 (2008): 161–89; Roger Stahl, "Why We 'Support the Troops': Rhetorical Evolutions," *Rhetoric & Public Affairs* 12, no. 4 (2009): 533–70.

10. Pateman, *Disorder of Women*; Mary Bernstein, "Identity Politics," *Annual Review of Sociology* 31 (2005): 47–74.

11. Carreon and Moghadam, "'Resistance Is Fertile.'"

5. RETURNING HOME

1. George Fink, *Stress of War, Conflict and Disaster* (San Diego: Academic Press, 2010).

2. "One in Five Iraq and Afghanistan Veterans Suffer from PTSD or Major Depression," RAND: National Defense Research Institute, accessed September 16, 2016, http://www.rand.org/news/press/2008/04/17.html.

3. Charles W. Hoge et al., "Combat Duty in Iraq and Afghanistan, Mental Health Problems, and Barriers to Care," *New England Journal of Medicine* 351, no. 1 (2004): 13–22.

4. Rajeev Ramchand et al., "Hidden Heroes," *Rand Health Quarterly* 4, no. 2 (June 1, 2014), http://www.ncbi.nlm.nih.gov/pmc/articles/PMC5052006.

5. Jerry Lembcke, *The Spitting Image: Myth, Memory, and the Legacy of Vietnam* (New York: New York University Press, 1998).

6. Hoge et al., "Combat Duty in Iraq and Afghanistan."

7. Committee on the Assessment of the Readjustment Needs of Military Personnel, Veterans, Board on the Health of Select Populations, and Institute of Medicine, *Screening, Assessment, and Treatment* (Washington, DC: National Academies Press, 2013), https://www.ncbi.nlm.nih.gov/books/NBK206857.

8. Hannah Fischer, *US Military Casualty Statistics: Operation New Dawn, Operation Iraqi Freedom, and Operation Enduring Freedom* (Washington, DC: Library of Congress Congressional Research Service, 2013).

9. "US & Allied Killed and Wounded | Costs of War," Watson Institute for International and Public Affairs, http://watson.brown.edu/costsofwar/costs/human/military.

10. "DoD Worldwide Numbers for TBI," Defense and Veterans Brain Injury Center, June 9, 2016, http://dvbic.dcoe.mil/dod-worldwide-numbers-tbi.

11. Institute of Medicine, Committee on the Initial Assessment of Readjustment Needs of Military Personnel, Veterans, and Their Families, *Returning Home from Iraq and Afghanistan: Preliminary Assessment of Readjustment Needs of Veterans, Service Members, and Their Families* (Washington, DC: National Academies Press, 2010), Part 2: *Operation Enduring Freedom and Operation Iraqi Freedom: Demographics and Impact*, https://www.ncbi.nlm.nih.gov/books/NBK220068.

12. Terri Tanielian et al., "Military Caregivers: Cornerstones of Support for Our Nation's Wounded, Ill, and Injured Veterans," RAND, 2013.

13. Steve Walsh, "Without Help, Navigating Benefits Can Be Overwhelming for Veterans," *National Public Radio*, http://www.npr.org/2015/01/14/374055310/indiana-s-veterans-service-officers-operate-on-a-shoe-string.

14. See for example FamilyofaVet.com, http://www.familyofavet.com/VA-links-for-Veterans-Caregivers.html.

15. "Profile of Post-9/11 Veterans: 2012," National Center for Veterans Analysis and Statistics, July 2015, https://www.va.gov/vetdata/docs/SpecialReports/Post_911_Veterans_Profile_2012_July2015.pdf.

16. Eric Christensen et al., *Economic Impact on Caregivers of the Seriously Wounded, Ill, and Injured* (Alexandria, VA: Center for Naval Analyses, 2009).

17. H. Stephen Kaye, Charlene Harrington, and Mitchell P. LaPlante, "Long-Term Care: Who Gets It, Who Provides It, Who Pays, and How Much?" *Health Affairs* 29, no. 1 (January 1, 2010): 11–21, https://doi.org/10.1377/hlthaff.2009.0535.

18. Deborah G. Schuss, "The 'Quicker and Sicker' Exit Strategy," *Boston.com*, July 30, 2009, http://archive.boston.com/bostonglobe/editorial_opinion/oped/articles/2009/07/30/the_quicker_and_sicker_exit_strategy.

19. Zoë H. Wool and Seth D. Messinger, "Labors of Love: The Transformation of Care in the Non-Medical Attendant Program at Walter Reed Army Medical Center," *Medical Anthropology Quarterly* 26, no. 1 (March 1, 2012): 26–48, https://doi.org/10.1111/j.1548-1387.2011.01195.x.

20. Bonnie J. Wakefield et al., "Strain and Satisfaction in Caregivers of Veterans with Chronic Illness," *Research in Nursing & Health* 35, no. 1 (February 1, 2012): 55–69, https://doi.org/10.1002/nur.21456.

21. Ramchand et al., "Hidden Heroes."

22. Ramchand et al., "Hidden Heroes."

23. Ramchand et al., "Hidden Heroes."

24. Wool and Messinger. "Labors of Love."

25. Ramchand et al., "Hidden Heroes."

26. Julie Robison et al., "A Broader View of Family Caregiving: Effects of Caregiving and Caregiver Conditions on Depressive Symptoms, Health, Work, and Social Isolation," *Journals of Gerontology* 64B, no. 6 (November 1, 2009): 788–98, https://doi.org/10.1093/geronb/gbp015.

27. Dana Priest and Anne Hull, "Soldiers Face Neglect, Frustration At Army's Top Medical Facility," *Washington Post*, February 18, 2007, http://www.washingtonpost.com/wp-dyn/content/article/2007/02/17/AR2007021701172.html.

28. Nancy Chodorow, *The Reproduction of Mothering: Psychoanalysis and the Sociology of Gender* (Berkeley: University of California Press, 1978).

29. Cynthia Enloe, *Maneuvers: The International Politics of Militarizing Women's Lives* (Austin, TX: Women's International News Gathering Service, 2000).

30. Ruth Lister, *Citizenship: Feminist Perspectives* (New York: New York University Press, 2003).

31. Pamela Herd and Madonna Harrington Meyer, "Care Work: Invisible Civic Engagement," *Gender and Society* 16, no. 5 (2002): 665–88.

6. THE FEW, THE PROUD, THE FORGOTTEN

1. Ruth Lister, *Citizenship: Feminist Perspectives* (New York: New York University Press, 2003); Theda Skocpol, *Protecting Soldiers and Mothers: The Political Origins of Social Policy in United States* (Cambridge, MA: Belknap, 1992).

2. Maxine Molyneux, "Mobilization without Emancipation? Women's Interests, the State, and Revolution in Nicaragua," *Feminist Studies* 11, no. 2 (1985): 227–54.

3. Pamela Herd and Madonna Harrington Meyer, "Care Work: Invisible Civic Engagement," *Gender and Society* 16, no. 5 (2002): 665–88.

4. Ruth Lister, "Women, Economic Dependency and Citizenship," *Journal of Social Policy* 19, no. 4 (2009): 445–67; Skocpol, *Protecting Soldiers and Mothers*.

5. Nancy A. Naples, *Grassroots Warriors: Activist Mothering, Community Work, and the War on Poverty* (New York: Routledge, 1998).

6. Mark C. Russell and Charles R. Figley, "Is the Military's Century-Old Frontline Psychiatry Policy Harmful to Veterans and Their Families? Part Three of a Systematic Review," *Psychological Injury and Law* 10, no. 1 (March 1, 2017): 72–95, https://doi.org/10.1007/s12207-016-9280-4.

7. Institute of Medicine, Board on the Health of Select Populations, and Committee on the Assessment of Resiliency and Prevention Programs for Mental and Behavioral Health in Service Members and Their Families, *Preventing Psychological Disorders in Service Members and Their Families: An Assessment of Programs* (Washington, DC: National Academies Press, 2014).

8. Russell and Figley, "Is the Military's Century-Old Frontline Psychiatry Policy Harmful?"

9. "VA Testimony of U.S. Department of Veteran's Affairs Panel before Congress on December 2, 2011—Office of Congressional and Legislative Affairs," accessed October 28, 2017, https://www.va.gov/OCA/testimony/hvac/sh/HVAC02DEC.asp.

10. "IAVA 2017 Member Survey: Iraq and Afghanistan Veterans of America," accessed October 28, 2017, http://iava.org/2017survey.

CONCLUSION

1. David Nakamura and Abby Phillip, "Trump Announces New Strategy for Afghanistan That Calls for a Troop Increase," *Washington Post*, August 21, 2017, https://www.washingtonpost.com/politics/trump-expected-to-announce-small-troop-increase-in-afghanistan-in-prime-time-address/2017/08/21/eb3a513e-868a-11e7-a94f-3139abce39f5_story.html; Bruce Drake, "More Americans Say U.S. Failed to Achieve Its Goals in Iraq," Pew Research Center, June 12, 2014, http://www.pewresearch.org/fact-tank/2014/06/12/more-americans-say-us-failed-to-achieve-its-goals-in-iraq.

2. Stephanie Condon, "10 Years Later: The Iraq War's Lasting Impact on U.S. Politics," *CBS News*, March 19, 2013, https://www.cbsnews.com/news/10-years-later-the-iraq-wars-lasting-impact-on-us-politics.

3. David R. Segal, *Recruiting for Uncle Sam* (Lawrence: University of Kansas, 1989); Peter A. Padilla and Mary R. Laner, "Trends in Military Influences on Army Recruitment Themes: 1954–1990," *Journal of Political and Military Sociology* 30, no. 1 (2002): 113–33; Bernard Rostker, *I Want You!: The Evolution of the All-Volunteer Force* (RAND, 2006); Maryann Rowland, "The Changing Face of the U.S. Military: A Textual Analysis of U.S. Army and U.S. Navy Recruiting and Advertisements from Pre-9/11 to Six Years into the Iraq War," master's thesis, University of Central Florida, 2006.

4. Cynthia Enloe, *Maneuvers: The International Politics of Militarizing Women's Lives* (Austin, TX: Women's International News Gathering Service, 2000); Cynthia Enloe, "The Recruiter and the Sceptic: A Critical Feminist Approach to Military Studies," *Critical Military Studies* 1, no. 1 (February 2, 2015): 3–10, https://doi.org/10.1080/23337486.2014.961746.

5. Enloe, "The Recruiter and the Sceptic."

6. Laura Sjoberg, *Gender, War, and Conflict* (Cambridge, UK: Polity, 2014).

7. Cynthia Enloe, "The Gendered Gulf," in *Collateral Damage: The New World Order at Home and Abroad*, ed. Susan Jeffords and Lauren Rabinovitz (New Brunswick, NJ: Rutgers University Press, 1994).

8. Joan W. Scott, "Gender: A Useful Category of Historical Analysis," *American Historical Review* 91, no. 5 (December 1986): 1053, https://doi.org/10.2307/1864376.

9. Michelle E. Carreon and Valentine M. Moghadam, "'Resistance Is Fertile': Revisiting Maternalist Frames across Cases of Women's Mobilization,"

Women's Studies International Forum 51 (July 2015): 19–30, https://doi.org/10.1016/j.wsif.2015.04.002.

10. Ann Marie Nicolosi, "Cindy Sheehan and the Politics of Motherhood: Politicized Maternity in the Twentieth and Twenty-First Centuries," *Genders* 58 (September 22, 2013); Adrienne Rich, *Of Woman Born: Motherhood as Experience and Institution* (New York: Norton, 1976); R.W. Connell, *Gender & Power* (Stanford, CA: Stanford University Press, 1987).

11. Carol Cohn and Ruth Jacobson, "Women and Political Activism," in *Women & War*, ed. Carol Cohn (Cambridge, UK: Polity, 2013), 104–23.

12. Enloe, *Maneuvers*; Joshua S. Goldstein, *War and Gender: How Gender Shapes the War System and Vice Versa* (Cambridge, UK: Cambridge University Press, 2001).

13. Lorraine Bayard de Volo, *Mothers of Heroes and Martyrs: Gender Identity Politics in Nicaragua, 1979–1999* (Baltimore: Johns Hopkins University Press, 2001); Rachel V. Kutz-Flamenbaum, "Code Pink, Raging Grannies, and the Missile Dick Chicks: Feminist Performance Activism in the Contemporary Anti-War Movement," *Feminist Formations* 19, no. 1 (2007): 89–105, https://doi.org/10.1353/nwsa.2007.0013; Rachel V. Kutz-Flamenbaum, "Maternalism and Feminism: Women's Organizing in the Contemporary Anti-War Movement," *NWSA Journal* 19, no. 1 (2007).

14. R.W. Connell, *Gender: Short Introductions* (Malden, MA: Blackwell, 2002); Mary Bernstein, "Identity Politics," *Annual Review of Sociology* 31 (2005): 47–74.

15. Carreon and Moghadam, "'Resistance Is Fertile.'"

16. Pamela Herd and Madonna Harrington Meyer, "Care Work: Invisible Civic Engagement," *Gender and Society* 16, no. 5 (2002): 665–88.

17. Rajeev Ramchand et al., "Hidden Heroes," *Rand Health Quarterly* 4, no. 2 (June 1, 2014), http://www.ncbi.nlm.nih.gov/pmc/articles/PMC5052006; Eric Christensen et al., *Economic Impact on Caregivers of the Seriously Wounded, Ill, and Injured* (Alexandria, VA: Center for Naval Analyses, 2009); Alison Howell and Zoë H. Wool, "The War Comes Home: The Toll of War and the Shifting Burden of Care," Brown University Watson Institute for International Studies, 2011, http://www.academia.edu/3363619/The_War_Comes_Home_The_Toll_of_War_and_the_Shifting_Burden_of_Care; "One in Five Iraq and Afghanistan Veterans Suffer from PTSD or Major Depression," RAND: National Defense Research Institute, accessed September 16, 2016, http://www.rand.org/news/press/2008/04/17.html; Terri Tanielian et al., "Military Caregivers: Cornerstones of Support for Our Nation's Wounded, Ill, and Injured Veterans," RAND, 2013; Peter Hussey et al., "Resources and Capabilities of the Department of Veterans Affairs to Provide Timely and Accessible

Care to Veterans," RAND, 2015, accessed August 31, 2017, https://
www.rand.org/pubs/research_reports/RR1165z2.html.

18. Mark C. Russell and Charles R. Figley, "Is the Military's Century-Old
Frontline Psychiatry Policy Harmful to Veterans and Their Families? Part
Three of a Systematic Review," *Psychological Injury and Law* 10, no. 1 (March
1, 2017): 72–95, https://doi.org/10.1007/s12207-016-9280-4.

APPENDIX

1. Kathy Charmaz, *Constructing Grounded Theory: A Practical Guide
through Qualitative Analysis* (London: Sage, 2006).

2. Charmaz, *Constructing Grounded Theory*, 46.

3. Charmaz, *Constructing Grounded Theory*, 57.

4. Catherine Kohler Riessman, *Narrative Analysis* (Newbury Park, CA:
Sage, 1993); Jane Elliott, *Using Narrative in Social Research: Qualitative and
Quantitative Approaches* (London: Sage, 2005).

5. Elliott, *Using Narrative in Social Research*.

6. Matthew B. Miles and Michael Huberman, *Qualitative Data Analysis:
An Expanded Sourcebook* (Thousand Oaks, CA: Sage, 1994); Anselm Strauss
and Juliet Corbin, *Basics of Qualitative Research: Techniques and Procedures
for Developing Grounded Theory*, 2nd ed. (London: Sage, 1998).

7. Patricia Bazeley and Lyn Richards, *The NVivo Qualitative Project Book*
(London: Sage, 2000).

8. Annette Markham, "Representation in Online Ethnographies: A Matter
of Context Sensitivity," in *Online Social Research: Theory, Methods, and Ethics*, ed. Sarina Chen, Jon Hall, and Mark Johns (New York: Peter Lang, 2003);
Annette Markham and Nancy Baym, "Introduction: Making Smart Choices on
Shifting Ground," in *Internet Inquiry: Conversations About Method*, ed. Annette N. Markham and Nancy Baym (Thousand Oaks, CA: Sage, 2009); Nicola
Illingworth, "Content, Context, Reflexivity and the Qualitative Research Encounter: Telling Stories in the Virtual Realm," *Sociological Research Online* 11,
no. 1 (2006); Dhiraj Murthy, "Digital Ethnography: An Examination of the Use
of New Technologies for Social Research," *Sociology* 42 (2008): 837–55.

9. Herbert J. Rubin and Irene S. Rubin, *Qualitative Interviewing: The Art
of Hearing Data* (Thousand Oaks, CA: Sage, 2004).

10. Markham and Baym, "Introduction"; Chris Mann and Fiona Stewart,
"Internet Interviewing," in *Inside Interviewing*, ed. Jaber F. Gubrium and
James A. Holstein (London: Sage, 2001), 241–65; Murthy, "Digital Ethnogra-
phy."

11. Rubin and Rubin, *Qualitative Interviewing*.

12. Rubin and Rubin, *Qualitative Interviewing*.

13. Kathleen M. Blee, "White-Knuckle Research: Emotional Dynamics in Fieldwork with Racist Activists," *Qualitative Sociology* 21, no. 4 (1998); Robert M. Emerson, *Contemporary Field Research: Perspectives and Formulations*, 2nd ed. (Prospect Heights, IL: Waveland, 2001).

14. Kevin F. Steinmetz, "Message Received: Virtual Ethnography in Online Message Boards," *International Journal of Qualitative Methods* 11, no. 1 (February 1, 2012): 26–39, https://doi.org/10.1177/160940691201100103; Mieke Schrooten, "Moving Ethnography Online: Researching Brazilian Migrants' Online Togetherness," *Ethnic and Racial Studies* 35, no. 10 (October 1, 2012): 1794–1809, https://doi.org/10.1080/01419870.2012.659271; Natalie Boero and C. J. Pascoe, "Pro-Anorexia Communities and Online Interaction: Bringing the Pro-Ana Body Online," *Body & Society* 18, no. 2 (June 1, 2012): 27–57, https://doi.org/10.1177/1357034X12440827.

15. Shani Orgad, "The Cultural Dimensions of Online Communication: A Study of Breast Cancer Patients' Internet Spaces," *New Media & Society* 8, no. 6 (2006): 877–99; Paul DiMaggio et al., "Social Implications of the Internet," *Annual Review of Sociology* 27 (2001): 307–36; Manuel Castells, *Networks of Outrage and Hope: Social Movements in the Internet Age* (Cambridge, UK: Polity, 2012); Melissa Wall, "'Blogs of War': Weblogs as News," *Journalism* 6, no. 2 (2005): 153–72; John W. Jordan, "Disciplining the Virtual Home Front: Mainstream News and the Web During the War in Iraq," *Communication and Critical/Cultural Studies* 4, no. 3 (2007): 276–302.

16. Marjorie DeVault, "Institutional Ethnography: A Feminist Sociology of Institutional Power," *Contemporary Sociology: A Journal of Reviews* 42, no. 3 (2013): 332–40.

17. Dorothy E. Smith, *Institutional Ethnography: A Sociology for People* (Lanham, MD: AltaMira, 2005).

18. Smith, *Institutional Ethnography*.

19. Bosah Ebo, "Internet or Outernet," in *Cyberghetto or Cybertopia?: Race, Class, and Gender on the Internet*, ed. Bosah Ebo (Westport, CT: Praeger, 1998).

20. Murthy, "Digital Ethnography."

21. Maxine Baca Zinn, "Insider Field Research in Minority Communities," *Social Problems* 27, no. 2 (1979): 209–19; Nancy A. Naples, "A Feminist Revisiting of the Insider/Outsider Debate: The 'Outsider Phenomenon' in Rural Iowa," *Qualitative Sociology* 19, no. 1 (1996); Patricia Hill Collins, "Shifting the Center: Race, Class and Feminist Theorizing about Motherhood," in *Mothering: Ideology, Experience, and Agency*, ed. Donna Bassin, Margaret Honey, and Meryle Mahrer Kaplan (New Haven, CT: Yale University Press, 1994).

22. Naples, "A Feminist Revisiting," 84.

23. Barbara Schading and Richard Schading, *A Civilian's Guide to the U.S. Military: A Comprehensive Reference to the Customs, Language and Structure of the Armed Forces* (Cincinnati, OH: Writer's Digest Books, 2006); Meredith Leyva, *Married to the Military: A Survival Guide for Military Wives, Girlfriends, and Women in Uniform* (New York: Simon & Schuster, 2009).

BIBLIOGRAPHY

Aducci, C. J., Joyce A. Baptist, Jayashree George, Patricia M. Barros, and Briana S. Nelson Goff. "The Recipe for Being a Good Military Wife: How Military Wives Managed OIF/OEF Deployment." *Journal of Feminist Family Therapy* 23, no. 3–4 (July 1, 2011): 231–49.

ACLU. *Soldiers of Misfortune: Abusive U.S. Military Recruitment and Failure to Protect Child Soldiers*. American Civil Liberties Union, 2008.

Albano, Sondra. "Military Recognition of Family Concerns: Revolutionary War to 1993." *Armed Forces & Society* 20, no. 2 (1994): 283.

Alexander, Michelle. *The New Jim Crow: Mass Incarceration in the Age of Colorblindness*. New York: New Press, 2012.

Amaya, Hector. "Dying American or the Violence of Citizenship: Latinos in Iraq." *Latino Studies* 5, no. 1 (2007): 3–24. https://doi.org/10.1057/palgrave.lst.8600240.

Asch, Beth J., Paul Heaton, and Bogdan Savych. "Recruiting Minorities: What Explains Recent Trends in the Army and Navy?" RAND: National Defense Research Institute, 2009. http://www.rand.org/content/dam/rand/pubs/monographs/2009/RAND_MG861.pdf.

Baldor, Lolita C. "Lower Standards Help Army Recruit More." *Washington Post*, October 10, 2006. http://www.washingtonpost.com/wp-dyn/content/article/2006/10/10/AR2006101000131.html.

Bazeley, Patricia, and Lyn Richards. *The NVivo Qualitative Project Book*. London: Sage, 2000.

Bennett, Stephen Earl, and Richard S. Flickinger. "Americans' Knowledge of U.S. Military Deaths in Iraq, April 2004 to April 2008." *Armed Forces & Society* 35, no. 3 (2009): 587–604.

Bernstein, Mary. "Identity Politics." *Annual Review of Sociology* 31 (2005): 47–74.

Bianchi, Suzanne M., and Melissa A. Milkie. "Work and Family Research in the First Decade of the 21st Century." *Journal of Marriage and Family* 72, no. 3 (June 2010): 705–25.

Bianchi, Suzanne M., John P. Robinson, and Melissa A. Milkie. *Changing Rhythms of American Family Life*. New York: Russell Sage, 2006.

Blee, Kathleen M. "White-Knuckle Research: Emotional Dynamics in Fieldwork with Racist Activists." *Qualitative Sociology* 21, no. 4 (1998).

Boero, Natalie, and C. J. Pascoe. "Pro-Anorexia Communities and Online Interaction: Bringing the Pro-Ana Body Online." *Body & Society* 18, no. 2 (June 1, 2012): 27–57. https://doi.org/10.1177/1357034X12440827.

Bouvard, Marguerite Guzman. *Revolutionizing Motherhood: The Mothers of the Plaza de Mayo*. Wilmington, DE: Scholarly Resources, 1994.

Bowyer, Richard. "Recruiting 21st Century Army Warriors: A Task Requiring National Attention." USAWC Strategy Research Project, 2007.

Brush, Lisa D. *Gender and Governance*. Walnut Creek, CA: AltaMira, 2003.

Bumiller, Elisabeth, and Thom Shanker. "Pentagon Set to Lift Ban on Women in Combat Roles." *New York Times*, January 23, 2013. https://www.nytimes.com/2013/01/24/us/pentagon-says-it-is-lifting-ban-on-women-in-combat.html.

Burk, James, and Evelyn Espinoza. "Race Relations Within the US Military." *Annual Review of Sociology* 38 (2012): 401–22.

Carreon, Michelle E., and Valentine M. Moghadam. "'Resistance Is Fertile': Revisiting Maternalist Frames across Cases of Women's Mobilization." *Women's Studies International Forum* 51 (July 2015): 19–30. https://doi.org/10.1016/j.wsif.2015.04.002.

Castells, Manuel. *Networks of Outrage and Hope: Social Movements in the Internet Age*. Cambridge, UK: Polity, 2012.

Cave, Damien. "Growing Problem for Military Recruiters: Parents." *New York Times*, June 3, 2005.

Charmaz, Kathy. *Constructing Grounded Theory: A Practical Guide through Qualitative Analysis*. London: Sage, 2006.

Chodorow, Nancy. *The Reproduction of Mothering: Psychoanalysis and the Sociology of Gender*. Berkeley: University of California Press, 1978.

Christensen, Eric, Candace Hill, Pat Netzer, DeAnn Farr, Elizabeth Schaefer, and Joyce McMahon. *Economic Impact on Caregivers of the Seriously Wounded, Ill, and Injured*. Alexandria, VA: Center for Naval Analyses, 2009.

Christensen, Wendy M. "The Black Citizen-Subject: Black Single Mothers in US Military Recruitment Material." *Ethnic and Racial Studies* 39, no. 14 (November 13, 2016): 2508–26. https://doi.org/10.1080/01419870.2016.1160139.

———. "Recruiting through Mothers: You Made Them Strong, We'll Make Them Army Strong." *Critical Military Studies* 2, no. 3 (September 1, 2016): 193–209. https://doi.org/10.1080/23337486.2016.1162975.

"CNN Poll: Afghanistan War Arguably Most Unpopular in U.S. History." Accessed August 23, 2017. http://politicalticker.blogs.cnn.com/2013/12/30/cnn-poll-afghanistan-war-most-unpopular-in-u-s-history.

Cockburn, Cynthia. "Gender Relations as Causal in Militarization and War." *International Feminist Journal of Politics* 12, no. 2 (2010): 139–57.

———. "War and Security, Women and Gender: An Overview of the Issues." *Gender & Development* 21, no. 3 (November 1, 2013): 433–52. https://doi.org/10.1080/13552074.2013.846632.

Cohn, Carol, and Ruth Jacobson. "Women and Political Activism." In *Women & War*, edited by Carol Cohn, 104–23. Cambridge, UK: Polity, 2013.

Collins, Patricia Hill. *Black Feminist Thought: Knowledge, Consciousness, and the Politics of Empowerment*. London: Harper Collins Academics, 1990.

———. "It's All In the Family: Intersections of Gender, Race, and Nation." *Hypatia* 13, no. 3 (1998): 62–82.

———. "Shifting the Center: Race, Class and Feminist Theorizing about Motherhood." In *Mothering: Ideology, Experience, and Agency*, edited by Donna Bassin, Margaret Honey, and Meryle Mahrer Kaplan, 45–65. New Haven, CT: Yale University Press, 1994.

Committee on the Assessment of the Readjustment Needs of Military Personnel, Veterans, Board on the Health of Select Populations, and Institute of Medicine. *Screening, Assessment, and Treatment*. Washington, DC: National Academies Press, 2013. https://www.ncbi.nlm.nih.gov/books/NBK206857.

Condon, Stephanie. "10 Years Later: The Iraq War's Lasting Impact on U.S. Politics." *CBS News*, March 19, 2013. https://www.cbsnews.com/news/10-years-later-the-iraq-wars-lasting-impact-on-us-politics.

Connell, R. W. "Arms and the Man: Using the New Research on Masculinity to Understand Violence and Promote Peace in the World." In *Male Roles, Masculinities and Violence: A*

Culture of Peace Perspective, edited by Ingeborg Breines, R. W. Connell, and Ingrid Eide, 21–33. Vendome: Presses Universitaires de France, 2000.

———. *Gender & Power*. Stanford, CA: Stanford University Press, 1987.

———. *Gender: Short Introductions*. Malden, MA: Blackwell, 2002.

Coy, Patrick G., Lynne M. Woehrle, and Gregory M. Maney. "Discursive Legacies: The U.S. Peace Movement and 'Support the Troops.'" *Social Problems* 55, no. 2 (2008): 161–89.

Cutright, Marc. "From Helicopter Parent to Valued Partner: Shaping the Parental Relationship for Student Success." *New Directions in Higher Education* 144 (2008): 38–48.

Davis, Jennifer, David B. Ward, and Cheryl Storm. "The Unsilencing of Military Wives: Wartime Deployment Experiences and Citizen Responsibility." *Journal of Marital and Family Therapy* 37, no. 1 (January 1, 2011): 51–63.

"Demographic Trends and Economic Well-Being." Pew Research Center, June 27, 2016. http://www.pewsocialtrends.org/2016/06/27/1-demographic-trends-and-economic-well-being.

Department of Defense Directive 1344.10 (amended February 19, 2008). *Political Activities by Members of the Armed Forces*. http://www.esd.whs.mil/DD.

DeVault, Marjorie. "Institutional Ethnography: A Feminist Sociology of Institutional Power." *Contemporary Sociology: A Journal of Reviews* 42, no. 3 (2013): 332–40.

de Volo, Lorraine Bayard. "Mobilizing Mothers for War: Cross-National Framing Strategies in Nicaragua's Contra War." *Gender & Society* 18, no. 6 (2004): 715–34.

———. *Mothers of Heroes and Martyrs: Gender Identity Politics in Nicaragua, 1979–1999*. Baltimore: Johns Hopkins University Press, 2001.

DiMaggio, Paul, Eszter Hargittai, Russell Neuman, and John P. Robinson. "Social Implications of the Internet." *Annual Review of Sociology* 27 (2001): 307–36.

"DoD Worldwide Numbers for TBI." Defense and Veterans Brain Injury Center, June 9, 2016. http://dvbic.dcoe.mil/dod-worldwide-numbers-tbi.

Drake, Bruce. "More Americans Say U.S. Failed to Achieve Its Goals in Iraq." Pew Research Center, June 12, 2014. http://www.pewresearch.org/fact-tank/2014/06/12/more-americans-say-us-failed-to-achieve-its-goals-in-iraq.

Ebo, Bosah. "Internet or Outernet." In *Cyberghetto or Cybertopia?: Race, Class, and Gender on the Internet*, edited by Bosah Ebo. Westport, CT: Praeger, 1998.

Einwohner, R. L., Jocelyn A. Hollander, and Toska Olson. "Engendering Social Movements: Cultural Images and Movement Dynamics." *Gender & Society* 14, no. 5 (2000): 679–99.

Elliott, Jane. *Using Narrative in Social Research: Qualitative and Quantitative Approaches*. London: Sage, 2005.

Elliott, Stuart. "Army's New Battle Cry Aims at Potential Recruits." *New York Times*, November 9, 2006. http://www.nytimes.com/2006/11/09/business/media/09adco.html.

———. "Army Tries a Reality Style for Recruitment." *New York Times*, May 21, 2013. http://www.nytimes.com/2013/05/22/business/media/army-tries-a-reality-style-for-recruitment.html.

Elshtain, Jean Bethke. *Women and War*. New York: Basic, 1987.

Emerson, Robert M. *Contemporary Field Research: Perspectives and Formulations*. 2nd ed. Prospect Heights, IL: Waveland, 2001.

Ender, Morten G., Marie Campbell, Toya J. Davis, and Patrick R. Michaelis. "Greedy Media: Army Families, Embedded Reporting, and War in Iraq." *Sociological Focus* 40, no. 1 (2007).

Enloe, Cynthia. "The Gendered Gulf." In *Collateral Damage: The New World Order at Home and Abroad*, edited by Susan Jeffords and Lauren Rabinovitz. New Brunswick, NJ: Rutgers University Press, 1994.

———. *Maneuvers: The International Politics of Militarizing Women's Lives*. Austin, TX: Women's International News Gathering Service, 2000.

———. *The Morning After: Sexual Politics at the End of the Cold War*. Berkeley: University of California Press, 1993.

———. "The Recruiter and the Sceptic: A Critical Feminist Approach to Military Studies." *Critical Military Studies* 1, no. 1 (February 2, 2015): 3–10. https://doi.org/10.1080/23337486.2014.961746.

Fink, George. *Stress of War, Conflict and Disaster*. San Diego: Academic Press, 2010.

Fischer, Hannah. *US Military Casualty Statistics: Operation New Dawn, Operation Iraqi Freedom, and Operation Enduring Freedom*. Washington, DC: Library of Congress Congressional Research Service, 2014.

"From Representation to Inclusion: Diversity Leadership for the 21st-Century Military." Military Leadership Diversity Commission, 2011.

Furstenberg, Frank F. "On a New Schedule: Transitions to Adulthood and Family Change." *Future Child* 20, no. 1 (2010): 67–87.

———. "The Sociology of Adolescence and Youth in the 1990s: A Critical Commentary." *Journal of Marriage and Family* 62, no. 4 (2004): 896–910.

Gartner, Scott Sigmund. "The Multiple Effects of Casualties on Public Support for War: An Experimental Approach." *American Political Science Review* 102, no. 01 (February 2008): 95–106. https://doi.org/10.1017/S0003055408080027.

———. "Ties to the Dead: Connections to Iraq War and 9/11 Casualties and Disapproval of the President." *American Sociological Review* 73, no. 4 (August 2008): 690–95. https://doi.org/10.1177/000312240807300408.

Glenn, Evelyn Nakano. "Constructing Citizenship Exclusion, Subordination, and Resistance." *American Sociological Review* 76, no. 1 (February 1, 2011): 1–24.

———. "Social Constructions of Mothering: A Thematic Overview." In *Mothering: Ideology, Experience, and Agency*, edited by Evelyn Nakano Glenn, Grace Chang, and Linda Rennie Forcey. New York: Routledge, 1994.

———. *Unequal Freedom: How Race and Gender Shaped American Citizenship and Labor*. Cambridge, MA: Harvard University Press, 2002.

Goldstein, Joshua S. *War and Gender: How Gender Shapes the War System and Vice Versa*. Cambridge, UK: Cambridge University Press, 2001.

Gordon, Linda. *Pitied but Not Entitled: Single Mothers and the History of Welfare 1890–1935*. Reprint edition. Cambridge, MA: Harvard University Press, 1998.

Gray, Herman. *Watching Race: Television and the Struggle for Blackness*. Minneapolis: University of Minnesota Press, 2004.

Herd, Pamela, and Madonna Harrington Meyer. "Care Work: Invisible Civic Engagement." *Gender and Society* 16, no. 5 (2002): 665–88.

Higate, Paul, and John Hopton. "War, Militarism, and Masculinities." in *Handbook of Studies on Men and Masculinities*, edited by Michael S. Kimmel, Jeff R. Hearn, and Raewyn W. Connell, 432–47. Thousand Oaks, CA: Sage, 2005.

Hochschild, Arlie Russell. *The Managed Heart: Commercialization of Human Feeling, Twentieth Anniversary Edition, With a New Afterword*. Berkeley: University of California Press, 2003.

Hoge, Charles W., Carl A. Castro, Stephen C. Messer, Dennis McGurk, Dave I. Cotting, and Robert L. Koffman. "Combat Duty in Iraq and Afghanistan, Mental Health Problems, and Barriers to Care." *New England Journal of Medicine* 351, no. 1 (2004): 13–22.

Howell, Alison, and Zoë H. Wool. "The War Comes Home: The Toll of War and the Shifting Burden of Care." Brown University Watson Institute for International Studies, 2011. http://www.academia.edu/3363619/The_War_Comes_Home_The_Toll_of_War_and_the_Shifting_Burden_of_Care.

Hulse, Carl, and Marjorie Connelly. "Poll Shows a Shift in Opinion on Iraq War." *New York Times*, August 23, 2006. https://www.nytimes.com/2006/08/23/washington/23poll.html.

Hussey, Peter, Jeanne Ringel, Sangeeta Ahluwalia, Rebecca Anhang Price, Christine Buttorff, Thomas W. Concannon, Susan L. Lovejoy, et al. "Resources and Capabilities of the Department of Veterans Affairs to Provide Timely and Accessible Care to Veterans." RAND, 2015. https://www.rand.org/pubs/research_reports/RR1165z2.html.

"IAVA 2017 Member Survey: Iraq and Afghanistan Veterans of America." Accessed October 28, 2017. http://iava.org/2017survey.

Illingworth, Nicola. "Content, Context, Reflexivity and the Qualitative Research Encounter: Telling Stories in the Virtual Realm." *Sociological Research Online* 11, no. 1 (2006).

Institute of Medicine, Board on the Health of Select Populations, and Committee on the Assessment of Resiliency and Prevention Programs for Mental and Behavioral Health in

Service Members and Their Families. *Preventing Psychological Disorders in Service Members and Their Families: An Assessment of Programs.* Washington, DC: National Academies Press, 2014.

Institute of Medicine, Committee on the Initial Assessment of Readjustment Needs of Military Personnel, Veterans, and Their Families. *Returning Home from Iraq and Afghanistan: Preliminary Assessment of Readjustment Needs of Veterans, Service Members, and Their Families.* Washington, DC: National Academies Press, 2010. Part 2: *Operation Enduring Freedom and Operation Iraqi Freedom: Demographics and Impact.* https://www.ncbi.nlm.nih.gov/books/NBK220068.

Jones, Jacqueline. *Labor of Love, Labor of Sorrow: Black Women, Work, and the Family, from Slavery to the Present.* New York: Basic, 2009.

Jordan, John W. "Disciplining the Virtual Home Front: Mainstream News and the Web During the War in Iraq." *Communication and Critical/Cultural Studies* 4, no. 3 (2007): 276–302.

Kaplan, E. Ann. *Motherhood and Representation: The Mother in Popular Culture and Melodrama.* New York: Routledge, 1992.

Kaufman, Joyce P., and Kristen P. Williams. *Women, the State, and War: A Comparative Perspective on Citizenship and Nationalism.* Lanham, MD: Lexington, 2007.

Kaye, H. Stephen, Charlene Harrington, and Mitchell P. LaPlante. "Long-Term Care: Who Gets It, Who Provides It, Who Pays, and How Much?" *Health Affairs* 29, no. 1 (January 1, 2010): 11–21. https://doi.org/10.1377/hlthaff.2009.0535.

Kelty, Ryan, Meredith A. Kleykamp, and David R. Segal. "The Military and the Transition to Adulthood." *Armed Forces & Society* 20, no. 1 (2010).

Kiel, John Loran. "When Soldiers Speak Out: A Survey of Provisions Limiting Freedom of Speech in the Military." *Parameters* 37, no. 3 (September 22, 2007): 69.

Kiley, David. "McCann-Erickson Wins Army Ad Biz. Good News for IPG." *Bloomberg,* December 7, 2005.

Kleykamp, Meredith A. "College, Jobs or the Military? Enlistment During Times of War." *Social Science Quarterly* 87, no. 2 (2006): 272–90.

Kutz-Flamenbaum, Rachel V. "Code Pink, Raging Grannies, and the Missile Dick Chicks: Feminist Performance Activism in the Contemporary Anti-War Movement." *Feminist Formations* 19, no. 1 (2007): 89–105. https://doi.org/10.1353/nwsa.2007.0013.

———. "Maternalism and Feminism: Women's Organizing in the Contemporary Anti-War Movement." *NWSA Journal* 19, no. 1 (2007).

Leitz, Lisa. *Fighting for Peace: Veterans and Military Families in the Anti–Iraq War Movement.* Minneapolis: University of Minnesota Press, 2014.

Lembcke, Jerry. *The Spitting Image: Myth, Memory, and the Legacy of Vietnam.* New York: New York University Press, 1998.

Leyva, Meredith. *Married to the Military: A Survival Guide for Military Wives, Girlfriends, and Women in Uniform.* New York: Simon & Schuster, 2009.

Levy, Yagil. "A Revised Model of Civilian Control of the Military: The Interaction between the Republican Exchange and the Control Exchange." *Armed Forces & Society* 38, no. 4 (October 1, 2012): 529–56. https://doi.org/10.1177/0095327X12439384.

Lister, Ruth. *Citizenship: Feminist Perspectives.* New York: New York University Press, 2003.

———. "Women, Economic Dependency and Citizenship." *Journal of Social Policy* 19, no. 4 (2009): 445–67.

Lundquist, Jennifer Hickes. "Ethnic and Gender Satisfaction in the Military: The Effect of a Meritocratic Institution." *American Sociological Review* 73, no. 3 (2008).

Lutz, Amy. "Who Joins the Military?: A Look at Race, Class, and Immigration Status." *Journal of Political and Military Sociology* 36, no. 2 (January 1, 2008): 167–88.

Managhan, Tina. *Gender, Agency and War: The Maternalized Body in US Foreign Policy.* New York: Routledge, 2012.

Mann, Chris, and Fiona Stewart. "Internet Interviewing." In *Inside Interviewing,* edited by Jaber F. Gubrium and James A. Holstein, 241–65. London: Sage, 2001.

Markham, Annette. "Representation in Online Ethnographies: A Matter of Context Sensitiv-ity." In *Online Social Research: Theory, Methods, and Ethics*, edited by Sarina Chen, Jon Hall, and Mark Johns. New York: Peter Lang, 2003.

Markham, Annette, and Nancy Baym. "Introduction: Making Smart Choices on Shifting Ground." In *Internet Inquiry: Conversations About Method*, edited by Annette N. Mark-ham and Nancy Baym. Thousand Oaks, CA: Sage, 2009.

Marshall, T. H. *Citizenship and Social Class: And Other Essays*. Cambridge, UK: University Press, 1950.

Maxfield, Betty. "Blacks in the U.S. Army." Office of Army Demographics, 2010.

Miles, Matthew B, and Michael Huberman. *Qualitative Data Analysis: An Expanded Sourcebook*. Thousand Oaks, CA: Sage, 1994.

Moffett, Ryan. "The Transformation of the Demographic Differential Between the U.S. Military and the U.S. Population." Master's thesis, University of California–Berkeley, 2009.

Molyneux, Maxine. "Mobilization without Emancipation? Women's Interests, the State, and Revolution in Nicaragua." *Feminist Studies* 11, no. 2 (1985): 227–54.

Moskos, Charles C., and John S. Butler. *All That We Can Be: Black Leadership and Racial Integration the Army Way*. New York: Basic, 1996.

Murthy, Dhiraj. "Digital Ethnography: An Examination of the Use of New Technologies for Social Research." *Sociology* 42 (2008): 837–55.

Nakamura, David, and Abby Phillip. "Trump Announces New Strategy for Afghanistan That Calls for a Troop Increase." *Washington Post*, August 21, 2017. https://www.washingtonpost.com/politics/trump-expected-to-announce-small-troop-increase-in-afghanistan-in-prime-time-address/2017/08/21/eb3a513e-868a-11e7-a94f-3139abce39f5_story.html.

Naples, Nancy A. "A Feminist Revisiting of the Insider/Outsider Debate: The 'Outsider Phenomenon' in Rural Iowa." *Qualitative Sociology* 19, no. 1 (1996).

———. *Grassroots Warriors: Activist Mothering, Community Work, and the War on Pover-ty*. New York: Routledge, 1998.

Nicolosi, Ann Marie. "Cindy Sheehan and the Politics of Motherhood: Politicized Maternity in the Twentieth and Twenty-First Centuries." *Genders* 58 (September 22, 2013).

"One in Five Iraq and Afghanistan Veterans Suffer from PTSD or Major Depression." RAND: National Defense Research Institute. Accessed September 16, 2016. http://www.rand.org/news/press/2008/04/17.html.

Orgad, Shani. "The Cultural Dimensions of Online Communication: A Study of Breast Cancer Patients' Internet Spaces." *New Media & Society* 8, no. 6 (2006): 877–99.

Padilla, Peter A., and Mary R. Laner. "Trends in Military Influences on Army Recruitment Themes: 1954–1990." *Journal of Political and Military Sociology* 30, no. 1 (2002): 113–33.

Pateman, Carole. *The Disorder of Women: Democracy, Feminism and Political Theory*. Cambridge, UK: Polity, 1989.

Phillips, Klaus. *War! What Is It Good For?: Black Freedom Struggles and the U.S. Military from World War II to Iraq*. Chapel Hill: University of North Carolina Press, 2012.

Population Representation in the Military Services. Arlington, VA: CNA. Accessed October 28, 2017. https://www.cna.org/research/pop-rep.

Priest, Dana, and Anne Hull. "Soldiers Face Neglect, Frustration at Army's Top Medical Facility." *Washington Post*, February 18, 2007. http://www.washingtonpost.com/wp-dyn/content/article/2007/02/17/AR2007021701172.html.

"Profile of Post-9/11 Veterans: 2012." National Center for Veterans Analysis and Statistics, July 2015. https://www.va.gov/vetdata/docs/SpecialReports/Post_911_Veterans_Profile_2012_July2015.pdf.

Quadagno, Jill. *The Color of Welfare: How Racism Undermined the War on Poverty*. New York: Oxford University Press, 1996.

Quester, Aline, and Robert Shuford. *Population Representation in the Military Services: Fiscal Year 2015 Summary Report*. Washington, DC: Center for Naval Analyses, 2017.

Ramchand, Rajeev, Terri Tanielian, Michael P. Fisher, Christine Anne Vaughan, Thomas E. Trail, Caroline Epley, Phoenix Voorhies, Michael Robbins, Eric Robinson, and Bonnie

Ghosh-Dastidar. "Hidden Heroes." *RAND Health Quarterly* 4, no. 2 (June 1, 2014). http://www.ncbi.nlm.nih.gov/pmc/articles/PMC5052006.

Rich, Adrienne. *Of Woman Born: Motherhood as Experience and Institution*. New York: Norton, 1976.

Riessman, Catherine Kohler. *Narrative Analysis*. Newbury Park, CA: Sage, 1993.

Robison, Julie, Richard Fortinsky, Alison Kleppinger, Noreen Shugrue, and Martha Porter. "A Broader View of Family Caregiving: Effects of Caregiving and Caregiver Conditions on Depressive Symptoms, Health, Work, and Social Isolation." *Journals of Gerontology* 64B, no. 6 (November 1, 2009): 788–98. https://doi.org/10.1093/geronb/gbp015.

Roeder, George Jr. *The Censored War: American Visual Experience During World War Two*. New Haven, CT: Yale University Press, 1995.

Rosen, Leora N., and Doris B. Durand. "Coping with the Unique Demands of Military Family Life." In *The Military Family: A Practice Guide for Human Service Providers*, edited by James A. Martin, Leora N. Rosen, and Linette R. Sparacino, 55–72. Westport, CT: Praeger, 2000.

Rosen, Leora N., Doris B. Durand, and James A. Martin. "Wartime Stress and Family Adaptation." In *The Military Family: A Practice Guide for Human Service Providers*, edited by James A. Martin, Leora N. Rosen, and Linette R. Sparacino, 123–38. Westport, CT: Praeger, 2000.

Rostker, Bernard. *I Want You!: The Evolution of the All-Volunteer Force*. RAND, 2006.

Rowland, Maryann. "The Changing Face of the U.S. Military: A Textual Analysis of U.S. Army and U.S. Navy Recruiting and Advertisements from Pre-9/11 to Six Years into the Iraq War." Master's thesis, University of Central Florida, 2006.

Rubin, Herbert J., and Irene S. Rubin. *Qualitative Interviewing: The Art of Hearing Data*. Thousand Oaks, CA: Sage, 2004.

Ruddick, Sara. *Maternal Thinking: Toward a Politics of Peace*. Boston: Beacon, 1995.

———. "Rethinking Maternal Politics." In *The Politics of Motherhood: Activist Voices from Left to Right*, edited by Alexis Jetter, Annelise Orleck, and Diana Taylor. Hanover: University Press of New England [for] Dartmouth College, 1997.

Russell, Mark C., and Charles R. Figley. "Is the Military's Century-Old Frontline Psychiatry Policy Harmful to Veterans and Their Families? Part Three of a Systematic Review." *Psychological Injury and Law* 10, no. 1 (March 1, 2017): 72–95. https://doi.org/10.1007/s12207-016-9280-4.

Sackett, Paul R., and Anne S. Mavor. "Evaluating Military Advertising and Recruiting: Theory and Methodology." National Research Council, March 29, 2004.

Sasson-Levy, Orna. "Contradictory Consequences of Mandatory Conscription: The Case of Women Secretaries in the Israeli Military." *Gender & Society* 21, no. 4 (August 1, 2007): 481–507. https://doi.org/10.1177/0891243207303538.

Schading, Barbara, and Richard Schading. *A Civilian's Guide to the U.S. Military: A Comprehensive Reference to the Customs, Language and Structure of the Armed Forces*. Cincinnati, OH: Writer's Digest Books, 2006.

Schrooten, Mieke. "Moving Ethnography Online: Researching Brazilian Migrants' Online Togetherness." *Ethnic and Racial Studies* 35, no. 10 (October 1, 2012): 1794–1809. https://doi.org/10.1080/01419870.2012.659271.

Schuss, Deborah G. "The 'Quicker and Sicker' Exit Strategy." *Boston.com*, July 30, 2009. http://archive.boston.com/bostonglobe/editorial_opinion/oped/articles/2009/07/30/the_quicker_and_sicker_exit_strategy.

Scott, Joan W. "Gender: A Useful Category of Historical Analysis." *American Historical Review* 91, no. 5 (December 1986): 1053. https://doi.org/10.2307/1864376.

———. "Some Reflections on Gender and Politics." In *Revisioning Gender*, edited by Myra Marx Ferree, Judith Lorber, and Beth B. Hess. New York: Rowman & Littlefield, 2000.

Segal, David R. *Recruiting for Uncle Sam*. Lawrence: University of Kansas Press, 1989.

Segal, Mady Wechsler. "The Military and the Family as Greedy Institutions." *Armed Forces & Society* 13 (1986): 9–38.

———. "Women's Military Roles Cross-Nationally: Past, Present, and Future." *Gender & Society* 9, no. 6 (1995).

Segal, Mady Wechsler, Meridith Hill Thanner, and David R. Segal. "Hispanic and African American Men and Women in the U.S. Military: Trends in Representation." *Race, Gender, and Class* 14, no. 3–4 (2007): 48–64.

Segal, David R., and Mady Wechsler Segal. "America's Military Population." *Population Bulletin* 59, no. 4 (2004).

Settersten, Richard A., and Barbara Ray. "What's Going on with Young People Today? The Long and Twisting Path to Adulthood." *Future of Children* 20, no. 1 (January 2010): 19–41.

Sisk, Richard. "US Doubles Number of Advisers in Iraq as Forces Push into Mosul." Military.com. Accessed August 30, 2017. http://www.military.com/daily-news/2017/01/04/us-doubles-number-advisers-in-iraq-forces-push-mosul.html.

Sjoberg, Laura. *Gender, War, and Conflict*. Cambridge, UK: Polity, 2014.

Skocpol, Theda. *Protecting Soldiers and Mothers: The Political Origins of Social Policy in United States*. Cambridge, MA: Belknap, 1992.

Slattery, Karen, and Ana C. Garner. "News Coverage of U.S. Mothers of Soldiers During the Vietnam War." *Journalism Practice* 9, no. 2 (March 4, 2015): 265–78. https://doi.org/10.1080/17512786.2014.924735.

Smith, Dorothy E. *Institutional Ethnography: A Sociology for People*. Lanham, MD: AltaMira, 2005.

"Social Media Fact Sheet." Pew Research Center, January 12, 2017. http://www.pewinternet.org/fact-sheet/social-media.

Stahl, Roger. "Why We 'Support the Troops': Rhetorical Evolutions." *Rhetoric & Public Affairs* 12, no. 4 (2009): 533–70.

Steinmetz, Kevin F. "Message Received: Virtual Ethnography in Online Message Boards." *International Journal of Qualitative Methods* 11, no. 1 (February 1, 2012): 26–39. https://doi.org/10.1177/160940691201100103.

Strauss, Anselm, and Juliet Corbin. *Basics of Qualitative Research: Techniques and Procedures for Developing Grounded Theory*. 2nd ed. London: Sage, 1998.

Tanielian, Terri, Rajeev Ramchand, Michael P. Fisher, Carra S. Sims, Racine S. Harris, and Margaret C Harrell. "Military Caregivers: Cornerstones of Support for Our Nation's Wounded, Ill, and Injured Veterans." RAND, 2013. https://www.rand.org/pubs/research_reports/RR244.html.

Tierney, Dominic. "Forgetting Afghanistan." *Atlantic*, June 24, 2015. https://www.theatlantic.com/international/archive/2015/06/afghanistan-war-memory/396701.

"US & Allied Killed and Wounded | Costs of War." Watson Institute for International and Public Affairs. http://watson.brown.edu/costsofwar/costs/human/military.

"U.S. Census Bureau QuickFacts Selected: United States." https://www.census.gov/quickfacts/fact/table/US/PST045216.

"VA Testimony of U.S. Department of Veteran's Affairs Panel before Congress on December 2, 2011—Office of Congressional and Legislative Affairs." Accessed October 28, 2017. https://www.va.gov/OCA/testimony/hvac/sh/HVAC02DEC.asp.

Wacquant, Loïc J. D. "From Slavery to Mass Incarceration: Rethinking the 'Race Question' in the US." *New Left Review* 13 (2002).

Wakefield, Bonnie J., Jeanne Hayes, Suzanne Austin Boren, Youngju Pak, and J. Wade Davis. "Strain and Satisfaction in Caregivers of Veterans with Chronic Illness." *Research in Nursing & Health* 35, no. 1 (February 1, 2012): 55–69. https://doi.org/10.1002/nur.21456.

Wall, Melissa. "'Blogs of War': Weblogs as News." *Journalism* 6, no. 2 (2005): 153–72.

Walsh, Steve. "Without Help, Navigating Benefits Can Be Overwhelming for Veterans." *National Public Radio*. http://www.npr.org/2015/01/14/374055310/indiana-s-veterans-service-officers-operate-on-a-shoe-string.

Wartman, Katherine Lynk, and Marjorie Savage. "Parental Involvement in Higher Education: Understanding the Relationship Among Students, Parents, and the Institution." *ASHE Higher Education Report* 33, No. 6 (2008).

Weinstein, Laurie Lee, and Christie C. White. *Wives and Warriors: Women and the Military in the United States and Canada*. Westport, CT: Bergin & Garvey, 1997.

"What Americans Don't Understand About Their Own Military." *Defense One*, May 6, 2015. http://www.defenseone.com/ideas/2015/05/what-americans-dont-understand-about-their-own-military/112042.

Winant, Howard. *The New Politics of Race: Globalism, Difference, Justice*. Minneapolis: University of Minnesota Press, 2004.

Wood, Suzanne, Jacquelyn Scarville, and Katherine S. Gravino. "Waiting Wives: Separation and Reunion among Army Wives." *Armed Forces & Society* 21, no. 2 (January 1995): 217–36.

Wool, Zoë H., and Seth D. Messinger. "Labors of Love: The Transformation of Care in the Non-Medical Attendant Program at Walter Reed Army Medical Center." *Medical Anthropology Quarterly* 26, no. 1 (March 1, 2012): 26–48. https://doi.org/10.1111/j.1548-1387.2011.01195.x.

Woolever, Daniel. "A Strategic Systems Model for Effective Recruiting." USAWC Strategy Research Project, 2003.

Yeung, Douglas, and Brian Gifford. "Potential Recruits Seek Information Online for Military Enlistment Decision Making: A Research Note." *Armed Forces & Society* 37, no. 3 (April 2010): 534–49.

Yuval-Davis, Nira. *Gender & Nation*. London: Sage, 1997.

Zinn, Maxine Baca. "Insider Field Research in Minority Communities." *Social Problems* 27, no. 2 (1979): 209–19.

INDEX

ABOUT THE AUTHOR

Wendy M. Christensen is associate professor in the Department of Sociology at William Paterson University in Wayne, New Jersey. She has published in journals such as *Ethnic and Racial Studies*, *Critical Military Studies*, and the *International Journal of Feminist Politics*. Her current research interests focus on how race, class, and gender inequalities shape political participation and grassroots political organization.